Lecture Notes in Computer Science   11017

Commenced Publication in 1973
Founding and Former Series Editors:
Gerhard Goos, Juris Hartmanis, and Jan van Leeuwen

More information about this series at http://www.springer.com/series/7409

Khalid Belhajjame · Ashish Gehani
Pinar Alper (Eds.)

Provenance and Annotation of Data and Processes

7th International Provenance
and Annotation Workshop, IPAW 2018
London, UK, July 9–10, 2018
Proceedings

 Springer

Editors
Khalid Belhajjame (iD)
Paris Dauphine University
Paris
France

Pinar Alper (iD)
University of Luxembourg
Belvaux
Luxembourg

Ashish Gehani (iD)
SRI International
Menlo Park, CA
USA

ISSN 0302-9743   ISSN 1611-3349   (electronic)
Lecture Notes in Computer Science
ISBN 978-3-319-98378-3   ISBN 978-3-319-98379-0   (eBook)
https://doi.org/10.1007/978-3-319-98379-0

Library of Congress Control Number: 2018951244

LNCS Sublibrary: SL3 – Information Systems and Applications, incl. Internet/Web, and HCI

This Springer imprint is published by the registered company Springer Nature Switzerland AG
The registered company address is: Gewerbestrasse 11, 6330 Cham, Switzerland

Preface

This volume contains the proceedings of the 7th International Provenance and Annotation Workshop (IPAW), held during July 9–10, 2018, at King's College in London, UK. For the third time, IPAW was co-located with the Workshop on the Theory and Practice of Provenance (TaPP). Together, the two leading provenance workshops anchored Provenance Week 2018, a full week of provenance-related activities that included a shared poster session and three other workshops on algorithm accountability, incremental re-computation, and security. The proceedings of IPAW include 12 long papers that report in-depth the results of research around provenance, two system demonstration papers, and 19 poster papers.

IPAW 2018 provided a rich program with a variety of provenance-related topics ranging from the capture and inference of provenance to its use and application. Since provenance is a key ingredient to enable reproducibility, several papers have investigated means for enabling dataflow steering and process re-computation. The modeling of provenance and its simulation has been the subject of a number of papers, which tackled issues that seek, among other things, to model provenance in software engineering activities or to use provenance to model aspects of the European Union General Data Protection Regulation. Other papers investigated inference techniques to propagate beliefs in provenance graphs, efficiently update RDF graphs, mine similarities between processes, and discover workflow schema-level dependencies. This year's program also featured extensions of the W3C Prov recommendation to support new features, e.g., versioning of mutable entities, or cater for new domain knowledge, e.g., astronomy.

In closing, we would like to thank the members of the Program Committee for their thoughtful reviews, Vasa Curcin and Simon Miles for the local organization of IPAW and the Provenance Week at King's College, London, and the authors and participants for making IPAW a successful event.

June 2018

Khalid Belhajjame
Ashish Gehani
Pinar Alper

Organization

Program Committee

Pinar Alper	University of Luxembourg, Luxembourg
Ilkay Altintas	SDSC, USA
David Archer	Galois, Inc., USA
Khalid Belhajjame	University of Paris-Dauphine, France
Vanessa Braganholo	UFF, Brazil
Kevin Butler	University of Florida, USA
Sarah Cohen-Boulakia	LRI, University of Paris-Sud, France
Oscar Corcho	Universidad Politécnica de Madrid, Spain
Vasa Curcin	King's College London, UK
Susan Davidson	University of Pennsylvania, USA
Daniel de Oliveira	Fluminense Federal University, Brazil
Saumen Dey	University of California, Davis, USA
Alban Gaignard	CNRS, France
Daniel Garijo	Information Sciences Institute, USA
Ashish Gehani	SRI International, USA
Paul Groth	Elsevier Labs, The Netherlands
Trung Dong Huynh	King's College London, UK
Grigoris Karvounarakis	LogicBlox, Greece
David Koop	University of Massachusetts Dartmouth, USA
Bertram Ludaescher	University of Illinois at Urbana-Champaign, USA
Tanu Malik	University of Chicago, USA
Marta Mattoso	Federal University of Rio de Janeiro, Brazil
Deborah McGuinness	Rensselaer Polytechnic Institute (RPI), USA
Simon Miles	King's College London, UK
Paolo Missier	Newcastle University, UK
Luc Moreau	King's College London, UK
Beth Plale	Indiana University Bloomington, USA
Satya Sahoo	Case Western Reserve University, USA
Stian Soiland-Reyes	The University of Manchester, UK
Jun Zhao	University of Oxford, UK

Additional Reviewers

Carvalho, Lucas Augusto Montalvão Costa	Pimentel, João
Cała, Jacek	Rashid, Sabbir
Chagas, Clayton	Souza, Renan
	Yan, Rui

Contents

Scientific Workflows

Applications

System Demonstrations

Joint IPAW/TaPP Poster Session

Reproducibility

Provenance Annotation and Analysis to Support Process Re-computation

Jacek Cała(✉) and Paolo Missier

School of Computing, Newcastle University, Newcastle upon Tyne, UK
{Jacek.Cala,Paolo.Missier}@ncl.ac.uk

Abstract. Many resource-intensive analytics processes evolve over time following new versions of the reference datasets and software dependencies they use. We focus on scenarios in which any version change has the potential to affect many outcomes, as is the case for instance in high throughput genomics where the same process is used to analyse large cohorts of patient genomes, or *cases*. As any version change is unlikely to affect the entire population, an efficient strategy for restoring the currency of the outcomes requires first to identify the *scope of a change*, i.e., the subset of affected data products. In this paper we describe a generic and reusable provenance-based approach to address this scope discovery problem. It applies to a scenario where the process consists of complex hierarchical components, where different input cases are processed using different version configurations of each component, and where separate provenance traces are collected for the executions of each of the components. We show how a new data structure, called a *restart tree*, is computed and exploited to manage the change scope discovery problem.

Keywords: Provenance annotations · Process re-computation

1 Introduction

Consider data analytics processes that exhibit the following characteristics. C1: are resource-intensive and thus expensive when repeatedly executed over time, i.e., on a cloud or HPC cluster; C2: require sophisticated implementations to run efficiently, such as workflows with a nested structure; C3: depend on multiple reference datasets and software libraries and tools, some of which are versioned and evolve over time; C4: apply to a possibly large population of input instances.

This is not an uncommon set of characteristics. A prime example is data processing for high throughput genomics, where the genomes (or exomes) of a cohort of patient cases are processed, individually or in batches, to produce lists of variants (genetic mutations) that form the basis for a number of diagnostic purposes. These *variant calling and interpretation* pipelines take batches of 20–40 patient exomes and require hundreds of CPU-hours to complete (C1). Initiatives like the 100K Genome project in the UK (www.genomicsengland.co.uk) provide a perspective on the scale of the problem (C4).

© Springer Nature Switzerland AG 2018
K. Belhajjame et al. (Eds.): IPAW 2018, LNCS 11017, pp. 3–15, 2018.
https://doi.org/10.1007/978-3-319-98379-0_1

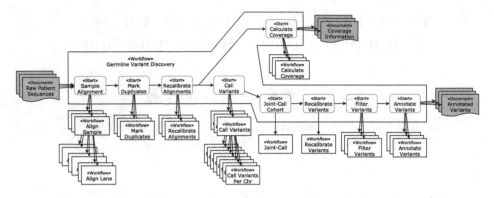

Fig. 1. A typical variant discovery pipeline processing a pool of input samples. Each step is usually implemented as a workflow or script that combines a number of tools run in parallel.

Figure 1, taken from our prior work [5], shows the nested workflow structure (C2) of a typical variant calling pipeline based on the GATK (Genomics Analysis Toolkit) best practices from the Broad Institute.[1] Each task in the pipeline relies on some GATK (or other open source) tool, which in turn requires lookups in public reference datasets. For most of these processes and reference datasets new versions are issued periodically or on an as-needed basis (C3). The entire pipeline may be variously implemented as a HPC cluster script or workflow. Each single run of the pipeline creates a hierarchy of executions which are distributed across worker nodes and coordinated by the orchestrating top-level workflow or script (cf. the "Germline Variant Discovery" workflow depicted in the figure).

Upgrading one or more of the versioned elements risks invalidating previously computed knowledge outcomes, e.g. the sets of variants associated with patient cases. Thus, a natural reaction to a version change in a dependency is to upgrade the pipeline and then re-process all the cases. However, as we show in the example at the end of this section, not all version changes affect each case equally, or in a way that completely invalidates prior outcomes. Also, within each pipeline execution only some of the steps may be affected. We therefore need a system that can perform more selective re-processing in reaction to a change. In [6] we have described our initial results in developing such a system for selective re-computation over a population of cases in reaction to changes, called ReComp. ReComp is a *meta-process* designed to detect the scope of a single change or of a combination of changes, estimate the impact of those changes on the population in scope, prioritise the cases for re-processing, and determine the minimal amount of re-processing required for each of those cases. Note that, while ideally the process of upgrading P is controlled by ReComp, in reality we must also account for upgrades of P that are performed "out-of-band" by developers, as we have assumed in our problem formulation.

---

[1] https://software.broadinstitute.org/gatk/best-practices.

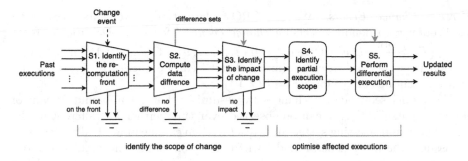

Fig. 2. Schematic of the ReComp meta-process.

Briefly, `ReComp` consists of the macro-steps shown in Fig. 2. The work presented in this paper is instrumental to the `ReComp` design, as it addresses the very first step (S1) indicated in the figure, in a way that is generic and agnostic to the type of process and data.

1.1 Version Changes and Their Scope

To frame the problem addressed in the rest of the paper, we introduce a simple model for version changes as triggers for re-computation. Consider an abstract process P and a population $X = \{x_1 \ldots x_N\}$ of inputs to P, referred to as *cases*. Let $\mathcal{D} = [D_1 \ldots D_m]$ be an ordered list of *versioned* dependencies. These are components, typically software libraries or reference data sets, which are used by P to process a case. Each D has a version, denoted $D.v$, with a total order on the sequence of versions $D.v < D.v' < D.v'' < \ldots$ for each D.

An *execution configuration* for P is the vector $V = [v_1 \ldots v_m]$ of version numbers for $[D_1 \ldots D_m]$. Typically, these are the latest versions for each D, but configurations where some D is "rolled back" to an older version are possible. The set of total orders on the versions of each $D \in \mathcal{D}$ induce a partial order on the set of configurations:

$$[v_1 \ldots v_m] \prec [v_1' \ldots v_m'] \text{ iff } \{v_i \leq v_i'\}_{i:1\ldots m} \text{ and } v_i < v_i' \text{ for at least one } v_i.$$

We denote an *execution* of P on input $x_i \in X$ using configuration V by $E = P(x, V)$, where P may consist of multiple components $\{P_1 \ldots P_k\}$, such as those in our example pipeline. When this is the case, we assume for generality that one execution $P(x, V)$ given x and V is realised as a collection $\{E_i = P_i(x, V)\}_{i:1\ldots k}$ of separate executions, one for each P_i. We use the W3C PROV [13] and ProvONE [7] abstract vocabularies to capture this model in which: $P, P_1 \ldots P_k$ are all instances of `provone:Program`, their relationships is expressed as

$$\{\texttt{provone:hasSubProgram}(P, P_i)\}_{i:1\ldots k}$$

and each execution E_i is associated with its program P_i using:

$$\{\texttt{wasAssociatedWith}(E_i, \_, P_i)\}_{i:1\ldots k}$$

Version Change Events. We use PROV derivation statements `prov:was-DerivedFrom` to denote a *version change event* C for some D_i, from v_i to v_i' : $C = \{D.v_i' \xrightarrow{\text{wDF}} D.v_i\}$. Given $V = [v_1 \ldots v_i \ldots v_m]$, C *enables* the new configuration $V' = [v_1 \ldots v_i' \ldots v_m]$, meaning that V' can be *applied* to P, so that its future executions are of form $E = P(x, V')$.

We model sequences of changes by assuming that an unbound stream of change events $C_1, C_2, \ldots$ can be observed over time, either for different or the same D_i. A re-processing system may react to each change individually. However, we assume the more general model where a set of changes accumulates into a window (according to some criteria, for instance fixed-time) and is processed as a batch. Thus, by extension, we define a composite change to be a set of elementary changes that are part of the same window. Given $V = [v_1 \ldots v_i \ldots v_j \ldots v_m]$, we say that $C = \{D.v_i' \xrightarrow{\text{wDF}} D.v_i, D.v_j' \xrightarrow{\text{wDF}} D.v_j, \ldots\}$ enables configuration $V' = [v_1 \ldots v_i' \ldots v_j' \ldots v_m]$. Importantly, all change events, whether individual or accumulated into windows, are merged together into the single *change front* CF which is the configuration of the latest versions of all changed artefacts.

Applying CF to $E = P(x, V)$ involves re-processing x using P to bring the outcomes up-to-date with respect to all versions in the change front. For instance, given $V = [v_1, v_2, v_3]$ and the change front $CF = \{v_1', v_2'\}$, the re-execution of $E = P(x, [v_1, v_2, v_3])$ is $E' = P(x, [v_1', v_2', v_3])$. It is important to keep track of how elements of the change front are updated as it may be possible to avoid rerunning some of P's components for which the configuration has not changed. Without this fine-grained derivation information, each new execution may use the latest versions but cannot be easily optimised using partial re-processing.

Clearly, processing change events as a batch is more efficient than processing each change separately, cf. $E' = P(x, [v_1', v_2, v_3])$ followed by $E'' = P(x, [v_1', v_2', v_3])$ with the example above. But a model that manages change events as a batch is also general in that it accommodates a variety of refresh strategies. For example, applying changes that are known to have limited impact on the outcomes can be delayed until a sufficient number of other changes have accumulated into CF, or until a specific high-impact change event has occurred. A discussion of specific strategies that are enabled by our scope discovery algorithm is out of the scope of this paper.

1.2   Problem Formulation and Contributions

Suppose P has been executed h times for some $x \in X$, each time with a different configuration $V_1 \ldots V_h$. The collection of past executions, for each $x \in X$, is:

$$\{E(P_i, x, V_j)_{i:1\ldots k, j:1\ldots h, x \in X}\} \tag{1}$$

The problem we address in this paper is to identify, for each change front CF, the smallest set of those executions that are affected by CF. We call this the *re-computation front* C relative to CF. We address this problem in a complex general setting where many types of time-interleaved changes are allowed, where many configurations are enabled by any of these changes, and where executions may reflect any of these configurations, and in particular individual cases x may be processed using any such different configurations. The example from the next section illustrates how this setting can manifest itself in practice.

Our main contribution is a generic algorithm for discovering re-computation front that applies to a range of processes, from simple black-box, single component programs where P is indivisible, to complex hierarchical workflows where P consists of subprograms P_i which may itself be defined in terms of subprograms.

Following a tradition from the literature to use provenance as a means to address re-computation [2,6,12], our approach also involves collecting and exploiting both execution provenance for each E, as well as elements of process–subprocess dependencies as mentioned above. To the best of our knowledge this particular use of provenance and the algorithm have not been proposed before.

1.3   Example: Versioning in Genomics

The problem of version change emerges concretely in Genomics pipelines in which changes have different scope, both within each process instance and across the population of cases. For example, an upgrade to the bwa aligner tool directly affects merely the alignment task but its impact may propagate to most of the tasks downstream. Conversely, an upgrade in the human reference genome directly affects the majority of the tasks. In both cases, however, the entire population of executions is affected because current alignment algorithms are viewed as "black boxes" that use the entire reference genome.

However, a change in one of the other reference databases that are queried for specific information only affects those cases where some of the changed records are part of a query result. One example is ClinVar, a popular variant database queried to retrieve information about specific diseases (phenotypes). In this case, changes that affect one phenotype will not impact cases that exhibit a completely different phenotype. But to detect the impact ReComp uses steps (S2) and (S3), which is out of scope of this paper.

Additionally, note that version changes in this Genomics example occur with diverse frequency. For instance, the reference genome is updated twice a years, alignment libraries every few months, and ClinVar every month.

2   Recomputation Fronts and Restart Trees

2.1   Recomputation Fronts

In Sect. 1.1 we have introduced a partial order $V \prec V'$ between process configurations. In particular, given V, if a change C enables V' then by definition $V \prec V'$. Note that this order induces a corresponding partial order between any two executions that operate on the same $x \in X$.

$$P(x, V) = E \ll E' = P(x, V') \text{ iff } V \prec V' \tag{2}$$

This order is important, because optimising re-execution, i.e. executing $P(x, V')$, may benefit most from the provenance associated with the latest execution according to the sequence of version changes, which is $E = P(x, V)$ (a discussion on the precise types of such optimisations can be found in [6]). For this reason in our implementation we keep track of the execution order explicitly using the `wasInformedBy` PROV relationship, i.e. we record PROV statement $E' \xrightarrow{\text{wIB}} E$ whenever re-executing E such that $E \ll E'$.

To see how these chains of ordered executions may evolve consider, for instance, $E_0 = P(x_1, [a_1, b_1]), E_1 = P(x_2, [a_1, b_1])$ for inputs x_1, x_2 respectively, where the a and b are versions for two dependencies D_1, D_2. The situation is depicted in Fig. 3/left. When change $C_1 = \{a_2 \xrightarrow{\text{wDF}} a_1\}$ occurs, it is possible that only x_1 is re-processed, but not x_2. This may happen, for example, when D_1 is a data dependency and the change affects parts of the data which were not used by E_1 in the processing of input x_2. In this case, C would trigger one single new execution: $E_2 = P(x_1, [a_2, b_1])$ where we record the ordering $E_0 \ll E_2$. The new state is depicted in Fig. 3/middle.

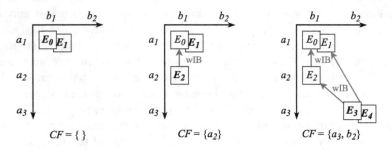

Fig. 3. The process of annotating re-execution following a sequence of events; in bold are executions on the re-computation front; a- and b-axis represent the artefact derivation; arrows in blue denote the `wasInformedBy` relation. (Color figure online)

Now consider the new change $C_2 = \{a_3 \xrightarrow{\text{wDF}} a_2, b_2 \xrightarrow{\text{wDF}} b_1\}$, affecting both D_1 and D_2, and suppose both x_1 and x_2 are going to be re-processed. Then, for each x we retrieve the latest executions that are affected by the change, in this case E_2, E_1, as their provenance may help optimising the re-processing of x_1, x_2 using the new *change front* $\{a_3, b_2\}$. After re-processing we have two new executions: $E_3 = P(x_1, [a_3, b_2]), E_4 = P(x_2, [a_3, b_2])$ which may have been optimised using E_2, E_1, respectively, as indicated by their ordering: $E_3 \ll E_2$, $E_4 \ll E_1$ (see Fig. 3/right).

To continue with the example, let us now assume that the provenance for a new execution: $E_5 = P(x_1, [a_1, b_2])$ appears in the system. This may have been triggered by an explicit user action independently from our re-processing system. Note that the user has disregarded the fact that the latest version of a_i is a_3. The corresponding scenario is depicted in Fig. 4/left. We now have two executions for x_1 with two configurations. Note that despite $E_0 \ll E_5$ holds it is not reflected by a corresponding $E_5 \xrightarrow{\text{wIB}} E_0$ in our re-computation system

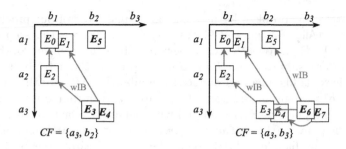

Fig. 4. Continuation of Fig. 3; in bold are executions on the re-computation front; a- and b-axis represent the artefact derivation; arrows in blue denote the `wasInformedBy` relation. (Color figure online)

because E_5 was an explicit user action. However, consider another change event: $\{b_3 \xrightarrow{\text{wDF}} b_2\}$. For x_2, the affected executions is E_4, as this is the single latest execution in the ordering recorded so far for x_2. But for x_1 there are now two executions that need to be brought up-to-date, E_3 and E_5, as these are the maximal elements in the set of executions for x_1 relative according to the order: $E_0 \ll E_2 \ll E_3, E_0 \ll E_5$. We call these executions the *recomputation front* for x_1 relative to change front $\{a_3, b_3\}$, in this case.

This situation, depicted in Fig. 4/right, illustrates the most general case where the entire set of previous executions need to be considered when re-processing an input with a new configuration. Note that the two independent executions E_3 and E_5 have merged into the new E_6.

Formally, the *recomputation front* for $x \in X$ and for a change front $CF = \{w_1 \ldots w_k\}, k \leq m$ is the set of maximal executions $E = P(x, [v_1 \ldots v_m])$ where $v_i \leq w_i$ for $1 \leq i \leq m$.

2.2 Building a Restart Tree

Following our goal to develop a generic re-computation meta-process, the front finding algorithm needs to support processes of various complexity – from the simplest black-box processes to complex hierarchical workflows mentioned earlier. This requirement adds another dimension to the problem of the identification of the re-computation front.

If process P has a hierarchical structure, e.g. expressed using the `provone:` `hasSubProgram` statement (cf. Sect. 1.1), one run of P will usually result in a collection of executions. These are logically organised into a hierarchy, where the top-level represents the execution of the program itself, and sub-executions (connected via `provone:wasPartOf`) represent the executions of the sub-programs. Following the principle of the separation of concerns, we assume the general case where the top-level program is not aware of the data and software dependencies of its parts. Thus, discovering which parts of the program used a particular dependency requires traversing the entire hierarchy of executions.

To illustrate this problem let us focus on a small part of our pipeline – the alignment step (Align Sample and Align Lane). Figure 5 shows this step modelled using ProvONE. P_0 denotes the top program – the Align Sample workflow, SP_0 is the Align Lane subprogram, SSP_0–SSP_3 represent the subsub-programs of bioinformatic tools like bwa and samtools, while SP_1–SP_3 are the invocations of the samtools program. Programs have input and output ports (the dotted grey arrows) and ports p_1–p_8 are related with default artefacts a_0, b_0, etc. specified using the provone:hasDefaultParam statement. The artefacts refer to the code of the executable file and data dependencies; e.g. e_0 represents the code of samtools. Programs are connected to each other via ports and channels, which in the figure are identified using reversed double arrows.

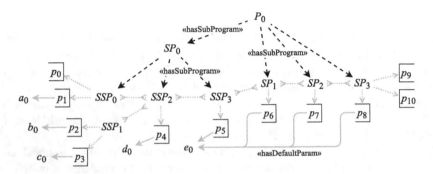

Fig. 5. A small part of the Genomics pipeline shown in Fig. 1 encoded in ProvONE. (- - ➤) denotes the hasSubProgram relation; (——➤) the has-DefaultParam statements; (······➤) hasInPort/hasOutPort; (➤·····◁) the sequence of the $\{P_i$ hasOutPort p_m connectsTo Ch_x, P_j hasInPort p_n connectsTo $Ch_x\}$ statements.

Running this part of the pipeline would generate the runtime provenance information with the structure resembling the program specification (cf. Fig. 6). The main difference between the static program model and runtime information is that during execution all ports transfer some data – either default artefacts indicated in the program specification, data provided by the user, e.g. input sample or the output data product. When introducing a change in this context, e.g. $\{b_1 \xrightarrow{\text{wDF}} b_0, e_1 \xrightarrow{\text{wDF}} e_0\}$, two things are important. Firstly, the usage of the artefacts is captured at the sub-execution level (SSE_1, SSE_3 and SE_1–SE_3) while E_0 uses these artefacts indirectly. Secondly, to rerun the alignment step it is useful to consider the sub-executions grouped together under E_0, which determines the end of processing and delivers data y_0 and z_0 meaningful for the user. We can capture both these elements using the tree structure that naturally fits the hierarchy of executions encoded with ProvONE. We call this tree the *restart tree* as it indicates the initial set of executions that need to be rerun. The tree also provides references to the changed artefacts, which is useful to perform further steps of the ReComp meta-process. Figure 6 shows in blue the restart tree generated as a result of change in artefacts b and e.

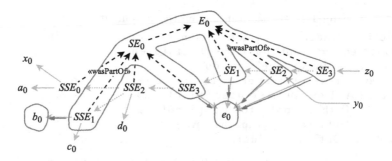

Fig. 6. An execution trace for the program shown in Fig. 5 with the restart tree and artefact references highlighted in blue. ($--\blacktriangleright$) – the `wasPartOf` relation between executions; ($\longrightarrow$) – the `used` statements; ($\cdots\cdots\blacktriangleright$) – the sequence of the E_j `used` z `wasGeneratedBy` E_i statements. (Color figure online)

Finding the restart tree involves building paths from the executions that used changed artefacts, all the way up to the top-level execution following the `was-PartOf` relation. The tree is formed by merging all paths with the same top-level execution.

3   Computing the Re-computation Front

Combining together all three parts discussed above, we present in Listing 1.1 the pseudocode of our algorithm to identify the re-computation front. The input of the algorithm is the change front CF that the ReComp framework keeps updating with every change observed. The output is a list of restart trees, each rooted with the top-level execution. Every node of the tree is a triple: (E, [$changedData$], [$children$]) that combines an execution with optional lists of changed data artefacts it used and sub-executions it coordinated. For executions that represent a simple black-box process the output of the algorithm reduces to the list of triples like: $[(E_i, [a_k, a_l, \ldots], [\,]), (E_j, [a_m, a_n, \ldots], [\,]), \ldots]$ in which the third element of each node is always empty. For the example of a hierarchical process shown above in Fig. 6 the output would be $[(E_0, [\,], [(SE_0, [\,], [(SSE_1, [b_0], [\,]), (SSE_3, [e_0], [\,])]), (SE_1, [e_0], [\,]), (SE_2, [e_0], [\,]), (SE_3, [e_0], [\,])])]$

The algorithm starts by creating the root node, OutTree, of an imaginary tree that will combine all independent executions affected by the change front. Then, it iterates over all artefacts in the ChangeFront set and for each artefact it traverses the chain of versions: Item $\xrightarrow{\text{wDF}}$ PredI $\xrightarrow{\text{wDF}}$ ... (line 4). For each version it looks up all the executions that used particular version of the data (line 5). The core of the algorithm (lines 6–7) is used to build trees out of the affected executions. In line 6 a path from the affected execution to its top-level parent execution is built. Then, the path is merged with the OutTree such that two paths with the same top-level execution are joined into the same subtree, whereas paths with different root become two different subtrees on the OutTree.children list.

Listing 1.1. An algorithm to find the re-computation front.

```
1   function find_recomp_front(ChangeFront) : TreeList
2     OutTree := (root,data := [],children := [])
3     for Item in ChangeFront do
4       for PredI in traverse_derivations(Item) do
5         for Exec in iter_used(PredI) do
6           Path := path_to_root(PredI,Exec)
7           OutTree.merge_path(Path)
8     return OutTree.childern
```

Listing 1.2 shows the path_to_root function that creates the path from the given execution to its top-level parent execution. First it checks if the given execution Exec has already been re-executed (lines 4–6). It does so by iterating over all wasInformedBy statements in which Exec is the informant checking if the statement is typed as recomp:re-execution. If such statement exists, path_to_root returns the empty path to indicate that Exec is not on the front (line 6). Otherwise, if none of the communication statements indicates re-execution by ReComp, Exec is added to the path (line 7) and algorithm moves one level up to check the parent execution (line 8). This is repeated until Exec is the top-level parent in which case get_parent(Exec) returns null and the loop ends. Note, get_parent(X) returns execution Y for which statement X wasPartOf Y holds.

Listing 1.2. Function to generate the path from the given execution to its top-level parent.

```
1    function path_to_root(ChangedItem, Exec) : Path
2      OutPath := [ChangedItem]
3      repeat
4        for wIB in iter_was_informed_by(Exec)
5          if typeof(wIB) is "recomp:re-execution" then
6            return []
7        OutPath.append(Exec)
8        Exec := get_parent(Exec)
9      until Exec = null
10     return OutPath
```

The discussion on other functions used in the proposed algorithm, such as traverse_derivations and iter_used, is omitted from the paper as they are simple to implement. Interested readers can download the complete algorithm written in Prolog from our GitHub repository.[2] Preliminary performance tests showed us execution times in the order of milliseconds when run on a 250 MB database of provenance facts for about 56k composite executions and a set of artefact documents of which two had 15 and 19 version changes. As expected, the response time was increasing with the growing length of the derivation chain.

---

[2] https://github.com/ReComp-team/IPAW2018.

4   Related Work

A recent survey by Herschel et al. [9] lists a number of applications of provenance like improving collaboration, reproducibility and data quality. It does not highlight, however, the importance of process re-computation which we believe needs much more attention nowadays. Large, data-intensive and complex analytics requires effective means to refresh its outcomes while keeping the re-computation costs under control. This is the goal of the ReComp meta-process [6]. To the best of our knowledge no prior work addresses this or a similar problem.

Previous research on the use of provenance in re-computation focused on the final steps of our meta-process: partial or differential re-execution. In [4] Bavoil et al. optimised re-execution of VisTrails dataflows. Similarly, Altintas et al. [2] proposed the "smart" rerun of workflows in Kepler. Both consider data dependencies between workflow tasks such that only the parts of the workflow affected by a change are rerun. Starflow [3] allowed the structure of a workflow and subworkflow downstream a change to be discovered using static, dynamic and user annotations. Ikeda et al. [10] proposed a solution to determine the fragment of a data-intensive program that needs rerun to refresh stale results. Also, Lakhani et al. [12] discussed rollback and re-execution of a process.

We note two key differences between the previous and our work. First, we consider re-computation in the view of a whole population of past executions; executions that may not even belong to the same data analysis. From the population, we select only those which are affected by a change, and for each we find the restart tree. Second, restart tree is a concise and effective way to represent the change in the context of a past, possibly complex hierarchical execution. The tree may be very effectively computed and also used to start partial rerun. And using the restart tree, partial re-execution does not need to rely on data cache that may involve high storage costs for data-intensive analyses [15].

Another use of provenance to track changes has been proposed in [8,11] and recently in [14]. They address the evolution of workflows/scripts, i.e. the changes in the process structure that affect the outcomes. Their work is complementary to our view, though. They use provenance to understand what has changed in the process e.g. to link the execution results together or decide which execution provides the best results. We, instead, observe changes in the environment and then react to them by finding the minimal set of executions that require refresh.

5   Discussion and Conclusions

In this paper we have presented a generic approach to use provenance annotations to inform a re-computation framework about the selection of past execution that require refresh upon a change in their data and software dependencies. We call this selection the re-computation front. We have presented an effective algorithm to compute the front, which relies on the information about changes and annotations of re-executions. The algorithm can handle composite hierarchical structure of processes and help maintain the most up-to-date version of the dependencies. Overall, it is a lightweight step leading to the identification of the scope of changes, i.e. computing difference and estimating the impact of the changes, and then to partial re-execution.

In line with [1], we note that a generic provenance capture facility which stores basic information about processes and data is often not enough to support the needs of applications. For our algorithm to work properly, we have to additionally annotate every re-execution with the `wasInformedBy` statement, so the past executions are not executed again multiple times. This indicates that the ProvONE model defines only a blueprint with minimal set of meta-information to be captured which needs to be extended within each application domain.

References

1. Alper, P., Belhajjame, K., Curcin, V., Goble, C.: LabelFlow framework for annotating workflow provenance. Informatics **5**(1), 11 (2018)
2. Altintas, I., Barney, O., Jaeger-Frank, E.: Provenance collection support in the Kepler scientific workflow system. In: Moreau, L., Foster, I. (eds.) IPAW 2006. LNCS, vol. 4145, pp. 118–132. Springer, Heidelberg (2006). https://doi.org/10.1007/11890850_14
3. Angelino, E., Yamins, D., Seltzer, M.: StarFlow: a script-centric data analysis environment. In: McGuinness, D.L., Michaelis, J.R., Moreau, L. (eds.) IPAW 2010. LNCS, vol. 6378, pp. 236–250. Springer, Heidelberg (2010). https://doi.org/10.1007/978-3-642-17819-1_27
4. Bavoil, L., et al.: VisTrails: enabling interactive multiple-view visualizations. In: VIS 05. IEEE Visualization, 2005, No. Dx, pp. 135–142. IEEE (2005)
5. Caƚa, J., Marei, E., Xu, Y., Takeda, K., Missier, P.: Scalable and efficient whole-exome data processing using workflows on the cloud. Future Gener. Comput. Syst. **65**, 153–168 (2016)
6. Caƚa, J., Missier, P.: Selective and recurring re-computation of Big Data analytics tasks: insights from a Genomics case study. Big Data Res. (2018). https://doi.org/10.1016/j.bdr.2018.06.001. ISSN 2214-5796
7. Cuevas-Vicenttín, V., et al.: ProvONE: A PROV Extension Data Model for Scientific Workflow Provenance (2016)
8. Freire, J., Silva, C.T., Callahan, S.P., Santos, E., Scheidegger, C.E., Vo, H.T.: Managing rapidly-evolving scientific workflows. In: Proceedings of the 2006 International Conference on Provenance and Annotation of Data, pp. 10–18 (2006)
9. Herschel, M., Diestelkämper, R., Ben Lahmar, H.: A survey on provenance: what for? what form? what from? VLDB J. **26**(6), 1–26 (2017)
10. Ikeda, R., Das Sarma, A., Widom, J.: Logical provenance in data-oriented workflows. In: 2013 IEEE 29th International Conference on Data Engineering (ICDE), pp. 877–888. IEEE (2013)
11. Koop, D., Scheidegger, C.E., Freire, J., Silva, C.T.: The provenance of workflow upgrades. In: McGuinness, D.L., Michaelis, J.R., Moreau, L. (eds.) IPAW 2010. LNCS, vol. 6378, pp. 2–16. Springer, Heidelberg (2010). https://doi.org/10.1007/978-3-642-17819-1_2
12. Lakhani, H., Tahir, R., Aqil, A., Zaffar, F., Tariq, D., Gehani, A.: Optimized rollback and re-computation. In: 2013 46th Hawaii International Conference on System Sciences, No. I, pp. 4930–4937. IEEE (Jan 2013)

13. Moreau, L., et al.: PROV-DM: the PROV data model. Technical report, World Wide Web Consortium (2012)
14. Pimentel, J.F., Murta, L., Braganholo, V., Freire, J.: noWorkflow: a tool for collecting, analyzing, and managing provenance from python scripts. Proc. VLDB Endow. **10**(12), 1841–1844 (2017)
15. Woodman, S., Hiden, H., Watson, P.: Applications of provenance in performance prediction and data storage optimisation. Future Gener. Comput. Syst. **75**, 299–309 (2017)

Provenance of Dynamic Adaptations in User-Steered Dataflows

Renan Souza[1,2(✉)] and Marta Mattoso[1]

[1] COPPE, Federal University of Rio de Janeiro, Rio de Janeiro, Brazil
renanfs@cos.ufrj.br
[2] IBM Research, Rio de Janeiro, Brazil

Abstract. Due to the exploratory nature of scientific experiments, computational scientists need to steer dataflows running on High-Performance Computing (HPC) machines by tuning parameters, modifying input datasets, or adapting dataflow elements at runtime. This happens in several application domains, such as in Oil and Gas where they adjust simulation parameters, or in Machine Learning where they tune models' hyperparameters during the training. This is also known as computational steering or putting the "human-in-the-loop" of HPC simulations. Such adaptations must be tracked and analyzed, especially during long executions. Tracking adaptations with provenance not only improves experiments' reproducibility and reliability, but also helps scientists to understand, online, the consequences of their adaptations. We propose PROV-DfA, a specialization of W3C PROV elements to model computational steering. We provide provenance data representation for online adaptations, associating them with the adapted domain dataflow and with execution data, all in the same provenance database. We explore a case study in the Oil and Gas domain to show how PROV-DfA supports scientists in questions like "who, when, and which dataflow elements were adapted and what happened to the dataflow and execution after the adaptation (*e.g.*, how much execution time or processed data was reduced)", in a real scenario.

Keywords: Computational steering · Human-in-the-loop
Dynamic workflow provenance

1 Introduction

It is known that certain actions are better performed by humans than by machines, especially when the actions require very specific domain or application knowledge [1]. Due to the exploratory nature of scientific experiments, this often happens in computational experiments modeled as scientific workflows, where computational scientists (the *users* in this work, who are specialists in application-specific systems, such as engineers, bioinformaticians, data scientists etc.) need to dynamically adapt online workflows while they are running on High-Performance Computing (HPC) machines, *i.e.*, without stopping, modifying, and resubmitting the execution [2].

The data dependencies between programs composing the scientific workflow form the dataflow. Many elements of the dataflow (*e.g.*, data elements, datasets, attribute

K. Belhajjame et al. (Eds.): IPAW 2018, LNCS 11017, pp. 16–29, 2018.
https://doi.org/10.1007/978-3-319-98379-0_2

values, data transformations) can be modified, online, by humans. This occurs in several application domains. For instance, in Oil and Gas HPC simulations where users need to fine tune parameters of a solver [3]; in Machine Learning model training, where data scientists use their knowledge on the data and on the methods to determine better ranges of values for hyperparameters, after analyzing their impact on the performance (*e.g.*, accuracy); or in Uncertainty Quantification iterative simulations where users control loop stop conditions [4]. Online data analysis and online adaptation steered by humans comprise "computational steering", often referred to as "human-in-the-loop" of HPC applications [2]. In that context, each adaptation occurred for a reason (best known by the user), in a certain time, influenced elements of the dataflow, and had effects in the running workflow, like data or execution time reduction [5]. Therefore, adaptations generate major improvement on performance, resource consumption, and quality of results [6], and thence need to be tracked.

Not tracking such adaptations has impactful disadvantages. It may compromise experiment reproducibility as users hardly remember what and how dataflow elements were modified (especially modifications in early stages), and what happened to the execution because of a specific adaptation. This is more critical when users adapt several times in long experiments, which may last for weeks. In addition to losing track of changes, one misses opportunities to learn from the *user steering data* (*i.e.*, data generated when humans adapt a certain dataflow element) with the associated dataflow. For example, by registering user steering data, one may query the data and discover that when input parameters are changed to certain range of values, the output result improves by a defined amount. Moreover, opportunities to use the data for AI-based recommendations on what to adapt next, based on a database of adaptations, are lost.

Although data provenance in HPC workflows has improved significantly over the past years, adding online data analyses integrating domain and execution data [7] to reproducibility [8], provenance of computational steering in HPC workflows remains an open challenge [6]. Provenance data management and computational steering in HPC are still worlds apart, despite the increasingly need for joint contribution. Indeed, in two recent surveys [6, 9], the authors highlight online provenance capture and human-in-the-loop of HPC simulations as research and development needed. We believe that a provenance representation able to model dynamic interactions in a computational steering system will facilitate data representation, understanding, and standardization among systems. To the best of our knowledge, such model does not exist yet.

In this work, we propose PROV-DfA, a data provenance representation for modeling online human adaptations in HPC workflows, built on W3C PROV standards. It allows for explicit representation of the dataflow and provenance of user-steered dataflow adaptations. PROV-DfA can be implemented in provenance databases of Parallel Scientific Workflow Management Systems (WMS) [2], or computational steering frameworks [10], or standalone HPC applications that allow for user-steered online adaptation. It can represent typical adaptations in HPC applications, while integrating with data for provenance, execution, and domain dataflow, all in a same data representation. We specialize PROV-DfA for provenance parameter tuning, loop control of iterative simulations, and data reduction. To validate our approach, we explore a case study in an Oil and Gas HPC workflow, where the user adapted online elements of the dataflow. We show how those adaptations can be represented using PROV-DfA to answer "who", "what", "when", and "how" queries in a relational provenance database to show, for example, the impact on the results after specific dataflow adaptations.

Paper Organization. Related work is presented in Sect. 2 and background in Sect. 3. PROV-DfA is presented in Sect. 4 and in Sect. 5 we specialize it for provenance of three dataflow adaptations. Section 6 shows the case study. Section 7 concludes.

2   Related Work

As mentioned in introduction, recent surveys [6, 9] bring up challenges of runtime provenance and human-in-the-loop of HPC workflows. Also, Atkinson *et al.* [11] discuss the future of scientific workflows, and they mention that *"monitoring and logging will be enhanced with more interactive components for intermediate stages of active workflows."* As a result, we found no related work for provenance representation of human-in-the-loop of HPC workflows. Thus, we analyze computational steering works that could highly benefit from provenance representation of human adaptation in dataflows.

Long lasting scientific applications require user steering [2, 10]. BSIT [12] is a platform tailored for seismic applications that supports adaptations in parameters, programs, datasets. Few parallel WMSs support human adaptation [13–15], but no provenance of adaptation. Chiron WMS [4, 5] enables users to change filter values, adapt loop conditions of iterative workflows, and reduce input datasets. These works show that online adaptations significantly reduce overall execution time, since users can identify a satisfactory result before the programmed number of iterations.

WorkWays [16] is a science gateway that enables users to dynamically adapt the workflow by reducing the range of parameters. It uses Nimrod/K as its underlying parallel workflow engine, which is an extension of the Kepler workflow system [17]. It presents tools for interaction, such as graphic interfaces, data visualization, and inter-operability among others. WINGS [18] is a WMS concerned with workflow composition and its semantics. It focuses on assisting users in automatic data discovery. It helps to generate and to execute multiple combinations of workflows based on user constraints, selecting appropriate input data, and eliminating workflows that are not viable.

Stamatogiannakis *et al.* [19] propose a provenance-based representation and analysis for unstructured processes, including representation of user interactions. However, their target applications are unstructured processes like editing in a content management system, which differ from our target HPC workflows applications, which are considered structured processes.

Bourhis *et al.* [20] propose a provenance-based solution for data-centric applications supporting queries like *"why such result was generated?"*, *"what would be the result if an application logic is modified?"*, and *"how can a user interact with the application to achieve a goal?"*, in the context of users interacting with the application in a "what-if" manner. However, no online user-steered dataflow adaptation in HPC workflows is tackled. Finally, we envision that AI-based systems recommending on what to adapt next [21], could highly benefit from a provenance database containing human user steering data to improve their models.

3 Workflows, Computational Steering and Data Provenance

3.1 Dataflow-Oriented Approach and Runtime Provenance

HPC computational experiments are often modeled as scientific workflows. While workflows are related to the execution flow control between chained activities (*e.g.*, scientific programs, processes, scripts, functions or parts of programs) [9], in dataflows datasets are transformed by the chaining of data transformations [22]. A workflow W has an associated *dataflow D*, which has a composition of n *data transformations* (DT), so that $D = \{DT_1, \ldots, DT_n\}$. Each DT_y, $1 \le y \le n$, is executed by a workflow activity, and consumes or produces *datasets*. Datasets are further specialized into *Input Datasets* (I_{DS}) and *Output Datasets* (O_{DS}). Each DT_y consumes one or more I_{DS} and produces one or more O_{DS}. Let $I_y = I_{DS1} \cup \ldots \cup I_{DSu}$ be a set containing all I_{DS} consumed by the DT_y and $O_y = O_{DS} \cup \ldots \cup I_{DSv}$ be a set containing all O_{DS} produced by the DT_y. Then, we have adapted from [22, 23]:

$$O_y \leftarrow DT_y(I_y), \text{ for all } DT_y \text{ of the dataflow } D.$$

Moreover, datasets are composed of data elements. Data elements in a given dataset DS have a data schema $\Sigma(DS) = \{attribute_1, \ldots, attribute_u\}$. The schema can be further specified as: $\Sigma(I_{DS}) = \{F_I, V_I, P_I, L_I\}$ and $\Sigma(O_{DS}) = \{F_o, V_o, C_o, L_O\}$, where:

- F_I and F_O contain attributes that represent pointers to input and output files, respectively. These files are often large raw (textual, imagery, matrices, binary data, etc.) scientific datasets in a wide variety of formats depending on the scientific domain (*e.g.*, FITS for astronomy, SEG-Y for seismic, NetCDF for fluid simulations).
- V_I and V_O contain attributes for extracted data or metadata from input and output files, respectively. In case of output data, some applications write calculated values, like the main results of a data transformation into files and they often need to be tracked. V_O represents these special resulting extracted data, which are often scalars, useful for domain data analyses [7, 22, 24]. V_I and V_O can be seen as a view over the actual large raw datasets, as users can have a big picture of the content of the large datasets through them.
- P_I contains attributes for general purpose input parameter values of the data transformation. For example, numerical solver parameters, thresholds, and any other parameter that can be adjusted.
- L_I contain attributes used in the data transformation in case it evaluates a loop [4]. Several applications modeled as scientific workflows have an iterative workflow execution model. Examples include uncertainty quantification and solvers from the Oil and Gas industry [4, 9]. In such workflows, typically there are loops like "*while*

$e >$ *threshold"* or *"while i < max"*. While P_I are for general purpose parameters, L_I contains parameters that are used for loop-stop conditions (*e.g.*, *"max"*, *"threshold"*).

- L_O contain output values related to an iteration in case of data transformations that evaluate a loop. In that case, each iteration may be modeled as a loop evaluation execution and produces an attribute value that has the current iteration counter.
- C_O contain attributes for any output values that are explicit data transformation results. For example, besides large scientific data files produced by data transformations, they may produce output quantities, often scalar values or simple arrays that are very meaningful for the result. Since they may be of high interest for the user, these values are typical provenance data that need to be registered.

A schema of a dataset *DS* may not have all these attributes, *i.e.*, they are optional. For example, if a data transformation consuming a dataset *DS* does not evaluate a loop, $\Sigma (DS)$ does not contain L_I or L_O.

Several real HPC workflows have been modeled and specified as previously described, allowing for enhanced provenance data representation [5, 7, 22, 24]. Thus, in addition to well-known advantages of collecting provenance in HPC workflows, such as for experiments' reproducibility and results' reliability [8], runtime provenance augments online data analytical potential and is especially useful for long-running workflows [2, 4, 5]. In addition to data analyses via *ad-hoc* analytical queries, visualization tools (*e.g.*, ParaView Catalyst) may be coupled to applications querying the database for a graphic view of the execution [24]. Based on online data analyses, the user may dynamically adapt dataflow elements, such as parameters, input data etc. [5]. This is known as computational steering or "human-in-the-loop" of HPC applications.

3.2   A Diagram for Runtime Provenance in HPC Workflows

In a previous work [25], we presented PROV-Wf, which is a PROV-DM [26] specialization. PROV-Wf models workflow provenance, domain-specific, and execution data, all in a same representation. ProvONE [27] has been compared to PROV-Wf in a previous work [28]. It has been implemented in provenance databases of existing WMSs, in real-world workflows [4, 5, 22].

More recently, we extended PROV-Wf into PROV-Df to explicitly represent the dataflow of a workflow [22]. Even without a WMS, runtime provenance can be extracted and integrated to domain data by instrumenting an application. Collecting provenance in standalone HPC applications without a WMS is desired, as there are applications that already employ highly efficient parallel libraries and the WMS scheduling conflicts with the HPC application execution control [24]. A diagram of PROV-Df extended, in this work, for registering human actions, is presented next (Sect. 2).

In this paper, we use "prov:" namespace to indicate PROV classes or relationships. Each ExecuteDataTransformation consumes (prov:used) and produces (prov:wasGeneratedBy) AttributeValues. These values may have been extracted by an ExecuteExtractor [7]. Data elements compose the dataset (Dataset). For prospective provenance, the dataset has an associated

DatasetSchema, which is composed of Attribute. Attributes describe the AttributeValues generated during execution. They have a data type (integer, text etc.) and may have extra fields in the Attribute class to allow for attribute specification (*i.e.*, determine if the attribute is in $\{F_I, F_O, V_I, V_O, P_I, L_I, L_O, C_O\}$). Such specifications enrich domain data analyses and allow for identifying attributes that can be adapted. Data about execution, such as duration and performance data (CPU, memory), linkage to subsequent and previous executions, and their related prospective provenance can be stored relating to instances of ExecuteDataTransformation.

We put this provenance representation into practice in a Bioinformatics HPC workflow to answer "what", "when", and "how" questions, useful for the bioinformatician [7]. She could query output domain data extracted from produced raw datasets, and relate domain data to performance data. However, despite the effort for data provenance in HPC workflows, there is no provenance representation for user steering data.

4 Provenance of Dynamic Adaptation in User-Steered Dataflows

During the execution of an HPC workflow, users analyze elements of a dataflow to steer the execution. In this work, we introduce PROV-DfA by specializing provenance data model classes to represent these dynamic adaptations. Instead of creating a completely new provenance model, we first begin by consolidating a base model using several past contributions to PROV-Wf and PROV-Df [5, 7, 22, 25] to build into PROV-DfA). PROV-DfA adds provenance of online dataflow adaptations to these previous PROV-extended models.

PROV-DfA introduces the classes SteeringAction, Analysis, Adaptation, and Adapter; and the relationship WasSteeredBy. We use a UML class diagram, where the <<stereotypes>> in classes specify PROV super-classes (mainly Agents, Entities, and Activities) and between classes specify relationships. Classes in white background represent prospective provenance, whereas in gray represent retrospective provenance. prov:Entity in yellow means that classes in PROV-DfA that are subclasses of prov:Entity (prospective or retrospective) can be used in place, as we explain next (Fig. 1).

Adaptation is a steering action performed by a human that causes a change in the flowing data elements in the dataflow. In PROV-DfA, it is represented by Adaptation, a subclass of SteeringAction, subclass of prov:Activity. An adaptation was steered by (wasSteeredBy) a prov:Person, occurred at a specified time (prov:startedAtTime), had an adaptation characteristic (adaptationCharacteristic) that can be "update" or "insert/delete". Users may add a plain description to the adaptation, to describe what was going on in the experiment when they decided to perform a specific change. Also, as inherited by SteeringAction, an Adaptation may have been informed by a previous Adaptation, hence the auto-relationship prov:wasInformedBy. This is the case, for example, of a rollback adaptation, requested by a user, that happened right after the user modified parameters in a simulation, which is another adaptation.

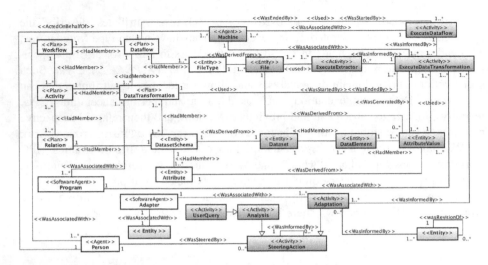

Fig. 1. PROV-DfA overview. A larger visualization is on GitHub [29].

Since adaptations in the dataflow occur while the workflow is executing, it is important to keep track of the execution state. The most representative PROV-DfA activity that represents the execution state is `ExecuteDataTransformation`. When an adaption occurs, these instances carry information about time, pointers to domain data values being consumed or produced, computational resources being consumed, etc. Thus, being able to track which specific data transformation was running at the moment of the adaptation may be very useful for extended analyses that integrates adaptation with provenance, domain, and execution data. For this, we relate which `ExecuteDataTransformation` instances were influenced (`prov:wasInformedBy`) by adaptations. How adaptations relate to `ExecuteDataTransformation`, as well as how `prov:Entities` are affected depend on characteristic of the online adaptation, as explained next.

Adapter is a software component that knows how to adapt the elements of the dataflow in a running workflow, making it a subclass of `prov:SoftwareAgent`. In any case, PROV-DfA is just responsible for registering the actions of an Adapter software. Thus, when the user decides to adapt an element of the dataflow, the Adapter is responsible for modifying the requested element. Any information that describes the Adapter software (*e.g.*, which element of the dataflow it adapts, where the program can be located, how it can be invoked etc.) may be stored relating to the `Adapter` class. `Adapter` relates to classes that are subclasses of `prov:Entity` and to the adaptation itself (via `prov:wasAssociatedWith`).

Characteristics of Online Adaptation. Adaptations may have a characteristic of either update (we say *U-adaptation*) or insert/delete (*I/D-adaptation*).

- *U-adaptations* are updates where the user adjusts, tunes, or modifies one or more dataflow elements. Examples are parameter tuning, loop control adaptations, etc. In PROV-DfA, when the user performs a U-adaptation, a new instance of `Adaptation` is created. Also, a new instance of one of the `prov:Entity` subclasses in PROV-Df is created (*e.g.*, `AttributeValue`, `DataTransformation` etc.) containing the new data, which will replace the old data in the dataflow. The newly created entity is related (`prov:wasInformedBy`) to the adaptation. Moreover, the newly created data is related to the old one via `prov:wasRevisionOf`, so that the track between the new and old data is maintained. Additionally, to relate the adaptation with execution state, PROV-DfA relates (`prov:wasInformedBy`) the `ExecuteDataTransformation` instances that were in *"running"* state at the moment of the adaptation. Finally, `Adapter` is related to the prospective entity (*e.g.*, `Attribute`, `DataTransformation`) that specifies the entity adapted.

- *I/D-adaptations* are steering actions that cause addition or deletion of data elements in the dataflow. Examples are data reduction or extension, data transformation or attribute addition or deletion etc. A new instance of `Adaptation` is created and there is a relationship (`prov:wasInformedBy`) between the `Adaptation` and the added or deleted instances of a `prov:Entity` subclass. In case of deletions, the entity is not physically deleted from the provenance database, for the sake of provenance. Rather, it is assumed that when an `Adaptation` is a deletion, the deleted instance is logically deleted from the dataflow. This enables tracking entities deleted online. Since adding or deleting elements affects the execution, the instances of `ExecuteDataTransformation` directly affected to the added or deleted elements of the dataflow are related (`prov:wasInformedBy`) to the `Adaptation` instance. For example, in a data reduction [5], data transformations that were supposed to execute were not executed because of a dynamic adaptation. These instances of `DataTransformationExecution` not executed are related to the adaptation. Finally, `Adapter` and `Adaptation` are related like in U-adaptations.

Furthermore, to use PROV-DfA in a real use case, it is expected that the user will work in collaboration with a data specialist, especially in PROV concepts. Together they specialize the diagram for the domain and application in use, and add provenance capture calls to the simulation via code instrumentation. Users analyze the data via provenance queries together with domain, execution, and user steering data.

In summary, in PROV-DfA, an `Adaptation` is a `prov:Activity` steered by a `prov:Person`, which influenced instances of classes that are subclasses of `prov:Entity`, and influenced instances of `ExecuteDataTransformation`. The `Adapter` program relates to the prospective entity being adapted and to the adaptation.

5   Specializing PROV-DfA Concepts

In this section, we specialize PROV-DfA concepts to represent online parameter tuning, changes in loop control, and data reduction as PROV-DfA's U and I/D-adaptations. We assume that there is a computational steering framework, such as the ones surveyed by Bauer *et al.* [10], or an underlying WMS engine, such as the ones surveyed by Mattoso *et al.* [2], or a standalone program adaptable online, as we show in a previous work [3].

5.1 Simulation Parameter Tuning

Parameter tuning refers to the action of steering parameters of a data transformation in a dataflow, like numerical solver parameters or machine learning model hyperparameters. In PROV-DfA, ParameterTuning is a specialization of Adaptation. Parameter tunings are adaptations in attribute values (AttributeValue) that are related to data elements (DataElement) related to I_{DS} (Dataset) of a certain data transformation (DataTransformation). The attribute value modified must have been derived from (prov:wasDerivedFrom) an Attribute whose attribute specification is P_I.

It is a U-adaptation. As such, a new instance of ParameterTuning is created and related to the new instance of its adapted entity, *i.e.*, AttributeValue, with the new value for the parameter. The new value is related to the old one via prov:wasRevisionOf. ExecuteDataTransformation instances running at the moment of the adaptation are related to the Adaptation instance. Finally, since users tune parameters of data transformations, the Adapter relates to the DataTransformation associated to DatasetSchema that had the Attribute modified.

5.2 Online Adaptation of Iterative Simulations

Workflows with an iterative workflow execution model have data transformations that evaluate loops. Using the dataflow-oriented approach concepts (Sect. 3.1), values for these loop-stop conditions may be modeled as an attribute in L_I of a data transformation that evaluates a loop and the iteration counter can be modeled as an attribute in L_O of the data transformation. Moreover, each iteration generates an instance in ExecuteDataTransformation for the loop evaluation. During execution of each iteration, a relationship between the output of this data transformation, containing the current iteration value, and the ExecuteDataTransformation instance is particularly useful for such workflows, as it identifies a specific part of the workflow execution, and often users can analyze results as the workflow iterates. Such control information is important for the adaptation, as users can associate their specific actions with execution data, such as which point in workflow elapsed time that action happened or what memory/CPU consumption were. In complex iterative simulation, capturing data at each iteration may be managed *in transit* by an efficient database management solution. In a recent work [24], we show an efficient database implementation using an analytics-optimized DBMS and asynchronous provenance capture, including extractions from large domain raw data files (like metadata V_I and V_O), and related to provenance data in a real iterative HPC simulation. The overall overheads accounted for less than 1% of simulation time and added data, which is considered negligible.

Therefore, in PROV-DfA, it is represented as LoopAdaptation, a subclass of Adaptation. Similarly to ParameterTuning, its instance is related to the new instance of AtributeValue, containing the new value for the loop control condition, relating (prov:wasRevisionOf) to the old one. The adapted instance of AttributeValue must be derived from an Attribute whose attribute specification is L_I. Additionally, the generated ExecuteDataTransformation instance related to the output of the last iteration (*i.e.*, last execution of the data transformation for loop evaluation) is related to the `LoopAdaptation` instance. Finally, the adapter must be able to dynamically modify the data transformation that represents the loop evaluation. That is, `Adapter` in this case relates to `DataTransformation`.

5.3   Data Reduction

Online user-steered data reduction are very useful for reducing execution time and amount of data to be processed during a simulation [5]. `DataReduction` is a subclass of `Adaptation`. In the dataflow-oriented approach, the datasets stored as large raw data files to be processed by a data transformation are represented by attributes composing data elements in an I_{DS}. Data files are represented as pointers in F_I, whereas V_I contain extracted domain values from those files specified in F_I. An approach to reduce data is to specify a criteria based on V_I values to eliminate files in F_I to be processed, enabling the adapter program to logically delete data elements in the I_{DS}. This makes the HPC application not to execute the data transformations for the removed elements [5].

Analogously, in PROV-DfA, reducing data means logically removing instances of `DataElement` (and consequently `AttributeValues`) of a Dataset (I_{DS}). This can be the result of an I/D adaptation. Thus, there is a relationship (`prov:wasInformedBy`) between the removed instances of `DataElement` and `AttributeValue` and the adaptation. The `ExecuteDataTransformation` instances that would use (`prov:used`) the removed `AttributeValue` instances are related to the `DataReduction` instance. Additionally, the criteria to remove data elements [5] is stored within the adaptation instance. Finally, as users remove data elements in I_{DS}, the adapter is related to the `DataTransformation` associated to the `Dataset` that had the `DataElement and AttributeValues` removed.

6   Case Study

In this section, we present PROV-DfA being used in a real case study in the Oil and Gas domain. In a previous work [24], we applied the domain dataflow-oriented approach (Sect. 3.1) in an HPC turbidity currents simulation, modeled as an iterative scientific workflow. Parts of the simulation code were identified as workflow activities, modeled as data transformations chained in a dataflow. Data and metadata extractors were developed, and the simulation source code was instrumented to call these domain values extractors, together with provenance data collectors, to populate the datasets in a provenance database at runtime. In Fig. 2, we show large raw input files (with mesh data) stored on disk, with pointers in the solver I_{DS}. The solver I_{DS} has over 70 parameters (*i.e.*, P_I attributes), among which only 2 are displayed in the figure (flow linear and non-linear tolerance). All these solver parameters are extracted from a configurations file, which is read at each iteration. Yet, the maximum number of iterations (t_max) is a L_I attribute of the data transformation solver. Some metadata (V_I) are extracted from input raw files at runtime to facilitate tracking their contents while they are processed. Elements of O_{DS} of each data transformation are also

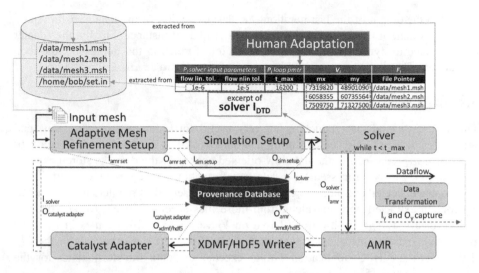

Fig. 2. Dataflow in the turbidity currents simulation [24].

collected (via raw data extractors and source code instrumentation) and stored in the database. For example, the solver O_{DS} contains calculated values, such as linear and non-linear results, as well as the current time iteration value. Moreover, the simulation was coupled to data analysis tools for *in-situ* data analysis while the workflow runs [24]. The entire simulation using 3D real data lasts for weeks, making online data analysis a requirement.

In addition to online data analyses, adapters were developed to enable online adaptation of the dataflow. Even though the user could adapt the running dataflow, the adaptations were not being tracked. There were several adaptations during the simulation, and the user lost their track, jeopardizing the experiment's reproducibility and results reliability, and missing opportunities to learn from the adaptations.

We developed a first prototype to instrument the source code of the simulation adapters to collect provenance of adaptation and store in a relational database [3]. However, we developed an *ad-hoc* provenance data model to represent a specific type of adaptation, *i.e.*, tuning some simulation parameters. In this section, we explore this case study to show parameter tuning and data reduction using PROV-DfA.

In Fig. 3, we present a visualization of an excerpt of the data in a provenance database implementing PROV-DfA. It shows a user tuning the *flow linear tolerance* parameter from `1e-5` to `1e-3` and a data reduction with criteria "`mx < 7e6`".

Using data in a relational provenance database implementing PROV-DfA, users can run the following queries (their SQL codes are on GitHub [29]).

Inspecting Parameter Tunings (*"who"*, *"when"*, *"what"*). *How many tunings did I do? Which parameters did I change? What were the values when I changed and what values did I change into? When did each adaptation happen?*

Understanding Consequences of a Tuning (*"how"*). *In parameter tuning 3, how was the main solver output values 10 iterations before and after?*

Data Reduction ("*how*", "*which*"). *On average, how long iterations were lasting before and after I reduced input files from the input data? Which files were affected?*

These queries show the potential of PROV-DfA for provenance databases keeping track of online dataflow adaptations in computational steering HPC workflows.

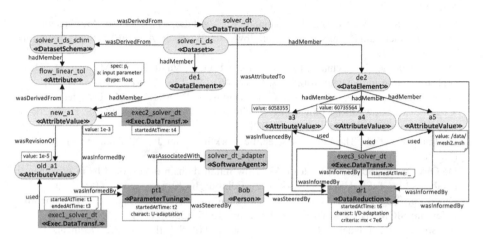

Fig. 3. Visualization of data using PROV-DfA.

7   Conclusion

In this work, we presented PROV-DfA, an extension of W3C PROV for provenance of dynamic adaptations in user-steered dataflows. Recent surveys [6, 9] call for research and development in human-in-the-loop of HPC workflows and dynamic data provenance. We believe PROV-DfA is an important step towards modeling provenance of dynamic adaptations in computational steering. To the best of our knowledge, no such model exists yet. Different dynamic dataflow adaptations may be modeled as PROV DfA's U- or I/D-adaptations. We showed it being used for modeling the track of parameter tuning, loop control of iterative simulations, and data reduction steered by users. We queried a provenance database implementing it to answer "who", "what", "when", "how" queries. In the context of computational steering and provenance, our approach contributes for reproducibility, results' reliability, online results understanding as consequences of adaptations, and adds a potential for users or AI-based systems to learn from dynamic interaction data. For future work, we plan to explore PROV-DfA to model the track of other dynamic adaptations and extend it with online data analyses steered by users. We plan to integrate it to ProvONE [27] as well. We expect it can be adopted by WMSs, computational steering frameworks, or standalone HPC applications with steering capabilities that need to keep track of human interactions.

Acknowledgement. This work was partially funded by CNPq, FAPERJ and HPC4E (EU H2020 and MCTI/RNP-Brazil).

References

1. Jagadish, H.V., et al.: Big data and its technical challenges. Commun. ACM **57**, 86–94 (2014)
2. Mattoso, M., et al.: Dynamic steering of HPC scientific workflows: a survey. FGCS **46**, 100–113 (2015)
3. Souza, R., Silva, V., Camata, J., Coutinho, A., Valduriez, P., Mattoso, M.: Tracking of online parameter tuning in scientific workflows. In: Works in ACM/IEEE Supercomputing Workshops (2017)
4. Dias, J., Guerra, G., Rochinha, F., Coutinho, A.L.G.A., Valduriez, P., Mattoso, M.: Data-centric iteration in dynamic workflows. FGCS **46**, 114–126 (2015)
5. Souza, R., Silva, V., Coutinho, A.L.G.A., Valduriez, P., Mattoso, M.: Data reduction in scientific workflows using provenance monitoring and user steering. FGCS 1–34 (2017). https://doi.org/10.1016/j.future.2017.11.028
6. Deelman, E., et al.: The future of scientific workflows. Int J HPC Appl. **32**(1), 159–175 (2018)
7. De Oliveira, D., Silva, V., Mattoso, M.: How much domain data should be in provenance databases? In: TaPP. USENIX Association, Edinburgh (2015)
8. Davidson, S.B., Freire, J.: Provenance and scientific workflows: challenges and opportunities. In: SIGMOD, New York, NY, USA, pp. 1345–1350 (2008)
9. da Silva, R.F., Filgueira, R., Pietri, I., Jiang, M., Sakellariou, R., Deelman, E.: A characterization of workflow management systems for extreme-scale applications. FGCS **75**, 228–238 (2017)
10. Bauer, A.C., Abbasi, H., Ahrens, J., Childs, H., Geveci, B., Klasky, S., et al.: In situ methods, infrastructures, and applications on high performance computing platforms. Comput. Graph. Forum Banner **35**, 577–597 (2016)
11. Atkinson, M., Gesing, S., Montagnat, J., Taylor, I.: Scientific workflows: past, present and future. FGCS **75**, 216–227 (2017)
12. Hanzich, M., Rodriguez, J., Gutierrez, N., de la Puente, J., Cela, J.: Using HPC software frameworks for developing BSIT: a geophysical imaging tool. In: Proceedings of WCCM ECCM ECFD, vol. 3, pp. 2019–2030 (2014)
13. Lee, K., Paton, N.W., Sakellariou, R., Fernandes, A.A.A.: Utility functions for adaptively executing concurrent workflows. CCPE **23**, 646–666 (2011)
14. Pouya, I., Pronk, S., Lundborg, M., Lindahl, E.: Copernicus, a hybrid dataflow and peer-to-peer scientific computing platform for efficient large-scale ensemble sampling. FGCS **71**, 18–31 (2017)
15. Jain, A., Ong, S.P., Chen, W., Medasani, B., Qu, X., Kocher, M., et al.: FireWorks: a dynamic workflow system designed for high-throughput applications. CCPE **27**, 5037–5059 (2015)
16. Nguyen, H.A., Abramson, D., Kipouros, T., Janke, A., Galloway, G.: WorkWays: interacting with scientific workflows. CCPE **27**, 4377–4397 (2015)
17. Abramson, D., Enticott, C., Altinas, I.: Nimrod/K: towards massively parallel dynamic grid workflows. In: Supercomputing, pp. 24:1–24:11. IEEE Press, Piscataway (2008)
18. Gil, Y., et al.: Wings: intelligent workflow-based design of computational experiments. IEEE Intell. Syst. **26**, 62–72 (2011)
19. Stamatogiannakis, M., Athanasopoulos, E., Bos, H., Groth, P.: PROV 2R: practical provenance analysis of unstructured processes. ACM Trans. Internet Technol. **17**, 37:1–37:24 (2017)

20. Bourhis, P., Deutch, D., Moskovitch, Y.: Analyzing data-centric applications: why, what-if, and how-to. In: ICDE, pp. 779–790 (2016)
21. Silva, B., Netto, M.A.S., Cunha, R.L.F.: JobPruner: a machine learning assistant for exploring parameter spaces in HPC applications. FGCS **83**, 144–157 (2018)
22. Silva, V., et al.: Raw data queries during data-intensive parallel workflow execution. FGCS **75**, 402–422 (2017)
23. Ikeda, R., Sarma, A.D., Widom, J.: Logical provenance in data-oriented workflows? In: ICDE, pp. 877–888 (2013)
24. Camata, J.J., Silva, V., Valduriez, P., Mattoso, M., Coutinho, A.L.G.A.: In situ visualization and data analysis for turbidity currents simulation. Comput. Geosci. **110**, 23–31 (2018)
25. Costa, F., Silva, V., de Oliveira, D., Ocaña, K., et al.: Capturing and querying workflow runtime provenance with PROV: a practical approach. In: EDBT/ICDT Workshops, pp. 282–289 (2013)
26. Moreau, L., Missier, P.: PROV-DM: The PROV Data Model. https://www.w3.org/TR/prov-dm/
27. ProvONE provenance model for scientific workflow. http://vcvcomputing.com/provone/provone.html
28. Oliveira, W., Missier, P., Oliveira, D., Braganholo, V.: Comparing provenance data models for scientific workflows: an analysis of PROV-Wf and ProvOne. In: Brazilian e-Science Workshop (2016)
29. PROV-DfA: PROV-DfA GitHub Repository. https://github.com/hpcdb/PROV-DfA

Classification of Provenance Triples for Scientific Reproducibility: A Comparative Evaluation of Deep Learning Models in the ProvCaRe Project

Joshua Valdez[1], Matthew Kim[2], Michael Rueschman[2],
Susan Redline[2], and Satya S. Sahoo[1(✉)]

[1] Department of Population and Quantitative Health Sciences,
School of Medicine, Case Western Reserve University,
Cleveland, OH 44106, USA
satya.sahoo@case.edu
[2] Department of Medicine, Brigham and Women's Hospital,
Beth Israel Deaconess Medical Center and Harvard Medical School,
Boston, MA, USA

Abstract. Scientific reproducibility is key to the advancement of science as researchers can build on sound and validated results to design new research studies. However, recent studies in biomedical research have highlighted key challenges in scientific reproducibility as more than 70% of researchers in a survey of more than 1500 participants were not able to reproduce results from other groups and 50% of researchers were not able to reproduce their own experiments. Provenance metadata is a key component of scientific reproducibility and as part of the Provenance for Clinical and Health Research (ProvCaRe) project, we have: (1) identified and modeled important provenance terms associated with a biomedical research study in the S3 model (formalized in the ProvCaRe ontology); (2) developed a new natural language processing (NLP) workflow to identify and extract provenance metadata from published articles describing biomedical research studies; and (3) developed the ProvCaRe knowledge repository to enable users to query and explore provenance of research studies using the S3 model. However, a key challenge in this project is the automated classification of provenance metadata extracted by the NLP workflow according to the S3 model and its subsequent querying in the Prov-CaRe knowledge repository. In this paper, we describe the development and comparative evaluation of deep learning techniques for multi-class classification of structured provenance metadata extracted from biomedical literature using 12 different categories of provenance terms represented in the S3 model. We describe the application of the Long Term Short Memory (LSTM) network, which has the highest classification accuracy of 86% in our evaluation, to classify more than 48 million provenance triples in the ProvCaRe knowledge repository (available at: https://provcare.case.edu/).

Keywords: Scientific reproducibility · Semantic provenance
Provenance for Clinical and Health Research · Provenance triple classification
Deep learning

© Springer Nature Switzerland AG 2018
K. Belhajjame et al. (Eds.): IPAW 2018, LNCS 11017, pp. 30–41, 2018.
https://doi.org/10.1007/978-3-319-98379-0_3

1 Introduction

Reproducibility is a key component of advancing scientific research that enables validation of both research protocols and study data [1, 2]. However, there is growing concern in the biomedical research domain regarding the lack of reproducible results due to missing information or lack of appropriate contextual metadata describing various aspects of a research study. For example, research study results published in peer-reviewed articles often lack details regarding the statistical models used to analyze data and the parameters used to select or discard study data for further analysis, which often leads to selection bias [2]. The lack of reproducibility has significant impact on the quality as well as integrity of published scientific results, potential misallocation of limited funding resources, and concern for patient safety during clinical trials [3]. A number of initiatives in the biomedical domain have focused on supporting scientific reproducibility, including the US National Institutes of Health (NIH) "Rigor and Reproducibility Guidelines" [4], and the Consolidated Standards of Reporting Trials (CONSORT) guidelines [5]. Provenance metadata representing essential contextual information about research studies is central to achieving the goals of the community-initiated guidelines and ensure scientific reproducibility [6].

The Provenance for Clinical and Health Research (ProvCaRe) project is developing a provenance-enabled framework to identify, characterize, and evaluate provenance metadata terms in support of scientific reproducibility [7]. The ProvCaRe project has developed: (1) the S3 model for representing multiple aspects of a research study by extending the W3C PROV Data Model (PROV-DM) [8]; (2) a provenance-focused Natural Language Processing (NLP) workflow for extracting structured provenance metadata from unstructured full-text articles from the National Center for Biotechnology Information (NCBI) PubMed [9]; and (3) the ProvCaRe knowledge repository consisting of 48.6 million provenance "triples" extracted from more than 435,000 full-text articles [7]. The ProvCaRe S3 model consists of three core concepts of:

(a) **Study Method** describing the research study protocols used for data collection, inclusion-exclusion criteria among other provenance information
(b) **Study Data** describing the categorical and continuous variables used in the research study dataset, including valid data range
(c) **Study Tool** describing the hardware and software tools used for recording and analyzing research study data

Detailed provenance metadata associated with a research study, for example study design, statistical data analysis techniques, among other terms are modeled as sub-categories of these three core concepts. The S3 model has been formalized in the ProvCaRe ontology that extends the W3C PROV Ontology (PROV-O) [10] with classes and properties representing various metadata information of research studies [7]. The ProvCaRe NLP workflow uses the S3 model to identify and extract provenance metadata associated with a research study described in a full-text published article. The extracted provenance information is transformed into a triple structure similar to the W3C Resource Description Framework (RDF) model [11] with mappings to the ProvCaRe ontology terms, for example *electroencephalogram* → *wasRecordedUsing* → *scalp electrodes*. These semantic provenance triples are aggregated to create provenance graphs, which can be analyzed for characterizing the reproducibility of research studies, in the ProvCaRe knowledge repository (accessible at: https://provcare.case.edu/). The ProvCaRe knowledge repository features multiple functionalities to allow users to query and explore provenance information associated with research studies, including a hypothesis-driven search interface and a provenance-based ranking technique to rank query results. The ProvCaRe knowledgebase stores the provenance triples generated by the NLP workflow after categorizing each triple according to the S3 model concepts, which allows users to easily view provenance metadata relevant to a specific aspect of research study. For example, researchers often analyze detailed information regarding the design of the study in the context of the research hypothesis of the study, the appropriateness of the sample size of the study, and validity of the conclusions derived from the study.

Motivation and Contribution. Figure 1 shows a screenshot of provenance triples extracted from a research study exploring the association between sleep disordered breathing and hypertension, which are classified according to the S3 model. However, the classification of provenance triples according to the S3 model is a significant challenge due to multiple issues, including:

1. **Complexity** of provenance metadata information modeled in each triple requires significant effort for accurate classification;
2. **Large volume** of provenance triples generated from the ProvCaRe NLP workflow (e.g., 48 million triples generated from 435,000 papers) requires the use of automated classification techniques.

The classification task for these semantic provenance triples [12] is similar to the well-known task of sentence classification in the NLP domain [13]. In particular, deep learning techniques have been used in NLP applications for classification of word vectors learned from unstructured text and have generated high quality results.

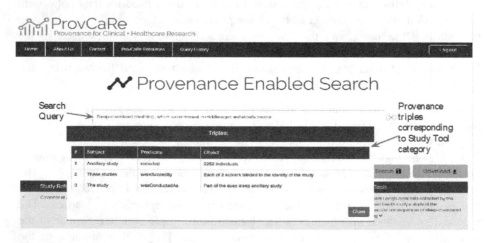

Fig. 1. A screenshot of the ProvCaRe knowledgebase interface with provenance triples corresponding to a user query

Therefore, we adapted deep learning architecture used for sentence classification to classify provenance triples in the ProvCaRe project. In this paper, we describe the extension of three deep learning techniques: (1) Convoluted Neural Network (CNN); (2) Recurrent Neural Network (RNN); and (3) a combined CNN/RNN-based approach, for multi-label classification of provenance triples in the ProvCaRe project.

2   Method

In this section, we describe the details of the S3 model used as the reference model for classification of the provenance triples, the provenance-specific training data, and details of the three deep learning models used in ProvCaRe. The deep learning models used in the ProvCaRe project were constructed using Google Tensorflow [14] and used hyperparameter tuning for classification of the provenance triples.

2.1   ProvCaRe S3 Model and Ontology

The ProvCaRe S3 model has been developed based on the NIH Rigor and Reproducibility guidelines that describe the essential components of a research study, which need to be reported in a transparent manner to support reproducibility [2]. The S3 model is modeled in a formal ontology by extending the three core classes of the W3C PROV Ontology, that is, `prov:Entity`, `prov:Activity`, and `prov:Agent` [10] (`prov` represents the W3C PROV namespace, http://www.w3.org/ns/prov). The ProvCaRe ontology represents various components of the S3 model in a class hierarchy, for example three different categories of research study design, `provcare:FactorialStudy`, `provcare:InterventionalStudy`, `provcare:ObservationalStudy`, are modeled as subclasses of randomized controlled trial class (`provcare` represents the namespace http://www.case.edu/ProvCaRe/provcare).

Figure 2 shows a subset of the ProvCaRe ontology class hierarchy representing various types of research study design. Although, the ProvCaRe ontology currently models more than 1300 provenance-specific classes, it is impractical to model provenance terms for different biomedical domains using only pre-coordinated class expressions [15]. Therefore, we have developed a post-coordinated compositional grammar syntax that can be used to represent new class expressions based on requirements of specific disciplines of biomedical research [16]. Similar to the SNOMED CT post coordinated grammar syntax, this provenance-specific compositional grammar syntax allows the re-use of existing ontology terms to create new provenance expressions. For example, the expression |Models|: |underwent| = |10-fold cross validation| describes the validation method for a model used in a prospective cohort study to evaluate association between sleep disordered breathing and hypertension [17]. Together with pre-coordinated classes, the post coordinated syntax enables the representation of a variety of provenance terms in the ProvCaRe ontology.

The ProvCaRe ontology is used as the reference knowledge model in the NLP workflow for named entity recognition (NER), generation of provenance triples from parse tree, and finally classification of the provenance triples before they are added to

Fig. 2. A screenshot of the ProvCaRe ontology representing different categories of research study design.

the ProvCaRe knowledgebase for user query. The classification of provenance triples using deep learning model enables easier visualization of query results for users.

2.2 Training of Deep Learning Models

We used two manually created datasets consisting of provenance metadata extracted from 75 full-text articles describing sleep medicine research studies to train the deep learning models. The 75 articles were selected by two members of the US NIH-funded National Sleep Research Resource (NSRR) project, which is creating the largest repository of sleep medicine study data from more than 40,000 sleep studies involving more than 36,000 participants [18]. They selected published articles describing research studies that are releasing their study data through the NSRR project. Therefore, the provenance information extracted from these articles can be used by the sleep medicine community to potentially reproduce the results reported in these published articles. These manually extracted provenance triples serve as gold standard in the ProvCaRe project and they are used to train the deep learning models.

As part of the training procedure, the first step involves defining a session and creation of a default Tensorflow graph in that session (a graph in Tensorflow can be understood as a structure that contains tensors and operations). The next step in the training process defines the Tensorflow network's loss function and optimizes the loss function using built-in Tensorflow Adam optimizer. Once the optimizer has been defined, a function is created to perform a single training step using the optimizer. This is implemented by allowing Tensorflow to automatically detect variables that can be trained and then calculate the gradients of these variables. In the next phase, the global step is defined and passed to the optimizer. This allows the count of the training steps to be computed automatically by Tensorflow. The final phase in the training process involves looping through the training steps defined above using specific number of training loops that iterate over the predefined batched data.

2.3 Deep Learning Model Architectures

In this section, we describe the details of the three deep learning models used to classify the provenance triples in the ProvCaRe project.

Convoluted Neural Network (CNN). The CNN model used for classification of provenance triples is similar to a CNN architecture proposed by Kim et al. [13]. This CNN model has been used in the NLP community and it has performed well on a variety of tasks ranging from sentiment analysis to classification. The architecture for this model comprises of a first layer that embeds each word of the sentence into a low-dimensional vector space using the pre-trained word-2-vec vectors. Following word embedding, the vectors are passed to a convolution layer which performs convolutions over the embedded vector using the specified filter sizes (standard filter sizes of 3, 4 and 5 were used in this project). Once the convolutions have been performed, the results are max-pooled into a single, large feature vector. In the next step, dropout regularization is added to stochastically turn-off a portion of the model to force the network to learn features individually and not together (drop out is only set during the training process and is disabled during prediction). Finally, the result is classified with a softmax layer and a prediction label is produced with the highest value by performing matrix multiplication operation. Figure 3 illustrates the components of a CNN model used in this project.

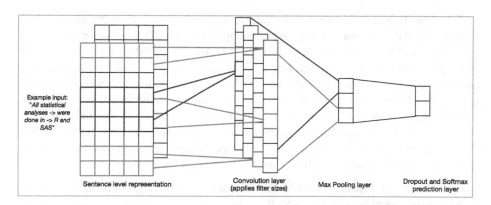

Fig. 3. Overview of the CNN model used in the ProvCaRe project

Recurrent Neural Network (RNN). RNN is the second deep learning model evaluated in the project for classification of the provenance triples. Like CNN's, RNN's are a type of neural network which have become more popular in recent years for natural language classification. Specifically, RNN's feedforward networks consist of recurrent connections. The advantage of this approach is that these connections afford the network the capacity to refer to previous states. This means that RNN's are able to process arbitrary sequences of input. RNN's model define and build a language model. This is implemented through a series steps. The first step in this process is to clean and store the training data. This is done according to several NLP techniques. To accomplish this in our model we tokenize the text, remove stop words as well as infrequent words and add special tokens to the beginning and end of the sentence. Figure 4 illustrates an overview of a RNN network.

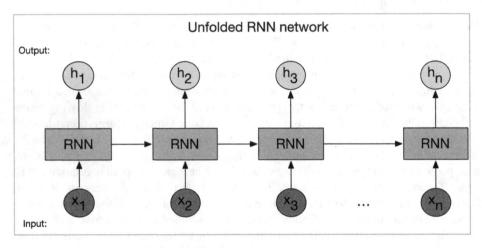

Fig. 4. Overview of the RNN model with input and output variables

Once the training data has been cleaned, the next step is to construct the data matrices that will hold our training data and map the words in the sentence to a vector representation. Once our vectors have been built on our training data, the next step is to feed our data into the RNN model. Our model represents each word from the training data as a "one-hot" vector. Once the data has been converted a Tensorflow RNN, it is initialized with the parameters specified above. During initialization, we allow for forward propagation, this returns both the calculated outputs and the hidden states which are used to calculate the gradients using Backpropagation Through Time (BPTT). Once this is done full the full training procedure is performed making use of stochastic gradient descent and BPTT the predicted label is produced.

Long-Short Term Memory (LSTM or CNN/RNN). Given the wide acceptance of neural network architectures in the NLP community, there has been recent interest in the use of a combined approach for classification tasks. To this end, we implemented a combined model consisting of our CNN and RNN approaches described above. This model is created with pre-trained vectors from word2vec, max pooling and LSTM recurrent unit. The model takes local features extracted by the CNN as input for the RNN. This is accomplished by first using the predefined word embedding as the input for the CNN. The output of this step are feature maps, which were described earlier as

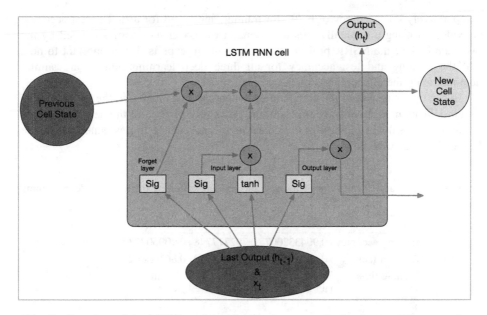

Fig. 5. Overview of the LSTM model with input, output, and other layers of the network

part of the CNN implementation and are formed during the convolutional windowing process. After convolution and pooling operations, the encoded feature maps are fed as input into the RNN. The output from the RNN are the learned sentence-level representations which are given to the network and the softmax output which produces the classification label (Fig. 5).

These three deep learning models were applied to classify the provenance triples generated by the ProvCaRe NLP workflow and the classified triples were added to the ProvCaRe knowledgebase.

3   Result and Discussion

In this section, we describe the results of a comparative evaluation of the three deep learning models for classification of provenance triples.

3.1   Classification Results

Table 1 shows the training and test accuracy of the three deep learning models in addition to the time taken to train the three models. The training and test results are evaluated using the following hyperparameter values: number of epochs (1); batch size (50); number of filters (32); filter sizes (3, 4, 5, 7); embedding dimension (200); evaluation loop (100); hidden unit (300); I1 regularization lamda (0); and dropout keep probability (0.5). The CNN and LSTM models have comparable accuracy in terms of training with score of 0.904 and 0.909 respectively. Similarly, the test accuracy for CNN and LSTM are 0.844 and 0.861 respectively. In contrast, the RNN model has comparatively low accuracy of 0.792 for training and 0.758 for test. The test accuracy is evaluated using a manually annotated dataset of provenance triples created by the two members of the NSRR project serving as domain experts. It is important to note that the training and test accuracy for all three deep learning models are similar demonstrating the effectiveness of the training process.

Based on the results of the comparative evaluation, we integrated the LSTM model for classification of provenance triples in the ProvCaRe project. In the next section, we describe the results of classifying five datasets of provenance triples generated by the ProvCaRe NLP workflow.

Table 1. Comparative evaluation of the test and training accuracy of the three deep learning models.

	CNN	RNN	CNN/RNN (LSTM)
Training accuracy	0.904332007	0.792777778	0.909607732
Test accuracy	0.844146341	0.758648649	0.86105042
Training time	14 min 47 s	13 min 05 s	16 min 23 s

3.2 Comparative Evaluation Results

The LSTM deep learning model was used to evaluate 5 datasets of provenance triples consisting of: (1) 20,000 triples; (2) 50,000 triples; (3) 100,000 triples; (4) 500,000 triples; and (5) 1 million triples, which were added to the ProvCaRe knowledgebase. To systematically evaluate the multi-label classification feature of the deep learning models, we used 12 subcategories of the S3 model. Table 2 shows the distribution of provenance triples across the 12 subcategories of the S3 model. The results show that Data Collection, Study Hypothesis, and terms describing Comparison (a component of the PICO(T) model used in evidence-based medicine [19]) are the three categories with highest number of provenance triples across all the five datasets. In contrast, the S3 subcategory describing software tools used in a research study have the lowest number of provenance triples. This is not surprising as only relatively few number of research studies use software tools, such as R or SAS-based libraries for data pre-processing or data analysis, therefore the occurrence of provenance triples describing software tools is relatively low.

Table 2. Results of classification of provenance triples according to the S3 model.

Triples	SV	SH	SM	S	P	RI	I	DP	DC	DA	C	TV
20000	798	3,154	1,861	39	1,572	2,233	904	425	3,157	1,819	3,821	217
50000	2926	7,094	4,645	655	4,728	4,219	3,077	1,857	6,787	3,998	9,213	801
100000	4652	12,003	10,295	903	10,243	7,428	7,164	2,914	14,399	8,986	18,896	2,117
500000	20876	61,399	49,488	5,502	52,339	37,224	31,359	16,898	70,853	42,597	98,755	12,710
1000000	39452	127,125	95,820	9,039	100,409	80,003	58,862	36,039	146,319	87,343	197,713	21,876

Table Legends: SV (Study Variables), SH (Study Hypothesis), SM (Statistical Model), S (Software), P (Population), RI (Recording Instrument), I (Intervention), DP (Data Preprocessing), DC (Data Collection), DA (Data Analysis), C (Comparison), TV (Time Value).

It is interesting to note that a high number of provenance triples are categorized into the important S3 subcategories of recording instruments and statistical models with 80,003 and 95,820 triples respectively. Provenance metadata describing the details of the recording instruments used in a research study is important to provide essential contextual information for interpreting the research study data. For example, provenance information describing the specific type of blood pressure measurement instrument used to record systolic and diastolic blood pressure of patients and scalp or intracranial electrodes used to record brain electrical activity are important for subsequent analysis of the recorded data. Similarly, a high number of provenance triples describe the details of research study population (100,409 provenance triples out of 1 million provenance triples), which is critical for evaluating the statistical significance of the results reported in a given study.

In contrast, the provenance triples describing the data variables used in a research study and time values associated with different aspects of a research study (e.g., recording of patient information) is relatively low. This may highlight the need for encouraging researchers to improve the quality of provenance metadata describing these two important aspects of a research study. Overall, this analysis of the distribution of provenance triples according to the S3 model subcategories clearly highlights the need for classification of provenance triples for analyzing the properties of provenance metadata extracted from published biomedical articles. In addition to the ease of query result visualization (as illustrated in Fig. 1), the classification of provenance triples using deep learning model (as described in this paper) makes it easier to characterize the provenance metadata available in published articles describing biomedical research studies.

4 Conclusion

The ProvCaRe project aims to advance the use of provenance metadata to meet the objectives of various community-based initiatives to improve scientific reproducibility in the biomedical research domain. In this paper, we described a comparative evaluation of deep learning models to address the critical challenge of automated and accurate classification of semantic provenance triples generated by the ProvCaRe NLP workflow. The three deep learning models were trained and evaluated using a manually curated dataset of provenance triples generated from 75 papers describing sleep medicine research studies (as part of the NSRR project).

The LSTM model featuring a combination of CNN and RNN outperformed both CNN and RNN models individually. The LSTM model was used to classify five dataset of provenance triples according to 12 subcategories of the S3 model, which were analyzed to demonstrate the importance of provenance triple classification for easier analysis and interpretation of provenance metadata extracted from published biomedical articles.

Acknowledgement. This work is supported in part by the NIH-NIBIB Big Data to Knowledge (BD2 K) 1U01EB020955 grant, NSF grant#1636850, and the NIH-NHLBI R24HL114473 grant.

References

1. Collins, F.S., Tabak, L.A.: Policy: NIH plans to enhance reproducibility. Nature **505**, 612–613 (2014)
2. Landis, S.C., et al.: A call for transparent reporting to optimize the predictive value of preclinical research. Nature **490**(7419), 187–191 (2012)
3. Prinz, F., Schlange, T., Asadullah, K.: Believe it or not: how much can we rely on published data on potential drug targets? Nat. Rev. Drug Discov. **10**(9), 712 (2011)
4. National Institutes of Health: Principles and Guidelines for Reporting Preclinical Research (2016). https://www.nih.gov/research-training/rigor-reproducibility/principles-guidelines-reporting-preclinical-research
5. Schulz, K.F., Altman, D.G., Moher, D.: CONSORT 2010 statement: updated guidelines for reporting parallel group randomised trials. J. Clin. Epidemiol. **63**(8), 834–840 (2010). CONSORT Group
6. Sahoo, S.S., Valdez, J., Rueschman, M.: Scientific reproducibility in biomedical research: provenance metadata ontology for semantic annotation of study description. In: American Medical Informatics Association (AMIA) Annual Symposium, Chicago, pp. 1070–1079 (2016)
7. Valdez, J., Kim, M., Rueschman, M., Socrates, V., Redline, S., Sahoo, S.S.: ProvCaRe semantic provenance knowledgebase: evaluating scientific reproducibility of research studies. Presented at the American Medical Informatics Association (AMIA) Annual Conference, Washington DC (2017)
8. Moreau, L., Missier, P.: PROV data model (PROV-DM). In: W3C Recommendation, World Wide Web Consortium W3C (2013)
9. Valdez, J., Rueschman, M., Kim, M., Redline, S., Sahoo, S.S.: An ontology-enabled natural language processing pipeline for provenance metadata extraction from biomedical text. Presented at the 15th International Conference on Ontologies, DataBases, and Applications of Semantics (ODBASE) (2016)
10. Lebo, T., Sahoo, S.S., McGuinness, D.: PROV-O: the PROV ontology. In: W3C Recommendation, World Wide Web Consortium W3C (2013)
11. Herman, I., Adida, B., Sporny, M., Birbeck, M.: RDFa 1.1 primer - second edition. In: W3C Working Group Note, World Wide Web Consortium (W3C) (2013). http://www.w3.org/TR/rdfa-primer/
12. Sahoo, S.S., Sheth, A., Henson, C.: Semantic provenance for escience: managing the deluge of scientific data. IEEE Internet Comput. **12**(4), 46–54 (2008)
13. Kim, Y.: Convolutional neural networks for sentence classification. arXiv preprint. https://arxiv.org/abs/1408.5882
14. TensorFlow. https://www.tensorflow.org/
15. Rector, A.L., Brandt, S., Schneider, T.: Getting the foot out of the pelvis: modeling problems affecting use of SNOMED CT hierarchies in practical applications. J. Am. Med. Inform. Assoc. **18**(4), 432–440 (2011)
16. Valdez, J., Rueschman, M., Kim, M., Arabyarmohammadi, S., Redline, S., Sahoo, S.S.: An extensible ontology modeling approach using post coordinated expressions for semantic provenance in biomedical research. In: 16th International Conference on Ontologies, DataBases, and Applications of Semantics (ODBASE), Rhodes, Greece (2017)

17. O'Connor, G.T., et al.: Prospective study of sleep-disordered breathing and hypertension: the sleep heart health study. Am. J. Respir. Crit. Care Med. **179**(12), 1159–1164 (2009)
18. Dean, D.A., et al.: Scaling up scientific discovery in sleep medicine: the national sleep research resource. Sleep **39**(5), 1151–1164 (2016)
19. Huang, X., Lin, J., Demner-Fushman, D.: Evaluation of PICO as a knowledge representation for clinical questions. Presented at the AMIA Annual Symposium Proceedings (2006)

Modeling, Simulating and Capturing Provenance

A Provenance Model for the European Union General Data Protection Regulation

Benjamin E. Ujcich[1,2]([✉]), Adam Bates[3], and William H. Sanders[1,2]

[1] Department of Electrical and Computer Engineering,
University of Illinois at Urbana-Champaign, Urbana, IL 61801, USA
{ujcich2,whs}@illinois.edu
[2] Information Trust Institute, University of Illinois at Urbana-Champaign,
Urbana, IL 61801, USA
[3] Department of Computer Science, University of Illinois at Urbana-Champaign,
Urbana, IL 61801, USA
batesa@illinois.edu

Abstract. The European Union (EU) General Data Protection Regulation (GDPR) has expanded data privacy regulations regarding personal
data for over half a billion EU citizens. Given the regulation's effectively
global scope and its significant penalties for non-compliance, systems
that store or process personal data in increasingly complex workflows
will need to demonstrate how data were generated and used. In this
paper, we analyze the GDPR text to explicitly identify a set of central
challenges for GDPR compliance for which data provenance is applicable;
we introduce a data provenance model for representing GDPR workflows;
and we present design patterns that demonstrate how data provenance
can be used realistically to help in verifying GDPR compliance. We also
discuss open questions about what will be practically necessary for a
provenance-driven system to be suitable under the GDPR.

Keywords: Data provenance · General Data Protection Regulation
GDPR · Compliance · Data processing · Modeling · Data usage
W3C PROV-DM

1 Introduction

The European Union (EU) General Data Protection Regulation (GDPR) [1], in
effect from May 2018, has significantly expanded regulations about how organizations must store and process EU citizens' personal data while respecting
citizens' privacy. The GDPR's effective scope is global: an organization offering services to EU citizens must comply with the regulation regardless of the
organization's location, and personal data processing covered under the regulation must be compliant regardless of whether or not it takes place within the
EU [1, Art. 3]. Furthermore, organizations that do not comply with the GDPR

© Springer Nature Switzerland AG 2018
K. Belhajjame et al. (Eds.): IPAW 2018, LNCS 11017, pp. 45–57, 2018.
https://doi.org/10.1007/978-3-319-98379-0_4

can be penalized up to €20 million or 4% of their annual revenue [1, Art. 83], which underscores the seriousness with which organizations need to take the need to assure authorities that they are complying.

A recent survey [2] of organizations affected by the GDPR found that over 50% believe that they will be penalized for GDPR noncompliance, and nearly 70% believe that the GDPR will increase their costs of doing business. The same survey noted that analytic and reporting technologies were found to be critically necessary for demonstrating that personal data were stored and processed according to data subjects' (*i.e.*, citizens') consent.

Achieving GDPR compliance is not trivial [3]. Given that data subjects are now able to withhold consent on what and how data are processed, organizations must implement controls that track and manage their data [4]. However, "[organizations] are only now trying to find the data they should have been securing for years," suggesting that there is a large gap between theory and practice, as the GDPR protections have "not been incorporated into the operational reality of business" [5]. Hindering that process is the need to reconcile high-level legal notions of data protection with low-level technical notions of data usage (access) control in information security [3].

In this paper, we show how *data provenance* can aid greatly in complying with the GDPR's analytical and reporting requirements. By capturing how data have been processed and used (and by whom), data controllers and processors can use data provenance to reason about whether such data have been in compliance with the GDPR's clauses [6–8]. Provenance can help make the compliance process accountable: data controllers and processors can demonstrate to relevant authorities that they stored, processed, and shared data in a compliant manner. Subjects described in the personal data can request access to such data, assess whether such data were protected, and seek recourse if discrepancies arise.

Our contributions include: (1) explicit codification of where data provenance is applicable to the GDPR's concepts of rights and obligations from its text (Sect. 2.1); (2) adaptation of GDPR ontologies to map GDPR concepts to W3C PROV-DM [9] (Sect. 3); and (3) identification of provenance design patterns to describe common events in our model in order to answer compliance questions, enforce data usage control, and trace data origins (Sect. 4). We also discuss future research to achieve a provenance-aware system in practice (Sect. 5).

2   Background and Related Work

2.1   GDPR Background

The GDPR "[protects persons] with regard to the processing of personal data and . . . relating to the free movement of personal data" by "[protecting] fundamental rights and freedoms" [1, Art. 1]. The regulation expands the earlier Data Protection Directive (DPD) [10], in effect in the EU since 1995, by expanding the scope of whose data are protected, what data are considered personally identifiable and thus protected, and which organizations must comply. As a result, it mandates "that organizations [must] know exactly what information they hold and where it is stored" [2]. Although the law does not prescribe particular mechanisms to ensure compliance, the law does necessitate thinking about such mechanisms at systems' design time rather than retroactively [2,4].

The GDPR defines data *subjects* identified in the personal data, data *controllers* who decide how to store and process such data, and data *processors* who process such data on the controllers' behalf [1, Art. 4]. *Recipients* may receive such data as allowed by the subject's *consent*, which specifies how the personal data can be used. Controllers and processors are answerable to public *supervisory authorities* in demonstrating compliance.

For each GDPR concept that is a right of a subject or an obligation of a controller or processor, we summarize in Table 1 where data provenance can be applicable using the GDPR's text and where data provenance can help benefit all involved parties from technical and operational perspectives.

2.2   Related Work

The prior research most closely related to ours is that of Pandit and Lewis [8] and Bartolini *et al.* [3]. Both efforts develop GDPR ontologies to structure the regulation's terminology and definitions. Pandit and Lewis [8] propose GDPRov, an extension of the P-Plan ontology that uses PROV's `prov:Plan` to model expected workflows. Rather than use plans that require pre-specification of workflows, we opted instead for creating relevant GDPR subclasses of PROV-DM agents, activities, and entities and encoding GDPR semantics into PROV-DM relations. Our model allows for more flexible specifications of how data can be used (*i.e.*, under consent for particular purposes while being legally valid for a period of time). Furthermore, our model focuses on temporal reasoning and online data usage control, whereas it is not clear how amenable GDPRov is to such reasoning or enforcement. The ontology of Bartolini *et al.* [3] represents knowledge about the rights and obligations that agents have among themselves. We find that a subset of that ontology is applicable in the data provenance context for annotating data, identifying justifications for data usage, and reasoning temporally about whether data were used lawfully. Bonatti *et al.* [7] propose transparent ledgers for GDPR compliance. Basin *et al.* [11] propose a data purpose approach for the GDPR by formally modeling business processes. Gjermundrød *et al.* [12] propose an XML-based GDPR data traceability system.

Aldeco-Pérez and Moreau [13] propose provenance-based auditing for regulatory compliance using the United Kingdom's Data Protection Act of 1998 as a case study. Their methodology proposes a way to capture questions that provenance ought to answer, to analyze the actors involved, and to apply the provenance capture. For using provenance as access control, Martin *et al.* [6] describe how provenance can help track personal data usage and disclosure with a high-level example of the earlier DPD [10]. Bier [14] finds that usage control and provenance tracking can support each other in a combined architecture via policy decision and enforcement points. Existing systems such as Linux Provenance Modules [15] and CamFlow [16] can collect provenance for auditing, access control, and information flow control for Linux-based operating systems.

Table 1. GDPR Concepts of Rights and Obligations as Applicable to Provenance.

Concept	Explanation	**Provenance Applicability**
Right to Consent [1, Arts. 6–8]	Controllers and processors can lawfully process personal data when subjects have given consent "for one or more specific purposes"	Provenance can model the personal data for which consent has been given, the purposes for which consent is lawful, and the extent to which derived data are affected
Right to Withdrawal [1, Art. 7]	Subjects can withdraw consent regarding their personal data's use going forward but without affecting such data's past use	Provenance can verify past compliance from before the withdrawal and prevent future use
Right to Explanation [1, Arts. 12–15]	Subjects may ask controllers for explanations of how their data have been processed "using clear and plain language"	Provenance-aware systems can naturally provide such explanations by capturing past processing
Right to Removal [1, Art. 17]	Controllers must inform processors if subjects wish to remove or erase their data	Provenance can track when such removal requests were made, what data such requests affect, and to what extent derived data are affected
Right to Portability [1, Art. 20]	Subjects can request their data from controllers or ask controllers to transmit their data to other controllers directly	A common provenance model would allow each controller to link its respective provenance records with others' records
Obligation of Minimality [1, Art. 25]	Controllers must not use any more data than necessary for a process	Provenance can help analyze such data uses with respect to processes

3   GDPR Data Provenance Model

Motivated by data provenance's applicability to GDPR concepts as outlined in Table 1, we define a GDPR data provenance model based on the data-processing components of prior ontologies [3,8]. Our model is controller-centric because the GDPR requires that controllers be able to demonstrate that their data processing is compliant, though we imagine that both controllers and processors will collect provenance data. Figure 1 graphically represents the GDPR data provenance model's high-level classes and their relations.

Tables 2, 3, and 4 explain the high-level classes shown in Fig. 1 for Agent, Activity, and Entity W3C PROV-DM classes, respectively. Some high-level classes

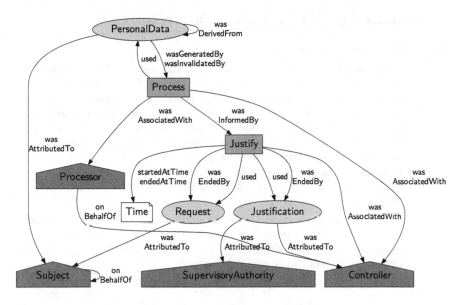

Fig. 1. GDPR data provenance model with high-level classes. House symbols represent agents (Table 2); rectangles represent activities (Table 3); ellipses represent entities (Table 4); arrows represent relations (Table 5); and notes represent other properties.

Table 2. GDPR Data Provenance Model Agent Classes.

Class	Explanation and Subclasses
Subject	An "identifiable natural person . . . who can be identified, directly or indirectly, in particular by reference to an identifier" [1, Art. 4]. *Subclasses*: Child subjects who cannot consent on their own and Parent subjects who can consent on their behalf [1, Art. 8]
Controller	An organization "which . . . determines the purposes and means of the processing of personal data" [1, Art. 4]. *Subclasses*: EURecipient controllers (with country subclasses), NonEURecipient controllers (with country subclasses). (Data processing or transmission that leaves the EU is subject to additional regulations [1, Arts. 44–50])
Processor	An organization "which processes personal data on behalf of the controller" [1, Art. 4]
Supervisory Authority	"An independent public authority" [1, Arts. 4, 51–59] that can "monitor and enforce the application of" the GDPR and "handle complaints lodged by a data subject . . . and investigate" [1, Art. 57]

Table 3. GDPR Data Provenance Model Activity Classes.

Class	Explanation and Subclasses
Process	"Any operation or set of operations which is performed on personal data or on sets of personal data, whether or not by automated means" [1, Art. 4]. *Subclasses*: Collect, Store, Retrieve, Combine, Disclose to another controller or processor via transmission; Erase to destroy personal data to fulfill the right to erasure [1, Art. 17]; Profile using "any form of automated processing … to evaluate certain personal aspects relating to a natural person" [1, Art. 4]; or Pseudonymize by "processing of personal data [so that it] can no longer be attributed to a specific data subject without the use of additional information" [1, Art. 4]
Justify	The rationale that a controller uses in taking some action on personal data, which includes temporal notions of "start" and "end" times. *Subclasses*: a subject's Consent [1, Arts. 6–7]; a controller's Obligation, Interest, or Authority [1, Art. 6]

Table 4. GDPR Data Provenance Model Entity Classes.

Class	Explanation and Subclasses
PersonalData	An "identifier [of a subject] such as a name, an identification number, location data, an online identifier or to one or more factors specific to the … identity of that natural person" [1, Art. 4]. *Subclasses*: DerivedData simplifies identification of data derived wholly or in part from PersonalData objects (by some Process)
Request	A request sent from a Subject to a Controller. *Subclasses*: ConsentRequest [1, Art. 6], WithdrawRequest [1, Art. 7], AccessRequest [1, Art. 15], CorrectionRequest [1, Art. 16], ErasureRequest [1, Art. 17], or a RestrictionRequest [1, Art. 18]
Justification	A justification (beyond a subject's consent) for lawful processing. *Subclasses*: LegalObligation "to which the controller is subject," a VitalInterest "of the data subject or of another natural person," a "performance of a task" in the PublicInterest, an OfficialAuthority "vested in the controller," a LegitimateInterest "pursued by the controller," or a Contract "to which the data subject is party" [1, Art. 6]

(*e.g.,* the Process activity) include subclasses (*e.g.,* the Combine activity) either because their notions are explicitly mentioned in the GDPR text or because they align with Bartolini *et al.*'s ontology for representing GDPR knowledge. We assigned more specific semantic meanings to several W3C PROV-DM relations; those meanings are summarized in Table 5.

Table 5. GDPR Data Provenance Model Relation Semantics.

From	Relation	To	Semantic Meaning
Process	wasInformedBy	Justify	Data processing actions under the GDPR require justification; we can reason about why data exist or why data were removed
PersonalData	wasDerivedFrom	PersonalData	Data updates, such as corrections submitted by the subject as part of the right to rectification [1, Art. 16]
PersonalData	wasGeneratedBy or wasInvalidatedBy	Process	Personal data have lifespans. For instance, a subject may request that personal data be deleted. Both generation and invalidation require reasoning, so we use both relations
Justify	used or wasEndedBy	Request or Justification	Justifications also have lifespans. For instance, a subject may withdraw his or her consent through a WithdrawRequest, which stops further data processing activities from using the Justify activity related to the withdraw request
Justify	wasAssociated With	Controller	Justify activities are associated with controllers since controllers must keep such records for authorities; however, the information used to make the justification legal (*i.e.*, a Request or Justification entity) can be attributed directly to the source that produced it (*e.g.*, a Subject)

We found that the GDPR includes strong temporal notions throughout its text that affect whether processing is considered lawful. For instance, the notion of consent with respect to data usage may be valid only for a particular period of time. We use data provenance not only for capturing data derivations, but also for temporally reasoning about data usage, as we detail in Sect. 4.

4   Using the GDPR Data Provenance Model

Although the GDPR data provenance model describes *what* provenance to collect, it does not explain *how* to use such provenance. We present design patterns that modelers and practitioners can use to describe common events. We use a running example based on the examples from prior works [8,11] that involve collecting personal data for a retail shop. We assume that a customer, Alice, interacts with the retailer by registering, making purchases, and subscribing to marketing information. We assume that each node and relation has a timestamp of its insertion into the graph so that we can perform temporal queries.

4.1   Design Patterns

Data Collection and Consent by a Subject. At time τ, Alice registers with and provides her personal data to the retail shop, along with her consent. Figure 2 shows the provenance generated from these activities. Our design pattern decouples the personal data collected (PersonalData entities) from the subject's consent about such data (ConsentRequest entities), as personal data may be updated or rectified [1, Art. 16] independently of the giving of consent.

The GDPR specifies that processing is lawful when consent has been given "for one or more specific purposes" [1, Art. 6]. We represent this consent for personal data in relation to purposes as a design pattern in the provenance graph

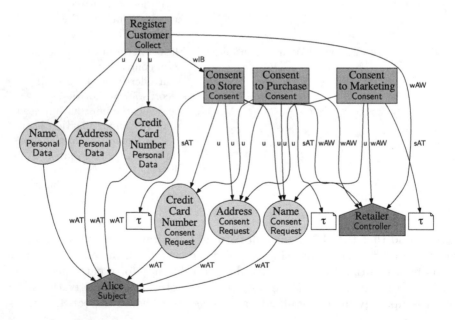

Fig. 2. Alice registers her personal data with a retail shop and consents to use of her data for storage, purchases, and marketing. Note that Alice does *not* consent to use of her credit card number for being shared for marketing purposes.

by mapping Consent activities to ConsentRequest entities with the used relation. As shown in Fig. 2, Alice does not consent to use of her credit card information for marketing, but she does allow it to be used for making purchases or for being stored by the retail shop (*e.g.*, to simplify future purchases).

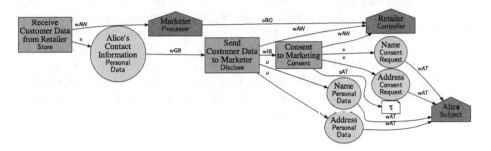

Fig. 3. The retail shop uses Alice's data for marketing purposes by employing a third-party marketer. The retail shop uses Alice's consent to receive marketing in allowing the processor to receive Alice's name and address. (For simplicity, portions of the provenance graph from Fig. 2 that are not relevant are not shown.)

Data Transfers Among Controllers and Processors. At time $\tau + 1$, suppose that the retail shop wishes to use a third-party marketing company to send marketing information to Alice. Figure 3 shows the provenance generated from the data transfer from the retail shop (the controller) to the marketing company (the processor). We model the transfer as a Disclose activity (by the controller) by which Alice's data are stored with a Store activity (by the processor).

Withdrawal by a Subject. At time $\tau + 2$, suppose that Alice no longer wishes to receive any further marketing from the retail shop. Figure 4 shows the provenance generated by her withdrawal of consent to receive marketing. We link the WithdrawRequest entity to the marketing Consent activity through the wasEndedBy relation to indicate that any prior Process that wasInformedBy the justification was valid, but that future uses will not be, after time $\tau + 2$. That ensures that "withdrawal of consent shall not affect the lawfulness of processing based on consent before its withdrawal" [1, Art. 7].

4.2 Verifying Compliance

We can now use provenance to reason about several GDPR requirements, either at run time when a decision about data usage is being made (*i.e.*, access control) or after the fact during an audit. The choice of *when* to verify will depend on design decisions on what provenance information a controller or processor has the ability to access. We can answer compliance questions by querying a provenance graph such as the graph in Fig. 4, as follows.

– *Was Alice's personal data used for marketing purposes after Alice withdrew her consent?* The "Send Customer Data to Marketer" activity was justified because it occurred during a time in which its justification activity, "Consent to Marketing," was valid (*i.e.*, after τ and before $\tau+2$). If subsequent activities used the "Consent to Marketing" as justification after $\tau+2$, then the controller would be noncompliant.

– *Who and what used Alice's address data?* One of the new operational and technical challenges with the GDPR is that of understanding where data "live" and what derived data are affected [2]. To answer this question, we start in Fig. 4 at the PersonalData entity representing Alice's address and work backward from the relations. We find that her address was used during registration and was sent to and stored by the marketing processor as a bundled piece of contact information.

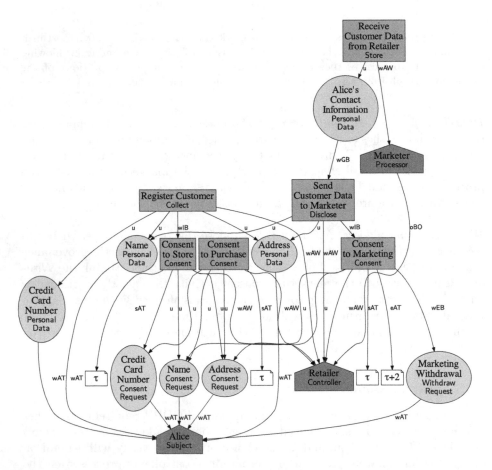

Fig. 4. Alice no longer wishes to receive marketing information, so she withdraws her consent for use of her personal data for marketing purposes. Future marketing activities that attempt to use the "Consent to Marketing" as justification will be noncompliant.

– *From the processor's perspective, under what usage conditions can Alice's address be used?* Processors are allowed to process data only if given the ability to do so by the controller. To answer this question, we start in Fig. 4 at the "Receive Customer Data from Retailer" activity to find any paths in the graph that end at a Consent activity that, at the time of querying, have not yet ended. We find that the processor can use Alice's address to send marketing on behalf of the controller.

Our questions presented here are necessarily incomplete, but we find that provenance can be highly flexible in answering questions that subjects and supervisory authorities will have when controllers or processors are audited.

5   Discussion

Privacy. Given that provenance collection includes metadata about *all* data processing activities, it introduces new privacy issues that will require that the metadata also be GDPR-compliant. That may require that PersonalData objects and Subject identifiers be stored as hashes of personal data and references to the personal data's actual locations rather than through embedding of the personal data in the provenance. We imagine that a *data protection officer* [1, Arts. 37–39] will maintain access to the provenance graph for enforcing data usage control and for complying with audit requests. Subjects may be entitled to the portions of the controller's provenance graph related to their personal data [1, Arts. 12, 20]. Challenges arise, however, in ensuring a balance among the subject's fundamental rights [1, Art. 1], the privacy of the controller's own (proprietary) processes, and the privacy of other subjects so that releasing such data "shall not adversely affect the rights and freedoms of others" [1, Art. 20].

Standardization. For inter-controller audits, we imagine that supervisory authorities will request provenance data from multiple controllers and processors so as to stitch together the relevant pieces of each's provenance graph. This will necessitate further standardization of (1) the granularity at which controllers and processors must collect provenance suitable for auditing; (2) the extent to which provenance collection mechanisms are built-in or retrofitted; and (3) tamper-proof and fraud-resistant provenance collection mechanisms.

Limitations. Provenance collection and querying alone are not sufficient for meeting GDPR compliance, though we believe that automated provenance annotations will simplify much of the work involved in reasoning about data processing. The GDPR will always require some human activity to support reasoning about whether compliance was met or not [11]. Annotation of existing workflows and application processes (*e.g.,* reads and writes in databases) is generally a non-trivial and implementation-dependent process, though retrofitting of applications to collect provenance for information security [17] shows promise.

6   Conclusion

We outlined how data provenance can help with GDPR compliance by supporting reasoning about how data were collected, processed, and disseminated; reasoning about whether such collection and processing complied with subjects' intents; enforcing data usage control; and aiding auditing by authorities to check compliance. We presented a GDPR data provenance model and showed how our model can be used. Although many practical issues will need to be considered, we believe that provenance can reduce the burden on practitioners and make systems more accountable to the subjects from whom controllers collect data.

Acknowledgments. The authors would like to thank Jenny Applequist for her editorial assistance, the members of the PERFORM and STS research groups at the University of Illinois at Urbana-Champaign for their advice, and the anonymous reviewers for their helpful comments. This material is based upon work supported by the Maryland Procurement Office under Contract No. H98230-18-D-0007 and by the National Science Foundation under Grant Nos. CNS-1657534 and CNS-1750024. Any opinions, findings, and conclusions or recommendations expressed in this material are those of the authors and do not necessarily reflect the views of the National Science Foundation.

References

1. Council of the European Union, Regulation (EU) 2016/679 of the European Parliament and of the Council of 27 April 2016 (General Data Protection Regulation). Official J. Eur. Union **L 119**, 1–88 (2016)
2. Tankard, C.: What the GDPR means for businesses. Netw. Secur. **2016**(6), 5–8 (2016)
3. Bartolini, C., Muthuri, R., Santos, C.: Using ontologies to model data protection requirements in workflows. In: Otake, M., Kurahashi, S., Ota, Y., Satoh, K., Bekki, D. (eds.) New Frontiers in Artificial Intelligence. JSAI-isAI 2015. LNCS, vol. 10091, pp. 233–248. Springer, Cham (2017). https://doi.org/10.1007/978-3-319-50953-2_17
4. Vijayan, J.: 6 ways to prepare for the EU's GDPR. InformationWeek, September 2016
5. Ashford, W.: Much GDPR prep is a waste of time, warns PwC, ComputerWeekly, October 2017
6. Martin, A., Lyle, J., Namilkuo, C.: Provenance as a security control. In: Proceedings of the Theory and Practice of Provenance 2012. USENIX (2012)
7. Bonatti, P., Kirrane, S., Polleres, A., Wenning, R.: Transparent personal data processing: the road ahead. In: Tonetta, S., Schoitsch, E., Bitsch, F. (eds.) SAFECOMP 2017. LNCS, vol. 10489, pp. 337–349. Springer, Cham (2017). https://doi.org/10.1007/978-3-319-66284-8_28
8. Pandit, H.J., Lewis, D.: Modelling provenance for GDPR compliance using linked open data vocabularies. In: Proceedings of Society, Privacy and the Semantic Web - Policy and Technology 2017 (2017)
9. World Wide Web Consortium, PROV-DM: The PROV data model, April 2013. https://www.w3.org/TR/prov-dm/

10. Council of the European Union, Directive 95/46/EC of the European Parliament and of the Council of 24 October 1995 (Data Protection Directive), Official J. Eur. Union **L 281**, 31–50 (1995)
11. Basin, D., Debois, S., Hildebrandt, T.: On purpose and by necessity: compliance under the GDPR. In: Proceedings of Financial Cryptography and Data Security 2018, March 2018
12. Gjermundrød, H., Dionysiou, I., Costa, K.: privacyTracker: a privacy-by-design GDPR-compliant framework with verifiable data traceability controls. In: Casteleyn, S., Dolog, P., Pautasso, C. (eds.) ICWE 2016. LNCS, vol. 9881, pp. 3–15. Springer, Cham (2016). https://doi.org/10.1007/978-3-319-46963-8_1
13. Aldeco-Pérez, R., Moreau, L.: Provenance-based auditing of private data use. In: Proceedings of Visions of Computer Science 2008, pp. 141–152 (2008)
14. Bier, C.: How usage control and provenance tracking get together - A data protection perspective. In: Proceedings of IEEE 4th International Workshop on Data Usage Management, pp. 13–17, May 2013
15. Bates, A., Tian, D., Butler, K.R.B., Moyer, T.: Trustworthy whole-system provenance for the Linux kernel. In: Proceedings of USENIX Security 2015, pp. 319–334 (2015)
16. Pasquier, T., Singh, J., Eyers, D., Bacon, J.: CamFlow: managed data-sharing for cloud services. IEEE Trans. Cloud Comput. **5**(3), 472–484 (2017)
17. Bates, A., et al.: Transparent web service auditing via network provenance functions. In: Proceedings of the 26th International Conference on World Wide Web, pp. 887–895 (2017)

Automating Provenance Capture in Software Engineering with UML2PROV

Carlos Sáenz-Adán[1][⊠], Luc Moreau[2], Beatriz Pérez[1], Simon Miles[2],
and Francisco J. García-Izquierdo[1]

[1] Department of Mathematics and Computer Science, University of La Rioja,
Logroño, La Rioja, Spain
{carlos.saenz,beatriz.perez,francisco.garcia}@unirioja.es
[2] Department of Informatics, King's College London, London, UK
{luc.moreau,simon.miles}@kcl.ac.uk

Abstract. UML2PROV is an approach to address the gap between application design, through UML diagrams, and provenance design, using PROV-Template. Its original design (i) provides a mapping strategy from UML behavioural diagrams to templates, (ii) defines a code generation technique based on Proxy pattern to deploy suitable artefacts for provenance generation in an application, (iii) is implemented in Java, using XSLT as a first attempt to implement our mapping patterns. In this paper, we complement and improve this original design in three different ways, providing a more complete and accurate solution for provenance generation. First, UML2PROV now supports UML structural diagrams (Class Diagrams), defining a mapping strategy from such diagrams to templates. Second, the UML2PROV prototype is improved by using a Model Driven Development-based approach which not only implements the overall mapping patterns, but also provides a fully automatic way to generate the artefacts for provenance collection, based on Aspect Oriented Programming as a more expressive and compact technique for capturing provenance than the Proxy pattern. Finally, there is an analysis of the potential benefits of our overall approach.

Keywords: Provenance data modeling and capture
PROV-Template · UML

1 Introduction

The diversity of provenance models used by existing software products (such as PASS [1], PERM [2], or Taverna [3]) to capture provenance has motivated the creation of PROV [4], an extensible provenance model created to exchange and integrate provenance captured among different provenance models. By giving support to PROV, these tools facilitate the software engineer's task of creating, storing, reading and exchanging provenance; however, they do not help decide which provenance data should be included, nor how software should be designed

© Springer Nature Switzerland AG 2018
K. Belhajjame et al. (Eds.): IPAW 2018, LNCS 11017, pp. 58–70, 2018.
https://doi.org/10.1007/978-3-319-98379-0_5

to allow its capture. In this context, the ability to consider the intended use of provenance during software development has become crucial, especially in the design phase, to support software designers in making provenance-aware systems.

Several design methodologies have been proposed to shorten the development time of software products. In particular, the Unified Modeling Language (UML) [5] has become a standard notation for OO software design. However, it does not offer support for provenance. In fact, our experience in developing software applications enhanced with support for provenance is that including provenance within the design phase can entail significant changes to an application design [6]. Against this background, PROV-Template [7] has been proposed as a declarative approach that enables software engineers to develop programs that generate provenance compatible with the PROV standard. Provenance *templates* are provenance documents expressed in a PROV-compatible format and containing placeholders (referred as *variables*), for values. PROV-Template includes an *expansion algorithm* by means of which, given a template and a set of *bindings* (associating variables to values), replaces the placeholders by the concrete values, generating a provenance record in one of the standardized PROV representations. Although this approach reduces the development and maintenance effort, it still requires designers to have provenance knowledge.

To overcome these challenges, we introduced *UML2PROV* [8], an approach to address the gap between application design, through UML behavioural diagrams, and provenance design, using PROV-Template. Briefly speaking, we (i) provided a mapping strategy from UML State Machine and Sequence diagrams to *templates*, (ii) defined a code generation technique based on the Proxy pattern to deploy suitable artefacts for provenance generation in an application, and (iii) developed a first prototype of UML2PROV in Java, using XSLT as a first attempt to implement our mapping patterns. In this paper, we complement and improve our previous approach by providing a more complete and accurate solution for provenance generation. First, we mainly give support to UML structural diagrams (UML Class Diagrams), by establishing a mapping strategy from such type of diagrams to templates. Our approach for capturing provenance data included on a system's class diagram provides a mean of storing lower level factors from objects' internal structure, factors not given by the previously considered behavioural diagrams. Overall, we provide an effective mechanism that integrates provenance data regarding both structural and behavioural aspects of a system, allowing for more realistic software designs to be supported. Second, we improve our first prototype by using a Model Driven Development (MDD)-based approach which implements the overall mapping patterns, and provides a fully automatic way to generate the artefacts for provenance collection based on Aspect Oriented Programming (AOP). Finally, we analyse the potential benefits of our overall approach in terms of time it takes to generate the templates, run-time overhead given by bindings collection, development and maintenance.

This paper is organized as follows: Sect. 2 gives an overview of UML2PROV. Section 3 describes our overall approach to translate UML Class diagrams to templates. A detailed description of the new implementation we propose for

our first UML2PROV prototype is described in Sect. 4. We analyse our overall
approach in Sect. 5, while Sect. 6 discusses related work. Finally, conclusions and
further work are set out in Sect. 7.

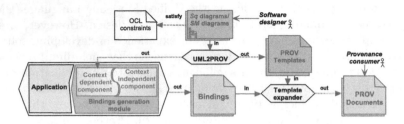

Fig. 1. The UML2PROV approach. The red and blue colours are used to refer to *design
time* and *runtime* documents of the approach, respectively. (Color figure online)

2   Overview: The UML2PROV Approach

To lay the foundation for a more in-depth understanding of the following sections,
we provide an overview of the UML2PROV architecture presented in [8]. We
illustrate our explanations using Fig. 1 which identifies the key facets of our
proposal together with the different stakeholders involved on the process. The
overall process consists of both *design time* (red) and *runtime* (blue) elements.

Design Time Facets. They correspond to the *UML diagrams* modelling the system, the associated *PROV templates* generated from those diagrams, and the
bindings generation module. In particular, this module is composed by: a *context-
independent component*, which contains the bindings' generation code that is
common to all applications, and a *context-dependent component*, which is generated from the system's UML diagrams and includes the bindings' generation
code specific to the concrete application. The starting point of the overall process corresponds to the UML system design, created by the *software designers* as
stated by the concrete domain's requirements. Among the two major categories
of UML diagrams (*structural* and *behavioural*) [5], in [8] we focused on these latter ones given the strong relation that provenance bears with all behavioural data
taking part in producing a final item. Having defined the UML diagrams, and
before applying our UML2PROV proposal, the diagrams are checked against a
set of OCL [9] constraints we have defined to ensure that they are consistent with
each other (see [10] for details about these constraints). Then, the UML2PROV
proposal takes as input the UML diagrams and automatically generates: (1) the
PROV *templates* with the design of the provenance to be generated, relying on
the information extracted from such diagrams, and (2) the *context-dependent
component* aimed at capturing provenance according to the PROV templates.

Runtime Execution Facets. They consist of the values logged by the application,
in the form of *bindings*, and the *PROV documents*. As far as the process is concerned, taking as source both the *templates* and the *bindings* previously created,

the *provenance consumer* uses the provenance *template expander* included in the PROV Template proposal to generate the final *PROV documents* (see Fig. 1).

3 From Class Diagrams to Templates

Our class diagrams to templates mapping takes *operations* as cornerstone elements. Translating data implicit on *operations* provides us with a complete background including not only the internal structure of the object before and after the execution (values of the *attributes*), but also information showing the internal changes (e.g. setting a new attribute, adding/removing an element in a collection). This represents a significant new capability since we were not able to extract these lower-level aspects from Sequence/State Machine Diagrams in [8].

Aimed at defining concrete operation transformation patterns, their different nature must be taken into account if we want to provide meaningful provenance which explains the nuances of each type of operation's execution. For instance, the key factors involved in the execution of an operation such as *getName* (which would return information about a data member) are different from the ones related to a *setName* operation (which would set a data member). Thus, the provenance data to be generated in both cases would be expected to be different. For this reason, we have first established a taxonomy of UML Class Diagrams' operations (Subsect. 3.1) to identify the different types of operations. Second, based on such a classification, we have defined different transformation mappings (Subsect. 3.2) depending on each type of operation.

Table 1. Extension of the taxonomy of methods' stereotypes given in [11].

Stereotype category	Stereotype name	Description
Structural *Accessor*	get	Returns a data member.
	*get-collection	Returns an element from a data member collection.
	predicate	Returns a Boolean value which is not a data member.
	property	Returns information about data members.
	void-accessor	Returns information through a parameter.
Structural *Mutator*	set	Sets a data member.
	*set-add-collection	Adds an element within a data member collection.
	*set-remove-collection	Removes an element within a data member collection.
	command	Perform a complex change to the object's state.
	non-void-command	
Creational	constructor/destructor	Creates/Destroys objects.
Collaborational	collaborator	*Works with objects (parameter, local variable and return object).*
	controller	*Changes an external object's state.*
Degenerate	incidental	*Does not read/change the object's state.*
	empty	*Has no statements.*

3.1 A Taxonomy of Operations Stereotypes

More than a nuance in terminology, the distinction between *operation* and *method* is important to lay the foundations of this section. *Operations* are characterized by their declaration, including name or parameters [5]. *Methods* are made up of the declaration (given by the *operation*) as well as the behaviour. From now on, we use the term *operation* and *method* interchangeably, always referring to the behaviour. In particular, we refer to the low-level behaviour related to the internal structure of the object's class to which the operation belongs.

In order to establish a taxonomy of operations that allows us to identify the different transformation patterns, we have undertaken a literature search looking for different categorizations of operations. Among the different works, the presented by Dragan et al. [11] stands out for being one of the most complete. Such a taxonomy is showed in Table 1 where, as we explain later, we have also included additional stereotypes needed in our proposal (marked with an asterisk). Their taxonomy establishes five categories of methods by defining stereotypes for their categorization, three of which have been included in our proposal (*Structural Accessor*, *Structural Mutator* and *Creational*). An explanation of these categories together with their specific transformation will be presented in Subsect. 3.2.

Whilst this taxonomy covers a wide range of behaviours, it lacks specific stereotypes for methods that manage collections of data members (e.g. search, addition or removal). Aimed at identifying this kind of methods on class diagrams to generate concrete provenance data, we have enriched the previous taxonomy with the additional stereotypes *get-collection*, *set-add-collection* and *set-remove-collection* (marked with an asterisk in Table 1). On the other hand, some stereotypes denote behaviours that cannot be faced without checking the source code (*empty*), or behaviours already provided by Sequence/State Machine Diagrams. In particular, Sequence Diagrams allow us to know if an *operation* works with objects (*collaborator*), and State Machine Diagrams provide us with information regarding external (*controller*) and internal (*incidental*) state changes. Thus, we have not considered *Collaborational* and *Degenerate* categories.

3.2 Class Diagrams to Templates Transformation Patterns

Our transformations are focused on *operations* customized by stereotypes so that, depending on the stereotype applied to an operation, they translate such an *operation* into the corresponding PROV template representing the *object*'s state. We define the *state* of an object as its internal structure, consisting of the object's properties (attributes and relationships) together with the values of those properties. The set of mappings comprises 8 transformation patterns identified *CDP1-8*, referred to as *Class Diagram Pattern*. Table 2 shows patterns *CDP1-6*, while patterns referring to collections, *CDP7* (*set-remove-collection*) and *CDP8* (*set-add-collection*), are presented in [10] due to space reasons. Table 2 has three columns: the first one shows each pattern together with the corresponding provenance template; the second and third columns depict the provenance document generated after expansion, and the provenance information collected during the operation's execution (*bindings*), respectively. The information shown in these two last columns corresponds to the case study we use in [8] referring to a system that manages the enrolment and attendance of students to seminars of

Table 2. Patterns *CDP1-CDP6* including the proposed provenance templates, together with the expanded template and the values of the variables (*bindings*).

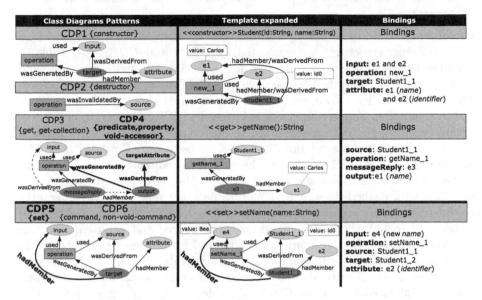

a University course. We have used the *Student*'s class constructor and the self-explained *getName* and *setName* operations to exemplify *CDP1*, *CDP3*, and *CDP5*. In Table 2: (1) the stereotypes (i.e. the types of operations) tackled by each pattern are showed between curly brackets, and (2) the prov:Entities created as a result of the operation's execution are in dark yellow, while prov:Entities assumed to exist before the operation's invocation are in light yellow.

All patterns share common transformations. First, all the *operations* are translated into a prov:Activity identified by `var:operation`. Second, when applicable, the object's initial state is given by a prov:Entity identified by `var:source`. Third, each *input operation*'s *argument* is mapped to a prov:Entity named `var:input`. Finally, when applicable, two prov:used relationships link `var:operation` with `var:source` and `var:input` to represent that the operation "uses" an initial state of the object (`var:source`), and a set of *input arguments* (`var:input`).

Creational. The operations included in this category, which are *constructor* and *destructor*, are addressed by *CDP1* and *CDP2*, respectively. Following *CDP1*, a *constructor* operation (identified by `var:operation`) creates a new object using (or not) *input arguments* (identified by `var:input`). Such a new object is translated into a prov:Entity identified by `var:target`, together with its set of data members, represented by the prov:Entity named `var:attribute`. Additionally, to show that the new object (`var:target`) has been generated using the *input arguments* (`var:input`), we define a prov:wasDerivedFrom relationship between them. In turn, `var:target` is related to `var:operation` through prov:wasGeneratedBy to show that the new object (`var:target`) has been generated by the *constructor* operation (`var:operation`). Following *CDP2*, a *destructor* operation (identified by `var:operation`) destroys an object (identified by `var:source`), fact represented by the relationship prov:wasInvalidatedBy between `var:source` and `var:operation`.

Structural Accessors. The operations that do not change the state of an object (internal structure) are translated by *CDP3* and *CDP4* (see Table 2). In particular, these operations are used for retrieving information, represented by the prov:Entity identified by `var:output`. While the operations *get* and *get-collection* tackled by *CDP3* return the data member directly, the operations *predicate*, *property* and *void-accessor* addressed by *CDP4* generate new information based on the data member(s). To represent the return of information (not the generation of information) in *CDP3*, we use a prov:Entity identified by `var:messageReply`, which is created by the operation (`var:operation`), and encapsulates the retrieved information (`var:output`). These elements, highlighted in italic and with dashed lines in *CDP3* of Table 2, are related to `var:operation` by the relationship prov:wasGeneratedBy. The relationship prov:hadMember is also used to link them (`var:messageReply` as source and `var:output` as target). On the contrary, the information retrieved by the operations tackled in *CDP4* is generated by such operations, involving a data member which is represented by an prov:Entity identified by `var:targetAttribute`. These additional aspects, highlighted in bold in *CDP4* of Table 2, are represented by the relationships: prov:wasGeneratedBy, between `var:operation` and `var:output`, and prov:wasDerivedFrom, between `var:output` and `var:targetAttribute`.

Structural Mutators. For operations that change the state of an object, we distinguish (i) those that set a specific data member –*set* methods– together with those whose behaviour performs a complex change –*command* and *non-void-command* methods– (tackled by *CDP5* and *CDP6*); from (ii) those that manage data member collections –*set-remove-collection* and *set-add-collection* methods– (tackled by *CDP7* and *CDP8*, presented in [10]).

In addition to the set of transformations shared by all patterns as explained before, *CDP5* and *CDP6* also have a set of common transformations. The operations tackled by these patterns change the object's state (internal structure) through the modification of some of its data member(s). Hence, the new state of the object is represented by a prov:Entity identified by `var:target`, while each object's data member is translated using a prov:Entity identified by `var:attribute`. To represent that such attributes (`var:attribute`) belong to the new state of the object (`var:target`), we use the relationship prov:hadMember between them. In turn, `var:target` is also related to the operation (`var:operation`) through prov:wasGeneratedBy, representing that the new object's state has been generated by such an operation. Additionally, `var:target` is linked, by means of prov:wasDerivedFrom, with a prov:Entity identified by `var:source`, which represents the previous object's state. In addition to these elements, the *CDP5* pattern, which tackles *set* operations, includes the prov:hadMember relationship between `var:target` and `var:input` to show that the input parameter is set as a new data member (see the highlighted prov:hadMember relationship in Table 2).

4   Implementation

Here, we discuss our proposal for enhancing our first UML2PROV approach
[8], which is mainly characterized by: (1) the implementation of our transformation patterns from UML Diagrams to *provenance templates files*, and (2) the
generation of artefacts for provenance collection. Although both aspects were
reasonably tackled in our prototype, they were subject to improvement. Next,
we explain why and how we have enhanced our prototype leaning on Fig. 2.

4.1   Implementation of the Mapping Patterns

Given the wide range of contexts of application, a manual translation of the UML
Diagrams of a system to *templates* constitutes a time-consuming, error-prone and
not cost-effective task. To overcome these challenges, we originally developed an
XSLT-based prototype as first attempt to implement our mapping patterns [8].
Although being a powerful solution, the usage of XSLT for implementing mapping rules is no longer the best option, given the availability of mapping and
transformation languages created by the MDD community which have better
properties in terms of maintenance, reusability, and support to software development processes [12]. For this reason, in this paper, we propose to use an MDD
approach [13], focusing on models rather than computer programs, so that the
templates files are automatically generated using a refinement process from the
UML Diagrams (see the top of Fig. 2). Our solution for template's generation
follows an MDD-based tool chain, comprising transformations *T1* and *T2*.

First, *T1* performs a model–to–model (M2M) transformation, taking as
source the *UML diagram models* of the system (which conform to the UML metamodel) and generating the corresponding provenance *template models* (which
conform to the PROV metamodel (PROV-DM [14]). Among the different MDD-
based tools in the literature, we have implemented this transformation by means
of the ATL Eclipse plug–in [15]. We have defined an ATL module named *UML-
PROV* which automatically translates each diagram model (sequence, state
machine and class diagram) into the corresponding provenance *template models*. Second, *T2* carries out a model–to–text (M2T) transformation, taking the
provenance *template models* resulted previously, and generating the final *templates files* serialized in PROV-N notation. *T2* has been implemented in the

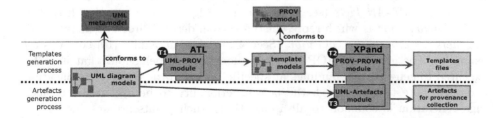

Fig. 2. MDD-based implementation proposal.

XPand tool [16] by means of a one-to-one transformation module named *PROV-PROVN*. This module takes the previously generated models and returns the *template files* in PROV-N.

By using the transformations defined in these two MDD–based tools, we are able to automatically generate, starting from the UML Diagrams of a system, the corresponding provenance *template files*. It is worth noting that the ATL and Xpand transformations can be applied to UML Diagrams (Sequence, State Machine, and Class Diagrams) in any context.

4.2 Generation of Artefacts

Having generated the template files, we need suitable code artefacts to create the bindings containing the pairs template variables–values. Programming the creation of bindings typically involves manually adding many lines of code repeated along the whole application's base code (obtaining the well-known *scattering* code), with its consequent loss of time on development and maintenance. Additionally, performing a manual creation of bindings requires the programmer to have a deep understanding of the design of both the application and the provenance to be generated. In [8] we faced this issue by following a Proxy pattern [17] approach as a first attempt to generate bindings with a minor programming intervention. Whilst the Proxy pattern approach facilitates such a generation by wrapping each object to extend its behaviour with extra lines of code, this solution still requires to manually modify the application's source code. In order to provide a fully automatic way for bindings generation, we instead propose to use the Aspect Oriented Programming (AOP) [18] paradigm. AOP aims at improving the modularity of software systems, by capturing inherently scattered functionality, often called *cross-cutting concerns* (thus, data provenance can be considered as a cross-cutting concern). Our solution exploits AOP to seamlessly integrate cross-cutting concerns into existing software applications without interference with the original system. The core of AOP is the *aspect*, which constitutes a separate module that describes the new functionality that should be executed at precise locations as the original program runs.

Taking this into account, we have followed an MDD-based approach for generating, starting from the source UML Diagrams, a context-dependent *aspect* in AspectJ (an AOP extension created for Java) together with other auxiliary components in Java, constituting what we have called *artefacts for provenance collection*. This new transformation *T3* has been implemented as an Xpand module named *UML-Artefacts* (see the bottom of Fig. 2) which, starting from the *UML diagram models* which represent the system design, directly generates the *artefacts for provenance collection* (Sect. 4 of online appendix [10] contains an example). The generated AOP *aspect* implements the behaviour that is to be executed to generate the bindings at specific points in the concrete application code. We note that, although the new functionality to be executed for bindings generation is common to all applications, such points are specific to the concrete application. With our proposal, the programmer just needs to include the resulted *artefacts* into the application, so that it will become automatically provenance-aware without requiring any other intervention.

5 Analysis and Discussion

We first analyses the strengths and weaknesses of UML2PROV taking into account (i) the automatically generation of *templates*, focusing on the time it takes to generate the *templates* and how much elements are included on the *templates*; and (ii) the collection of bindings during the execution of the application, discussing its run–time overhead. Finally, we highlight development and maintenance benefits of using UML2PROV.

As for the generation of the *templates*, since it is carried out during the design phase, it does not interfere in any way with the overall application performance. Regarding the amount of generated *templates*' elements, each *template* defines a fixed number of elements; thus, there is a linear association between the number of elements and the number of *templates* generated. Thus, in case of a huge amount of input/output arguments, and attributes, the number of elements after the expansion process grows proportionally to the length of these elements.

Another issue that may concern the users of UML2PROV is the run–time overhead. As a way of example, in Table 3 we provide a benchmark of seven execution experiments (identified from 1 to 7) using the *Stack* case study presented in [10]. In particular, it depicts the execution times with and without UML2PROV (see columns 2 and 3, respectively). We note that all experiments use retrieved information from a database. Based on the benchmarks showed in this table, as it would be expected, recording the provenance using our approach increases the original processing time by ∼14.5%. We can consider worthwhile this increment, taking into account that the approach herein captures provenance from all the elements modelled in the UML Diagrams with a high level of detail. In this line, an interesting aspect of future work would be to provide the UML designer with a mechanism to specify both the (i) the specific elements in the UML Diagrams to be traced, and (ii) the level of detail of the captured provenance for each selected element.

As said previously, UML2PROV makes the development and maintenance of provenance-aware systems a simple task, by automatically generating provenance templates and artefacts for provenance collection. In particular, the automation of template's generation entails direct benefits in terms of compatibility between the design of the application and the design of the provenance to be generated. Every time the design of the application changes, provenance design is updated automatically. As a consequence, since the artefacts for provenance collection

Table 3. Results obtained from seven experiments using the *Stack* case study [10].

ID	Without UML2PROV (ms)	With UML2PROV (ms)	Increment (%)	Number variables	Description	Legend:
						-ID: Experiment identifier.
1	48	56	16,67	2260	25 push operations from Stack	-Without UML2PROV: Average time taken by 50 executions
2	84	97	15,48	4510	50 push operations from Stack	without UML2PROV.
3	161	182	13,04	9010	100 push operations from Stack	-With UML2PROV: Average time taken by 50 executions
4	45	53	17,78	3160	25 pop operations from Stack	generating bindings with UML2PROV.
5	82	93	13,41	4710	50 pop operations from Stack	-Increment: Percentage of time increased by applying UML2PROV.
6	153	175	14,38	7810	100 pop operations from Stack	-Number variables: Total number of variables captured.
7	300	332	10,67	19952	Turn down a stack with size 100	-Description: Brief explanation of the experiment

* The experiments were run on a personal computer, Intel(R) Core(TM) i7 CPU, 2.8 GHz, running Windows 10 Enterprise. This computer runs Oracle JDK 1.8 together with MySQL 5.5

–which create bindings– are also automatically generated from the design of the application (as well as the templates), there are no problems with regard to incompatibility between templates and bindings. In fact, since these artefacts contain all the instructions to generate the *bindings*, programmers do not need to traverse the overall application's code, and include suitable instructions. Specifically, for each variable in a provenance template, a method call is needed to assign a value to it; thus, a programmer would need to write one line of code per each variable in a template. Although Table 2 shows that the templates are relatively small (e.g. *CDP4* –which is the biggest– comprises 6 nodes), we note that an application may encompass thousands of methods. Thus, our approach makes the collection of bindings a straightforward task.

6   Related Work

There is a huge amount of scientific literature about provenance, which has been collected and analysed by several surveys among different fields (see a complete review in [19]). Additionally, there are several works which particularly undertake the development of provenance-aware systems. For example, PASS [20], which is a storage systems supporting the collection and maintenance of provenance; PERM [2], which is a provenance-aware database middleware; or Taverna [3], Vistrails [21] and Kepler [22] which include provenance into workflow systems. Whilst these applications show efficacy in their research areas, they manually weave provenance generation instructions into programs, making the code maintenance a cumbersome task. In contrast to this strategy, some mechanisms for automatically provenance capture have been proposed in the literature. Among the systems in which the developers do not need to manually manipulate the code, Tariq et al. [23], noWorkflow [24] and Brauer et al. [25] stand out. Tariq et al. [23] automatically weave provenance capture instructions within the application before and after each function call during the compilation process. The noWorkflow tool [24] is registered as a listener in the Python profiling API, so that the profiler notifies when the functions have been activated in the source code. Brauer et al. [25] use AOP aspects for generating provenance. Our approach is similar in spirit with all these works, since UML2PROV transparently captures provenance in a non-intrusive way. Unlike these approaches which rely on the source code of the application, UML2PROV constitutes a generic solution based on the application's design. It identifies the design of the provenance to be generated (*templates*) and creates the context-dependent artefacts for provenance collection using the application design given by UML Diagrams. This fact unlinks the provenance capture with the specific implementation of the application, providing a generic solution for developing provenance-aware applications.

Finally, we note PrIMe [6] which, although being considered the first provenance-focused methodology, is standalone and is not integrated with existing software engineering methodologies. UML2PROV complements PrIMe, since it integrates the design of provenance by means of PROV-Templates enriched with UML.

7 Conclusions and Future Work

We have defined a comprehensive approach UML2PROV. First, we complete it by giving support to Class Diagrams, establishing a mapping strategy from such diagrams to templates. Second, we improve our first prototype by using an MDD-based approach which not only implements the overall mapping patterns, but also generates the AOP artefacts for provenance collection. Finally, there is an analysis of the potential benefits of our overall approach.

In addition to the future work advanced previously, another line of future work is the application of UML2PROV in a distributed system. We plan to tackle this goal by automatically generating an artefact for provenance collection able to capture provenance not only in a fully-in-memory system (as until now), but also in a system comprising distributed components. Finally, we may use some PROV attributes (e.g. prov:type, prov:role. . .) in the templates, in order to specialize concrete elements. With such specializations, we aim to improve the provenance consumption by creating less complex queries with higher accuracy, reducing the noise levels in the retrieved provenance information.

Acknowledgements. This work was partially supported by the spanish MINECO project EDU2016-79838-P, and by the U. of La Rioja (grant FPI-UR-2015).

References

1. Holland, D., Braun, U., Maclean, D., Muniswamy-Reddy, K.K., Seltzer, M.I.: Choosing a data model and query language for provenance. In: Proceedings of IPAW 2008, pp. 98–115 (2008)
2. Glavic, B., Alonso, G.: Perm: processing provenance and data on the same data model through query rewriting. In: Proceedings of the 25th IEEE International Conference on Data Engineering (ICDE 2009), pp. 174–185 (2009)
3. Wolstencroft, K.: The Taverna workflow suite: designing and executing workflows of Web Services on the desktop, web or in the cloud. Nucleic Acids Res. **41**, 557–561 (2013)
4. Groth P., Moreau L. (eds.): PROV-Overview. An Overview of the PROV Family of Documents. W3C Working Group Note prov-overview-20130430 (2013). http://www.w3.org/TR/2013/NOTE-prov-overview-20130430/
5. OMG. Unified Modeling Language (UML). Version 2.5: (2015) formal/03 Jan 2015. http://www.omg.org/spec/UML/2.5/. Last visited, March 2018
6. Miles, S., Groth, P.T., Munroe, S., Moreau, L.: Prime: a methodology for developing provenance-aware applications. ACM Trans. Softw. Eng. Methodol. **20**(3), 8:1–8:42 (2011)
7. Moreau, L., Batlajery, B.V., Huynh, T.D., Michaelides, D., Packer, H.: A templating system to generate provenance. IEEE Trans. Softw. Eng. (2017). http://eprints.soton.ac.uk/405025/
8. Sáenz-Adán, C., Pérez, B., Huynh, T.D., Moreau, L.: UML2PROV: automating provenance capture in software engineering. In: Proceedings of Sofsem 2018, pp. 667–681 (2018)
9. OMG: Object Constraint Language, Version 2.4 formal/02 March 2014 (2014). http://www.omg.org/spec/OCL/2.4/PDF

10. Supplementary material of UML2PROV (2018). https://uml2prov.github.io/
11. Reverse Engineering Method Stereotypes. In: Proceedings of the 22nd IEEE International Conference on Software Maintenance (2006)
12. Costa, C.M., Marcos Menárguez-Tortosa, J.T.F.B.: Clinical data interoperability based on archetype transformation. J. Biomed. Inform. **44**(5), 869–880 (2011)
13. Selic, B.: The pragmatics of model-driven development. IEEE Softw. **20**(5), 19–25 (2003)
14. Moreau, L., et al.: PROV-DM: The PROV Data Model. W3C Recommendation REC-prov-dm-20130430, World Wide Web Consortium (2013). http://www.w3.org/TR/2013/REC-prov-dm-20130430/
15. ATL - a model transformation technology, version 3.8, May 2017. http://www.eclipse.org/atl/. Last visited, March 2018
16. XPand: Eclipse platform (2018). https://wiki.eclipse.org/Xpand, Last visited, March 2018
17. Gamma, E., Helm, R., Johnson, R., Vlissides, J.: Design Patterns: Elements of Reusable Object-oriented Software. Addison Wesley, Reading (1995)
18. Kiczales, G., et al.: Aspect-oriented programming. In: Akşit, M., Matsuoka, S. (eds.) ECOOP 1997. LNCS, vol. 1241, pp. 220–242. Springer, Heidelberg (1997). https://doi.org/10.1007/BFb0053381
19. Pérez, B., Sáenz-Adán, C., Rubio, J.: A systematic review of provenance systems. Knowl. Inf, Syst (2018)
20. Glavic, B., Dittrich, K.R.: Data Provenance: A Categorization of Existing Approaches. In: Proceedings of Datenbanksysteme in Büro, Technik und Wissenschaft (BTW 2007), pp. 227–241 (2007)
21. Silva, C.T., Anderson, E., Santos, E., Freire, J.: Using vistrails and provenance for teaching scientific visualization. Comput. Graph. Forum **30**(1), 75–84 (2011)
22. Altintas, I., Barney, O., Jaeger-Frank, E.: Provenance collection support in the kepler scientific workflow system. In: Moreau, L., Foster, I. (eds.) IPAW 2006. LNCS, vol. 4145, pp. 118–132. Springer, Heidelberg (2006). https://doi.org/10.1007/11890850_14
23. Tariq, D., Ali, M., Gehani, A.: Towards automated collection of application-level data provenance. In: Proceedings of TaPP 2012 (2012)
24. Pimentel, J.F., Murta, L., Braganholo, V., Freire, J.: noworkflow: a tool for collecting, analyzing, and managing provenance from python scripts. In: Proceedings of VLDB 2017, vol. 10, pp. 1841–1844 (2017)
25. Brauer, P.C., Fittkau, F., Hasselbring, W.: The aspect-oriented architecture of the CAPS framework for capturing, analyzing and archiving provenance data. In: Ludäscher, B., Plale, B. (eds.) IPAW 2014. LNCS, vol. 8628, pp. 223–225. Springer, Cham (2015). https://doi.org/10.1007/978-3-319-16462-5_19

Simulated Domain-Specific Provenance

Pinar Alper[1], Elliot Fairweather[2(✉)], and Vasa Curcin[2]

[1] University of Luxembourg, Luxembourg City, Luxembourg
[2] King's College London, London, UK
elliot.fairweather@kcl.ac.uk

Abstract. The main driver for provenance adoption is the need to collect and understand knowledge about the processes and data that occur in some environment. Before analytical and storage tools can be designed to address this challenge, exemplar data is required both to prototype the analytical techniques and to design infrastructure solutions. Previous attempts to address this requirement have tried to use existing applications as a source; either by collecting data from provenance-enabled applications or by building tools that can extract provenance from the logs of other applications. However, provenance sourced this way can be one-sided, exhibiting only certain patterns, or exhibit correlations or trends present only at the time of collection, and so may be of limited use in other contexts. A better approach is to use a simulator that conforms to explicitly specified domain constraints, and generate provenance data synthetically, replicating the patterns, rules and trends present within the target domain; we describe such a constraint-based simulator here. At the heart of our approach are templates - abstract, reusable provenance patterns within a domain that may be instantiated by concrete substitutions. Domain constraints are configurable and solved using a Constraint Satisfaction Problem solver to produce viable substitutions. Workflows are represented by sequences of templates using probabilistic automata. The simulator is fully integrated within our template-based provenance server architecture, and we illustrate its use in the context of a clinical trials software infrastructure.

1 Motivations and Approach

A key requirement for the progression and adoption of provenance research is the availability of realistic provenance datasets. Such data is necessary to support the prototyping of new techniques or tools for provenance capture, analysis and visualisation. Thus far the community has tackled this requirement by using existing applications as data sources. One such effort is the ProvBench series of challenges [2,3] that built up a corpus from the output of a diverse selection of provenance-enabled applications, such as those used in scientific workflows and file systems.

Provenance sourced from a particular application is inherently tied to that domain, which can be limiting. Firstly, it may be one-sided and exhibit only certain patterns. For example, the Wikipedia corpus of the Reconstruction

© Springer Nature Switzerland AG 2018
K. Belhajjame et al. (Eds.): IPAW 2018, LNCS 11017, pp. 71–83, 2018.
https://doi.org/10.1007/978-3-319-98379-0_6

Challenge [4] focuses only on document revisions and not on delegation of author responsibilities. In reality data is often produced through processes involving multiple applications, such as security layers, content and collaboration management systems, local tools, and remote services. Focusing on a single element makes it difficult to obtain a full description of the provenance of data.

Secondly, the provenance data may exhibit trends and correlations that exist in the domain environment only at the time of collection. For example, the file system corpus [9] contains data traces taken from applications that are run only with a fixed default workload configuration. This only captures reality partially, as the applications experience changing workloads over time.

An alternative approach is to use a simulator and generate provenance synthetically. Synthetic data generation has been investigated in the context of relational databases [10,11] and graphs [17], but not as thoroughly in the context of provenance. In order for synthetic data to be useful for a particular domain, it needs to be *valid* (observe the allowed structure of the domain), and *realistic* (observe the data correlations present with in the domain). However it is important to note that true realism is only achievable by sampling distributions derived from real-world data, which is sometimes not possible.

In this paper we describe a simulator that is configurable to a particular domain and generates such data. Validity is achieved using *provenance templates*, an emerging approach for provenance recording and management, which represent abstract, reusable provenance fragments that may be instantiated using concrete data. Realism is approximated by providing the simulator with a set of constraints that represent the data correlations and trends of the target domain. Value sets for certain constraints are generated by sampling statistical distributions and we delegate the task of constraint solving to a Constraint Satisfaction Problem (CSP) solver.

Single templates are not however sufficient to generate meaningful traces. We therefore introduce the concept of processes to represent possible workflows. A process is a defined as a probabilistic finite automaton, in which each state is associated with a template. The simulator generates a path through the automaton that is used to produce a sequence of templates to be instantiated. The simulator is fully incorporated within our template-based provenance server.

2   Provenance Templates

A provenance template [5] is a abstract fragment of a provenance document, that may be instantiated using concrete substitutions for variables contained with the template. Variables are of two kinds; identifier variables inhabiting the `var` namespace which are placeholders for node or relation identifiers, and value variables under `vvar`, which can be used in the place of an attribute value. A provenance template is itself a valid provenance document and as such allows nodes to be semantically annotated, allowing the inclusion of domain-specific information. Concrete provenance fragments are generated by an algorithm that accepts as input a template and a substitution comprised of a set of variable-value *bindings*, and replaces variables for values in a copy of the template.

The template approach does not prescribe how one produces bindings, as this might differ across applications. This insulation from the application layer makes templates a suitable mechanism to represent the combined provenance of multiple applications.

Figure 1 gives an example of a template from the domain of health informatics. It outlines the provenance trace that is to be collected from the use of diagnostic support tool for the management of potential secondary stroke. An initial assessment is performed by a clinician at a GP practice. The assessment uses the available clinical guidelines and the patient's health record and produces a stroke prevention plan for that patient. The patient's progress with the plan is checked in a follow-up assessment and a revised plan is produced. The template illustrates the use of both identifier variables such as that for the entity var:record, and value variables, such as vvar:riskLevel given as the value of the attribute ex:priority.

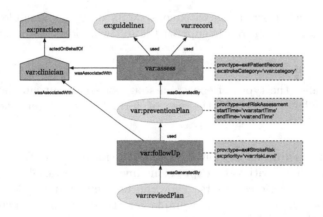

Fig. 1. Provenance template for stroke risk assessment

We require one extension to the published template model [5]. Nodes or relations using value variables must also be annotated with an attribute pgt:vvarTypes that contains a map from the names of the value variables present to their intended value type. The template model also provides the ability to define iterable sub-graphs within templates; we do not consider this functionality in this paper.

2.1   Variable Domains

Our first contribution is to introduce the concept of domains for template variables. Let V_T denote the set of variables occurring in the template T. For each variable $x \in V_T$, we may specify a set of values D_x specifying the values that may be used in bindings for x. If x is an identifier variable each element of the domain must be of type `prov:QUALIFIED _NAME`, and if it is a value variable the domain of each value must be of the type specified in the variable type map for that node or relation.

3   Domain-Specific Constraints for Templates

We now focus on constraints that ensure our simulated traces are not only valid, but also realistic. Application domains are often associated with restrictions or trends beyond those encoded in the data schema of an application. For instance, clinical guidelines contain rules restricting the ordering of events within a process, e.g. a patient follow-up assessment should occur between 30 and 90 days following the initial assessment. As another example, consider the extensive use of medical ontologies describing medical conditions and interventions - when multiple entities from ontologies are brought together in a particular context, their co-occurrence may require co-ordination (e.g. no pregnancy events in male patients).

We model such restrictions with constraints over the variables occurring within a template. We currently support the following kinds of constraints.

3.1   Constraint Types

We now formalise the types of constraints supported in our simulations. Note that, for simplicity, we avoid the use of formal medical terminologies and ontologies.

Relation Constraints. Relation constraints are formed from Boolean comparisons between binary arithmetic expressions involving the variables occurring in a template and numeric constants. They can be used to model domain-specific event ordering requirements. An example for the stroke assessment template would be as follows:

$$(preventionPlan.endTime - preventionPlan.startTime) > 30$$

Value-Dependency Constraints. Value-dependency constraints are conditional expressions that enforce a dependency between the possible values that two different variables may assume. A constraint of this type is constructed from set membership tests between the value $val(z)$ of a variable z and a subset of the values in the domain of that variable, $V_z \subset D_z$, such that:

$$\text{if } val(x) \in V_x \text{ then } val(y) \in V_y$$

Relations between domain-specific semantic attributes can be represented using value-dependency constraints. For example, stating that in our simulations diagnosis of diabetes should be followed by either a diet or insulin treatment or both, would be expressed as:

$$\text{if } val(diagnosisKind) \in \{Type1Diabetes,\ Type2Diabetes\}$$
$$\text{then } val(treatmentKind) \in \{CardioProtectiveDiet,\ InsulinTreatment\}$$

Distribution Constraints. Distribution constraints specify how domain values are picked for certain variables. They are configurations represented as triples of the form $\langle x, k, F_x \rangle$ where $x \in V_T$, and $k \in \{$ *uniform, exponential, pie* $\}$ denotes a distribution kind, and the set F_x represents the frequency of the occurrence of each possible domain value for the variable x. Each $f \in F_x$ is a pair $\langle d, p \rangle$, such that $d \in D_x$, where D_x denotes the domain of x, and a probability $p \in \mathbb{R}$.

We use frequency sets derived from discrete probability distributions and currently support three types of distribution: uniform distributions in which each domain value has equal probability, pie distributions in which each domain value has an associated probability, and the Zipf power law distribution.

Note that, in our implementation, any variables that have an associated relation or value-dependency constraint cannot also have a distribution constraint.

3.2   Solving Constraints

We make use of a Constraint Satisfaction Problem (CSP) solver [16] to solve the constraints given for a template. CSP solvers operate on problems of the form $\langle V, D, C \rangle$, where V is a set of variables, D is a set of domains for variables and C is a set of constraints. They use optimised search algorithms to find solutions to a given problem. A solution is a set of variable-value assignments, which ideally should be *consistent* and *complete*. A solution is consistent if it does not violate any of the constraints, and it is complete if it contains assignments for all variables.

We use the CSP solver in its most basic configuration; that is, where all constraints and variables are mandatory and a consistent and complete solution is sought. We create a problem with only integer variables. Each constraint type identified in the Sect. 3.1 can be mapped to a CSP constraint types as follows.

Binary CSP constraints are those involving two variables. Relation constraints with complex arithmetic expressions can be mapped to Binary CSP constraints through use of intermediary variables. Reified CSP constraints are those that involve constraints combined with logical operators. We use this mechanism to implement value-dependency constraints. Global CSP constraints are a portfolio of constraints that capture commonly encountered constraint patterns, and are defined over an arbitrary number of variables. Specifically, we use the Global Cardinality Constraint (gcc), which allows us to set the (min-max) number of times a value can be assigned to a set of variables.

4   Processes and Simulation

In order to produce simulated provenance traces, we first need to specify the processes involved, and map them onto templates.

4.1 Processes

Processes represent simple workflows constructed from the instantiation of sequences of templates, modelled as probabilistic finite automata, with each automata state associated with a template. When generating a trace the simulator first takes a possible path through the automata and outputs the respective sequence of transitions. This information is then used to determine a sequence of templates to be instantiated for that trace. The initial and terminal states of an automaton are not associated with a state and the initial state is chosen from a probability vector. Transition probabilities for each state sum to unity. An example is shown in Fig. 2.

When template instances are *merged* into the provenance document being constructed, any values given in bindings for variable identifiers that already exist in the document are reused and, if not present, are freshly created. This process by which nodes within template instances are *grafted* upon existing nodes is what enables larger documents to be constructed from the fragment documents created from the instantiation of templates. For more information on the document construction process and how it is carried out within the provenance server, see [7].

Whilst merging allows the natural building of complex documents under normal operation the simulator requires that graft points between the templates of a process be explicitly marked in order to control the way in which template instances are joined. This is achieved in the following way. Each transition of a process may be annotated with pairs of identifier variables called *anchors*. The lefthand-side of each pair is a variable from the preceding template and the righthand-side a variable from the subsequent template. Under simulation the righthand-side must be instantiated with the same value as the left, thus ensuring that a graft is created.

We also introduce the practice that a *partial substitution* may be associated with a given process state. This substitution will be pre-applied to the template of that state before the remaining bindings are generated. This allows more generic templates to be defined which may be reused in similar but distinct contexts.

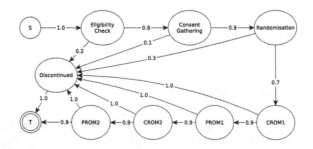

Fig. 2. Automaton for randomised clinical trial workflow

Figure 2 shows an example automaton describing the data workflow for a randomised clinical trial application. The eligibility check, consent gathering and randomisation states are each associated with a distinct template, whilst the Patient Reported Outcome Measure (PROM) and Clinician Reported Outcome Measure (CROM) states (representing the completion of form-based assessments) make use of the same single template, pre-applied with a partial substitution specifying whether the form is to be completed by the patient or clinician.

4.2 Simulation

To produce a simulated provenance trace, the simulator operates in conjunction with the provenance server. After reading the configuration, the given variable domains are mapped to integer values and stored for use by the CSP solver. The process configuration is then used to construct the described automaton, and the template used in each state is read from the provenance server database and stored. The variables for each template and any associated constraints are then mapped to their counterparts in the CSP solver, and any required distribution constraint value domains generated.

For each requested trace, the automaton is first used to generate a path, giving a sequence of templates to be instantiated. Then for each template in order, bindings for its variables are generated. If a distribution constraint exists for a variable, a sample is taken and together with any relation or value-dependency constraints upon the same variable, submitted to the CSP solver to be solved. If no constraint is present, a value is selected at random from the domain of the variable, or in the case that no domain is specified, a value of the correct type is generated at random.

These bindings are then submitted to the provenance server as a substitution, which constructs a new instance of the respective template and stores it in the database. Following the first instantiated template of a process the most recent bindings are stored and any values generated for anchored variables in the following transition reused.

5   Implementation and Architecture

The architecture of the simulator component and the template server are given in Fig. 3. The simulated process is represented by an XML configuration comprising the templates required, associated value domains for template variables, domain constraints, and transitions between process states. The configuration is passed to the simulator via the provenance server and template definitions are read from the server database. We use the Choco 4.0 solver [15] for CSP solving and the Apache Commons Mathematics library for distribution sampling.

Provenance documents are modelled as graphs in a formalism-agnostic way by the server's Model component. Interoperability with PROV is provided using ProvToolbox. The Model component provides templates, substitutions and the instantiation algorithm by which new provenance fragments are generated. The

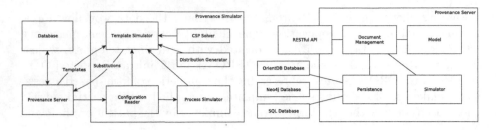

Fig. 3. Architecture of the simulator (left) and server (right)

Document Management component controls and executes the operations outlined in the document building workflow such as the creation of new target documents, namespace management, the registering of templates, and the generation and merging of new fragment documents. Storage of data in the system is abstracted by a persistence layer component to enable the use of different database technologies - at present Neo4J and OrientDB graph databases are supported, as is a relational SQL format. The management API may be accessed directly via a RESTful web interface. Analysis of target documents may be performed either at the database level, or otherwise by exporting target documents or fragments and using existing PROV tools.

The clients invoke the simulator via the management API by providing a configuration file, a target document and a number of iterations to be executed.

6 Evaluation

Following our initial work on decision support systems, we are now focusing on simulating clinical trial traces. Clinical trials have become increasingly reliant on contextual data sources that complement the data obtained directly from the patients, e.g. Electronic Health Record (EHR) systems are used to identify eligible patients and feed part of the required trial data into Electronic Case Report Forms (eCRFs). Tractability of such system is of essence in order to understand, evaluate and potentially improve the trial design. This requires the minute study details, e.g. eligibility criteria encodings, how they were applied to individual patients who presented to the clinician, data extracted from the EHR systems, data collected through eCRFs and the analysis performed on the collected data. Assembling the trace of the entire process requires provenance to be captured from the Clinical Trial Management System, EHR system and the patient/clinician data collection tools.

The overall goal is to use that provenance to demonstrate compliance of the software tasks executed during clinical trials with regulations such as US's 21 CFR Part 11 and Good Clinical Practice (GCP) standards. Techniques to validate the clinical trial provenance data against such standards need to be developed initially on simulated data and validated themselves before being attempted on real trial data, making it essential that synthetic data is structurally identical to real provenance traces.

The trials we are observing are based on the TRANSFoRm clinical trial infrastructure [6]. The key steps involve: (1) flagging up the patients eligible for the trial to the clinician by checking their EHR in the background; (2) obtaining patient consent; (3) randomising them into one arm of the trial; and (4) fill in a series of forms. Figure 4 shows the four templates used in this context. Our initial set of constraints states that:

- Forms must be completed between the start and end date of the trial: `vvar: formCompletionDate >= var:formStartDate`, `vvar:formCompletionDate <= var:formEndDate`
- We want an equal proportion of male and female participants: `vvar:patientSex` is a uniform distribution
- Ages should be uniform across age band values '18–30', '31–50', '51–70', '70+': `vvar:patientAge` is a pie distribution over the four categories defined.

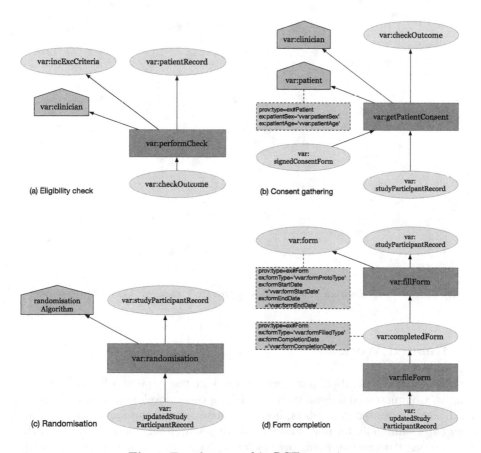

Fig. 4. Templates used in RCT scenario

With these constraints and templates in place, we run the simulation. Figure 5 shows an image from the Neo4j visualisation tool of a document built from five iterations of the RCT process, together with the original templates (yellow nodes) and the document metadata and indexing (green). The main subgraph shows the simulated trace under construction, with entities depicted in blue, activities in pink and agents in red. The trace can now be used to define various checks as required by the trial and have them validated and ready for the real data, once the trial starts.

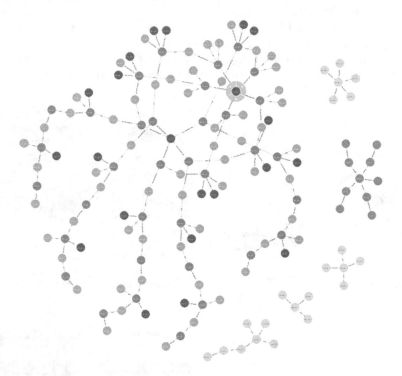

Fig. 5. Neo4j visualisation of five traces of the RCT process (Color figure online)

7   Related Work

Synthetic data generation has been studied in the context of databases and graphs. Commercial database systems such as those developed by Microsoft and IBM have associated generators, however these rely on random generation and only cater minimally for realism. One line of research has focused on generating test queries, data and verifying oracles for a given database schema [11], in order to create data with appropriate test coverage. Another approach is to generate data to be used against known query benchmarks [10] or applications [18]. The focus here is to have data with different (realistic or experimental) distributions.

These generators cater for dependencies such as foreign keys, but do not address constraints among other data elements.

Graph-based data is encountered in social networks, the internet, or the power grid. In order to assist the development of graph analysis and visualisation techniques, research has been undertaken on synthetic graph generation [13], focusing on statistical properties, with one recent work addressing the use of predefined patterns when generating graphs [17]. These patterns can somewhat be likened to templates, in that they constrain the structure of the generated graph. However, this work does not cater for constraints and allows the manipulations of the generated patterns to achieve statistical properties.

Two research groups are actively studying templates with similar approaches [14] and [5]. A detailed comparison of these is beyond the scope of this paper; but their difference mainly lies in the instantiation procedure. In [14] instantiation uses the Cartesian product of available bindings, whereas in [5] bindings can be given either simultaneously or incrementally using well-defined iteration zones.

To the best of our knowledge ProvGen [8] and DAGaholic [1] are the only approaches that have studied the generation of synthetic provenance data. These systems accept a seed graph as input, which identifies the PROV statements allowed to be emitted by the generator, in the context of a set of additional constraints. Constraints are restrictions that help enforce patterns or control statistical graph properties (such as vertex degree), but do not support the control of the domain-specific attributes of provenance elements. This highlights an important distinction to our approach, where provenance is an information model first, and its graph-based nature only of secondary importance. Hence we focus on restricting domain-specific attributes to indirectly control statistical graph properties.

Shapes Constraint Language (SHACL) [12] is a recent W3C specification for validating RDF data. SHACL has a comprehensive set of built-in constraints over RDF literals, such as regular expressions or integer ranges, and allows constraints involving complex graph patterns surrounding the focus node to be defined as SPARQL ASK and SELECT queries, the results of which are used to determine whether or not a constraint has been violated. We see SHACL as a complementary foundational technology for encoding templates. Our templates can be encoded as shape graphs, and our relation constraints as SPARQL constraints. However, SHACL has no means to represent value-dependency and distribution constraints and, furthermore does not support variables, which, for us are crucial abstractions for collecting and incrementally building provenance.

8   Conclusions and Future Work

In this paper we described a simulator for generating synthetic provenance in a way that observes domain-specific constraints. Our approach uses templates [5] to control and output provenance of a valid structure and three categories of constraints mapped to and solved by a CSP solver to help model domain-specific patterns in a realistic way. We described how workflows are modelled as probabilistic automata, traversals of which represent sequences of templates to be instantiated, and explained how the simulator fits within our provenance server architecture. Finally we illustrated our system with a case study based upon randomised clinical trials.

The implementation and testing of our simulator is ongoing. CSPs have high computational complexity, so an important next step for us is to determine the performance of our system for large output sizes in terms of number of variables, and number and types of constraints.

The clinical trial use case will be fully evaluated within the REST clinical trial (Runny Ear STudy: Immediate oral, immediate topical or delayed oral antibiotics for acute otitis media with discharge) later in 2018, before which provenance data will be synthesised in accordance with the design presented here, to be compared against the data collected.

References

1. David Allen, M., Chapman, A., Blaustein, B.: Engineering choices for open world provenance. In: Ludäscher, B., Plale, B. (eds.) IPAW 2014. LNCS, vol. 8628, pp. 242–253. Springer, Cham (2015). https://doi.org/10.1007/978-3-319-16462-5_25
2. Belhajjame, K., Chapman, A.: 2nd ProvBench: Benchmarking Provenance Management Systems (2014). https://sites.google.com/site/provbench/home/provbench-provenance-week-2014
3. Belhajjame, K., Zhao, J.: 1st ProvBench: Benchmarking Provenance Management Systems. In: Proceedings of the Joint EDBT/ICDT 2013 Workshops (2013)
4. Belhajjame, K., Zhao, J., Garijo, D., et al.: A workflow PROV-corpus based on Taverna and Wings. In: Proceedings of the Joint EDBT/ICDT 2013 Workshops, ProvBench: Provenance Benchmark Challenge (2013)
5. Curcin, V., Fairweather, E., Danger, R., et al.: Templates as a method for implementing data provenance in decision support systems. J. Biomed. Inform. **65** (2017)
6. Delaney, B., Curcin, V., Andreasson, A., et al.: Translational medicine and patient safety in Europe: TRANSFoRm - Architecture for the Learning Health System in Europe. Biomed Research Int., special edition on Improving Performance of Clinical Research: Development and Interest of Electronic Health Records (2015)
7. Fairweather, E., Alper, P., Porat, T., et al.: Architecture for Building Provenance Documents using Templates (2017). https://elliot.fairweather.eu/resources/ArchProvTemp.pdf
8. Firth, H., Missier, P.: ProvGen: generating synthetic PROV graphs with predictable structure. In: Ludäscher, B., Plale, B. (eds.) IPAW 2014. LNCS, vol. 8628, pp. 16–27. Springer, Cham (2015). https://doi.org/10.1007/978-3-319-16462-5_2
9. Gehani, A., Tariq, D.: Cross-platform provenance. In: Proceedings of the Joint EDBT/ICDT 2013 Workshops (2013)
10. Houkjær, K., Torp, K., Wind, R.: Simple and realistic data generation. In: Proceedings of the 32nd International Conference on Very Large Data Bases (2006)
11. Khalek, S. A., Elkarablieh, B., Laleye, Y. O. et al.: Query-aware test generation using a relational constraint solver. In: Proceedings of the 2008 23rd IEEE/ACM International Conference on Automated Software Engineering (2008)
12. Knublauch, H., Kontokostas, D.: Shapes constraint language (SHACL). Technical report, W3C (2017)

13. Leskovec, J., Chakrabarti, D., Kleinberg, J., Faloutsos, C.: Realistic, mathematically tractable graph generation and evolution, using kronecker multiplication. In: Jorge, A.M., Torgo, L., Brazdil, P., Camacho, R., Gama, J. (eds.) PKDD 2005. LNCS (LNAI), vol. 3721, pp. 133–145. Springer, Heidelberg (2005). https://doi.org/10.1007/11564126_17

14. Michaelides, D., Huynh, T. D., Moreau, L.: PROV-TEMPLATE: A template system for PROV documents (2014). https://provenance.ecs.soton.ac.uk/prov-template/

15. Prud'homme, C., Fages, J.-G., Lorca, X.: Choco Documentation (2016)

16. Rossi, F., van Beek, P., Walsh, T.: Handbook of Constraint Programming (Foundations of Artificial Intelligence). Elsevier Science Inc. (2006)

17. Shuai, H.-H., Yang, D.-N., Yu, P.S., et al.: On Pattern Preserving Graph Generation. In: 2013 IEEE 13th International Conference on Data Mining (2013)

18. Soltana, G., Sannier, N., Sabetzadeh, M., et al.: A model-based framework for probabilistic simulation of legal policies. In: 18th ACM/IEEE International Conference on Model Driven Engineering Languages and Systems (MoDELS 2015) (2015)

PROV Extensions

Versioned-PROV: A PROV Extension to Support Mutable Data Entities

João Felipe N. Pimentel[1]([✉]) [iD], Paolo Missier[2] [iD], Leonardo Murta[1] [iD],
and Vanessa Braganholo[1] [iD]

[1] Instituto de Computação, Universidade Federal Fluminense, Niteró, Brazil
{jpimentel,leomurta,vanessa}@ic.uff.br
[2] School of Computing, Newcastle University, Newcastle upon Tyne, UK
paolo.missier@newcastle.ac.uk

Abstract. The PROV data model assumes that entities are immutable and all changes to an entity e are represented by the creation of a new entity e'. This is reasonable for many provenance applications but may produce verbose results once we move towards fine-grained provenance due to the possibility of multiple binds (i.e., variables, elements of data structures) referring to the same mutable data objects (e.g., lists or dictionaries in Python). Changing a data object that is referenced by multiple immutable entities requires duplicating those immutable entities to keep consistency. This imposes an overhead on the provenance storage and makes it hard to represent data-changing operations and their effect on the provenance graph. In this paper, we propose a PROV extension to represent mutable data structures. We do this by adding reference derivations and checkpoints. We evaluate our approach by comparing it to plain PROV and PROV-Dictionary. Results indicate a reduction in the storage overhead for assignments and changes in data structures from $O(N)$ and $\Omega(R \times N)$, respectively, to $O(1)$ in both cases when compared to plain PROV (N is the number of members in the data structure and R is the number of references to the data structure).

Keywords: Provenance · Specification · Interoperability

1 Introduction

The PROV data model [6] is an extensible domain-agnostic model that describes the provenance of entities through their relationships with activities, agents, and other entities. An *entity* is a term used to represent any data, physical object, or concept whose provenance may be obtained. The *activity* term describes actions or processes that use entities and generate other entities. Finally, the *agent* term describes roles in activities.

PROV (and its predecessor, OPM [10]) has been applied to describe the provenance gathered from operating systems [11], workflow systems [2], and scripts [1]. Tools that collect operating system provenance map users as agents,

© Springer Nature Switzerland AG 2018
K. Belhajjame et al. (Eds.): IPAW 2018, LNCS 11017, pp. 87–100, 2018.
https://doi.org/10.1007/978-3-319-98379-0_7

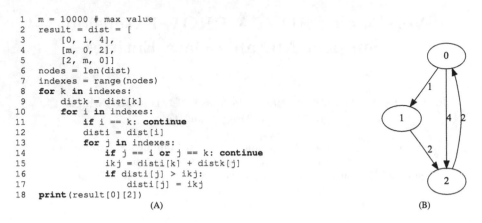

```
1    m = 10000 # max value
2    result = dist = [
3        [0, 1, 4],
4        [m, 0, 2],
5        [2, m, 0]]
6    nodes = len(dist)
7    indexes = range(nodes)
8    for k in indexes:
9        distk = dist[k]
10       for i in indexes:
11           if i == k: continue
12           disti = dist[i]
13           for j in indexes:
14               if j == i or j == k: continue
15               ikj = disti[k] + distk[j]
16               if disti[j] > ikj:
17                   disti[j] = ikj
18   print(result[0][2])
```

(A)   (B)

Fig. 1. *Floyd-Warshall* implementation (A) and encoded input graph (B).

file objects and program arguments as entities, and program executions and system calls as activities [11]. Workflow systems map data as entities and processing steps as activities [2]. Finally, tools that collect coarse-grained provenance from scripts map data in function arguments and data values obtained from return statements as entities, and function calls as activities [1].

In the aforementioned approaches, entities are immutable data that go through processing steps (modeled as activities) to produce new immutable data (modeled as entities). The assumption of immutable entities also exists in the PROV data model, where changes to an entity e are explicitly represented by the creation of a new entity e' generated by the activities that use the original e.

No known approaches use PROV to describe fine-grained provenance from scripts, with support for variables and mutable data structures. Our goal is to extend the well-known concepts of coarse-grained provenance for scripts, which is limited to function arguments and function calls, to (1) script variables, (2) expressions with operators, and (3) assignments, thus realizing fine-grained provenance for scripts. Specifically, we note that we can map script variables to entities, expressions with operators to activities that generate new entities, and assignments to activities that produce derivations, i.e., from expression results to variables. For example, a = b + c can be mapped as an activity + that uses the entities b and c to generate the derived entity sum, and an assignment activity that uses sum to generate the derived entity a.

This is a challenging goal because using PROV to represent fine-grained provenance suffers from two main problems: (P1) when an entity that represents a collection is changed (e.g., a list is updated to add an element), a new entity should be created, together with multiple new relationships, connecting the new entity to each of the existing or new entities that represent the elements of the collection; and (P2) when more than one variable is assigned to the same collection, and one of the variables changes, all other variables should also change, as they refer to the same memory area. This means that a new entity should be created for each variable that contains the collection, together with edges for all entities that represent the elements of the collection. As we show in Sect. 4, these problems lead to $O(N)$ and $\Omega(R \times N)$ extra elements in the provenance graph, respectively, for collections with N elements and R references.

PROV-Dictionary [8] improves the support for data structures in PROV by adding derivation statements that indicate that a new collection shares most elements of the old one, but with the insertion or removal of specific elements. This solves P1 since it reduces the number of edges to 1. However, it still suffers from P2, since it requires updating all entities that refer to the same collection when it changes, which leads to $\Omega(R)$ extra elements.

We propose Versioned-PROV, an extension that adds *reference sharing* and *checkpoints* to PROV. Checkpoints solve problem P1 in $O(1)$ by allowing the representation of multiple versions of collections with a single entity. Reference sharing solves problem P2 in $O(1)$ by allowing collections to be represented only once and referred to by other entities through reference derivations plus checkpoints to indicate states.

This paper is organized as follows. Section 2 presents a running example, which is based on the *Floyd-Warshall* algorithm [3]. Section 3 introduces Versioned-PROV. Section 4 evaluates the approach by comparing it to PROV and PROV-Dictionary. Section 5 discusses related work, and Sect. 6 concludes the paper.

2 Running Example

While Versioned-PROV intends to be generic enough for any situation that requires sharing references to mutable collections in PROV, we use fine-grained script provenance as a case study for presenting our extension. More specifically, we use the *Floyd-Warshall* algorithm [3] as a base to describe and evaluate the mapping of fine-grained provenance from scripts using Versioned-PROV. This algorithm has relevant applications, such as finding the shortest path between two addresses in a navigation system.

The algorithm calculates the length of the shortest path between all pairs of nodes in a weighted graph. It achieves this by updating the distance of the path from node i to node j if there is a node k for which the distance of the path from i to k plus the distance of the path from k to j is shorter than the distance from i to j. The result of *Floyd-Warshall* is the set of shortest distances among all pairs of nodes, but it does not produce the actual shortest paths. However, observing that the path between two nodes is defined by the sum of two other paths, here we show that we can use the fine-grained provenance of a given output distance to obtain the actual paths that have that distance.

Figure 1 presents a Python implementation of *Floyd-Warshall* with a predefined input graph. Line 18 prints the distance of the shortest path from 0 to 2. While there is a direct edge with cost 4, the actual result is 3, because the shortest path goes from 0 to 1, with cost 1, and then from 1 to 2, with cost 2. After the algorithm changes the result matrix, querying the provenance of `result[0][2]` in line 18 should indicate that it derives from `result[0][1]` and `result[1][2]`.

3   Versioned-PROV

Versioned-PROV adds the concepts of checkpoints, reference sharing, and accesses to PROV. Different from plain PROV, which assumes immutable entities, a Versioned-PROV entity may represent multiple versions of a data object. We present Versioned-PROV concepts in Sect. 3.1. In Sect. 3.2, we detail Versioned-PROV by presenting a mapping of a part assignment in the *Floyd-Warshall* algorithm, and contrasting it to PROV and PROV-Dictionary.

3.1   Concepts

The PROV data model is based on the idea of instantaneous transition events that describe usage, generation, and invalidation of entities [6]. These events are important to describe the provenance timeline without explicit time and ordering. Versioned-PROV builds on top of PROV events and determines that a version of a data object changes on a generation event, and is accessed on a usage event. Instead of relying on the implicit ordering of events from PROV, Versioned-PROV uses *checkpoint* attributes to tag events and changes on entities. Then, it uses the explicit ordering of *checkpoints* to obtain a version of a data object. Hence, we require a total order to be defined on the set of checkpoints. Our implementation of *Floyd-Warshall* uses *timestamps* as checkpoints, but the figures in this paper use *sequential numbers*. Both can be ordered.

As an extension of PROV, Versioned-PROV follows its semantics. Thus, despite the goal of representing multiple versions of a data object, an entity in PROV can only be generated once, according to the unique-generation constraint of PROV [6]. Thus, the only mutability on the Versioned-PROV entities occurs in the memberships of collection entities. A collection may have different members at different moments, but the operations that put and delete members from a collection are incremental. It means that if a collection c had an entity e1 at checkpoint 1 and an operation put the entity e2 into a different position of c at checkpoint 2, then c had both e1 and e2 at checkpoint 2.

Different from PROV and PROV-Dictionary that use copy-by-value to represent data-structure assignments and derivations, Versioned-PROV uses copy-by-reference. Hence, it defines the data structure once and uses *reference sharing* to indicate that more than one entity refers to the same data structure. When generating and using Versioned-PROV entities, one must indicate a checkpoint to unfold the specific version of the data structure for any given event. When an entity associated with a data structure changes at a given checkpoint, we can infer that all entities that share reference with it also changes at the same checkpoint, without any extra explicit statements.

Table 1. Versioned-PROV types.

Type	Statement	Meaning
Reference	wasDerivedFrom	The generated entity derived from the used entity by reference, indicating that both have the same numbers
Put	hadMember	Put a member into a collection *key* position at a given *checkpoint*. Using a placeholder as member indicates a deletion

Table 2. Versioned-PROV attributes.

Attribute	Range	Statement	Meaning
checkpoint	Sortable Value	hadMember	Checkpoint of the collection update. Required for *hadMember* with type *Put*
checkpoint	Sortable Value	Events (e.g., used, wasDerivedFrom)	Checkpoint of the event. Required for *wasDerivedFrom* with type *Reference*
key	String	hadMember	The position of *Put*
key	String	wasDerivedFrom	The position of the accessed *collection* entity
collection	Entity Id	wasDerivedFrom	Collection entity that was accessed or changed
access	'r' or 'w'	wasDerivedFrom	Indicates whether an access reads ('r') an element from a collection or writes ('w') into it

Versioned-PROV uses PROV optional attributes and defines types to extend PROV. Table 1 presents the Versioned-PROV types, and Table 2 presents the Versioned-PROV attributes. The attributes *key, collection,* and *access* of *wasDerivedFrom* may only be used when the derivation is related to an access or collection update. Similarly, the type *Put* can only appear in data structures, to define their items. Differently, the attribute *checkpoint* and the type *Reference* can appear anywhere, despite affecting only collection entities. This keeps the model consistent in all situations that involve using and generating entities.

3.2 Mapping Example

We use the script example of Sect. 2 to detail Versioned-PROV in contrast to PROV and PROV-Dictionary. We map the execution provenance of the *Floyd-Warshall* algorithm (Fig. 1) to these three approaches. Due to space constraints, we present only the first execution of the part assignment in line 17 of Fig. 1 (i.e., `disti[j] = ikj`). The complete mapping is available at [13].

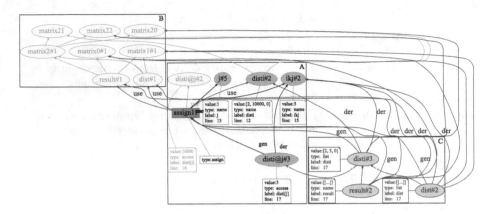

Fig. 2. Plain PROV mapping of `disti[j] = ikj`. (Color figure online)

Figures 2, 3, and 4 present the part assignment mapped to plain PROV, PROV-Dictionary, and Versioned-PROV, respectively. In our mappings, we name entities based on their textual representations. Since a textual element (e.g., a variable) can be represented by multiple entities, we enumerate them. Thus, `ikj#2` denotes the second entity that represents the variable `ikj` (as defined in line 15 of Fig. 1). In addition to this numbering, we change the notation of accesses to avoid using escaping characters to represent square brackets. Instead, we use the collection name followed by "@" and the accessed key. For instance, we use `disti@j` to represent `disti[j]` (lines 16–17 of Fig. 1). Note in region A of these figures that we have both `disti@j#2` in gray, representing `disti[j]` of line 16, and `disti@j#3` in yellow, representing `disti[j]` of line 17. The latter is the result of the part assignment.

We divide these figures into three regions: **A** represents the base part assignment that exists in all approaches; **B** represents a portion of the matrix that existed before this operation; and **C** represents the overhead entities (i.e., entities that are specific to an approach) that were generated as consequence of the part assignment. Note that Fig. 4 has no region C since Versioned-PROV does not have overhead entities. All the entities that exist in Versioned-PROV also exist in the other approaches.

We also use the color red to denote the overhead. Note that plain PROV has a bigger overhead than PROV-Dictionary, which has a bigger overhead than Versioned-PROV. This occurs due to the problems P1 and P2 mentioned in the introduction. Additionally, we use gray to indicate the portion of the provenance graph that is not related to the part assignment operation. As expected, all nodes and edges in region B are gray. The only gray node outside region B is `disti@j#2` in region A. This node appears due to the if condition in line 16 of Fig. 1. Hence, it is specific to this algorithm and not a generic node that occurs in all part assignments.

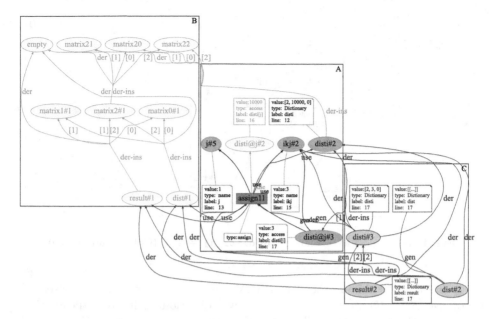

Fig. 3. PROV-Dictionary mapping of `disti[j] = ikj`. (Color figure online)

The operation `disti[j] = ikj` is putting the value of `ikj` into the position
j of `disti`. In region A of all figures, `ikj#2` represents the variable `ikj`; `j#5`
represents j; and `disti#2` represents `disti`. Additionally, `disti@j#3` represents
the resulting `disti[j]`. Note that `disti` in this execution is the same list as
`dist[2]`, represented by the entity `matrix2#1` (i.e., they point to the same
memory area). Note also that `dist` and `result` are the same matrix.

Since entities are immutable in PROV and PROV-Dictionary, an update
in a collection (`disti#2` in region A) requires the creation of a new collection
(`disti#3` in region C) that contains the updated members. PROV suffers from
P1, thus it reconstructs the membership of the new entity by using N *hadMember*
relationships in a collection with N members (3 in this case). We represent
these relationships by edges without labels in Fig. 2. PROV-Dictionary, on the
other hand, uses a single *derivedByInsertionFrom* (`der-ins` edges in Fig. 3) to
indicate that a collection was updated by the insertion of a member at a position
(`disti#3` derived from `disti#2` by the insertion of `disti@j#3` from region A at
position 1).

As stated before, `disti#2` represents the same value as `matrix2#1`. Thus,
we would have to update `matrix2#1` to reflect the change. This does not occur
because `matrix2#1` is out of the scope of the execution at this point and cannot be directly used without an access to `dist#1` or `result#1`. Due to P2,
plain PROV and PROV-Dictionary update `dist#1` and `result#1` by generating `dist#2` and `result#2` in region C and replacing `matrix2#1`, in the second
position, by `disti#3`.

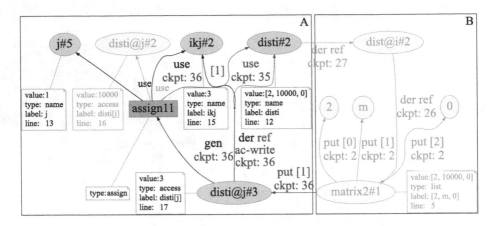

Fig. 4. Versioned-PROV mapping of `disti[j]` = `ikj`. (Color figure online)

In addition to this overhead in PROV and PROV-Dictionary, we use two extra *wasDerivedFrom* edges for every new collection entity to indicate that they derive both from the collection before the update and from the inserted value (`ikj#2`). Thus, in PROV, this operation has an overhead of 3 *entities*, 6 *wasDerivedFrom*, and 9 *hadMember*, and in PROV-Dictionary, this operation has an overhead of 3 *entities*, 6 *wasDerivedFrom*, and 3 *derivedByInsertionFrom*. Moreover, these overheads depend on the number of elements in the collections and the number of references to them.

Versioned-PROV does not suffer from these problems. It uses checkpoints to indicate multiple versions of a collection, and *derivations by reference* to indicate that two or more entities represent the same collection. In region C of Fig. 4, `matrix2#1` was defined at checkpoint 2 with the entities 2, m, 0 as members. This changed at checkpoint 36 since this part assignment put `disti@j#3` in the first position. Thus, `matrix2#1` has a version with the members 2, m, 0 between checkpoints 2 and 35, and a version with the members 2, `disti@j#3`, 0 after checkpoint 36. Note that in Fig. 4 we show the first value representation of collections for easy reading, but other Versioned-PROV implementations are free to decide on having the *value* attribute or not.

The aforementioned versions are valid for all the entities that derive by reference from `matrix2#1`. In Fig. 4, `dist@i#2` derived by reference from `matrix2#1`, and `disti#2` derived by reference from `dist@i#2`. By transitivity, `disti#2` derived by reference from `matrix2#1`. This derivation avoids the creation of `disti#3` and all the other entities and relationships that exist in the other mappings.

Since an entity can represent multiple versions of a collection in Versioned-PROV, we also use the *checkpoint* attribute in the use of `disti#2` to indicate the used version. Note in region A of Fig. 4 that this operation is using `disti#2` at checkpoint 35 to generate `disti@j#3` at checkpoint 36.

Every entity can only be derived by a single reference: if the algorithm assigns a new value to the variable `disti` (in line 12 of Fig. 1), we must create a new entity (e.g., `disti#3`) as a placeholder for the new value. That is, the checkpoint attribute does not apply for reusing an entity with different values. A variable entity in Versioned-PROV represents not just the variable name, but a pair consisting of the variable name and its value (memory area). Note that we do not need a new entity for `disti#2` in the part assignment as it still references the same memory area after the operation.

Finally, `disti@j#3` derived by reference from `ikj#2` in region A of Fig. 4. Since these entities are not collections, the derivation by reference has no impact on them - we use it just for consistency among all derivations. However, this specific derivation has other attributes in addition to *type* and *checkpoint*. We also indicate that it is a write *access* that puts the derived entity in the *key* position 1 of the collection `disti#2`. This information is required to answer the provenance query of *Floyd-Warshall* without encoding matrix positions into entities. Note that the members of `matrix2#1` in region B of Fig. 4 are the actual entities that exist in line 5 of Fig. 1, while the members of `matrix2#1` in Figs. 2 and 3 are dummy entities that encode the matrix position.

4   Evaluation

We evaluate the space overhead of Versioned-PROV in comparison to plain PROV and PROV-Dictionary by measuring the number or PROV-N statements each approach requires in similar situations. We analyze both the running example and the general case.

Space Overhead Analysis of the Running Example. For most operations, the storage requirements are the same in all three approaches. The only differences were observed in data structures definitions (lines 2–5 of Fig. 1), reference assignments or accesses (lines 2–5, 7, 9, 12, 18), and data structure updates (line 17).

In [13] we present the complete provenance graph of *Floyd-Warshall* in these three mappings, coloring only nodes and edges related to the list definitions, reference derivations, and part assignments, since these differ in the mappings. All nodes and edges that are common to all mappings are in light gray. PROV has many colored edges all over the graph due to the aforementioned problems P1 and P2. PROV-Dictionary has fewer scattered edges in the graph, but it has a huge concentration of Dictionary entities that derive from a single *EmptyDictionary* entity due to problem P2. Finally, Versioned-PROV has fewer colored nodes and edges since it does not suffer from these issues.

In Fig. 5(A) we count how many nodes are specific to each approach. Note that PROV and PROV-Dictionary use respectively 7.52 and 4.14 times the number of specific PROV-N statements used by Versioned-PROV to represent the same data structures. Additionally, Versioned-PROV does not impose any node overhead. All of its overhead occurs in edges that specify the membership of collections. On the other hand, PROV and PROV-Dictionary impose node overhead

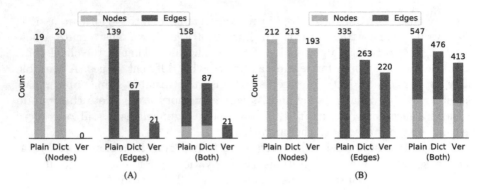

Fig. 5. Number of PROV, PROV-Dictionary, and Versioned-PROV PROV-N statements for list definitions, reference derivations, and part assignments (A) and total number of statements (B).

to indicate the position of elements in data structures and to derive immutable entities from existing ones. Moreover, by comparing Fig. 5(A) with Fig. 5(B), which shows the total number of statements, we can see that 29% of PROV statements, 18% of PROV-Dictionary statements, and 5% of Versioned-PROV statements are the overhead caused by collection operations.

These results refer to a small *Floyd-Warshall* execution, with a 3×3 matrix representing the input graph. Since the overheads of PROV and PROV-Dictionary grow in terms of the number of collection elements and the number of shared references, more complex input graphs and algorithms can cause a much larger overhead.

Space Overhead Analysis of the General Case. In Sect. 3, we describe the part assignment of PROV, PROV-Dictionary, and Versioned-PROV. Figure 6 presents the growth of statements in the three approaches for part assignments. Versioned-PROV has an overhead of **2 PROV-N statements**: the *hadMember* that puts the member in the collection, and the *used* that indicates the changed collection. Plain PROV has an overhead of $(3 + N) \times R$ **statements** for collections with N members and R references: it creates R *entities*, each of them with 2 *wasDerivedFrom* and N *hadMember*. Finally, PROV-Dictionary has an overhead of $4 \times R$ **statements**: it creates R *entities*, each with 2 *wasDerivedFrom* and 1 *derivedByInsertionFrom*. Note that both plain PROV and PROV-Dictionary also use the changed collection, but this *used* relationship can be inferred from one of the additional *wasDerivedFrom* statements. Hence, we count it only as an overhead for Versioned-PROV. The number of statements for PROV and PROV-Dictionary are lower bounds. If we update a collection x that is also a member of another collection y, we must also update all the references of y and apply this same rule with respect to references and number of elements. This occurs in our example of Sect. 3.2: the update of disti#2 with $R = 1$ and $N = 3$ motivates the update of dist#1 with $R = 2$ and $N = 3$.

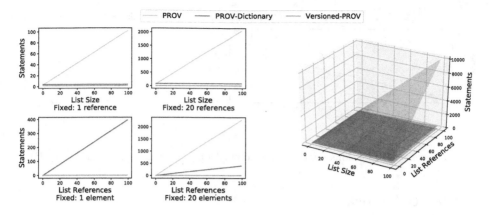

Fig. 6. Overhead functions of part assignments.

Besides part assignments, the approaches also differ in list definitions and derivations by reference. Figure 7(A) shows the overhead of defining a list in each approach. Versioned-PROV has an overhead of only N **hadMember statements** to define a list with N elements since they indicate the members with their positions in the list and we reference these positions in accesses. Thus, the provenance of *Floyd-Warshall* in Versioned-PROV includes the accessed positions, allowing us to use these positions to reconstruct the paths of the graph.

On the other hand, plain PROV and PROV-Dictionary have overheads of $3 \times N + 2$ **statements**, and 1 **(global)** $+ 2 \times N + 3$ **statements**, respectively. This occurs because these approaches do not indicate the access position and the access derivation directly from the member. Hence, we must encode the position information into entities. This encoding requires the creation of N dummy entities. Each one of these dummy entities derives from their respective entities (i.e., N *wasDerivedFrom*) by the application of a new *definelist* activity. The resulting list entity is also generated by this activity (i.e., 1 *wasGeneratedBy* and 1 list *entity* itself), and it has the dummy entities as members. PROV-Dictionary expresses the membership with a single *derivedByInsertionFrom* statement from a single global *EmptyDictionary*, while PROV additionally requires N *hadMember* statements to define the membership of all elements.

Figure 7(B) compares the growth of overhead in derivations by reference. Versioned-PROV imposes **no statement overhead** since it uses attributes of *wasDerivedFrom* to indicate the derivation. On the other hand, PROV and PROV-Dictionary have to recreate the membership of this new entity. PROV requires N **hadMember statements**, and PROV-Dictionary requires a **single derivedByInsertionFrom statement**. Note that both PROV-Dictionary and Versioned-PROV do not grow in terms of the number of elements, but Versioned-PROV still performs better than PROV-Dictionary, since the former does not require any extra statement.

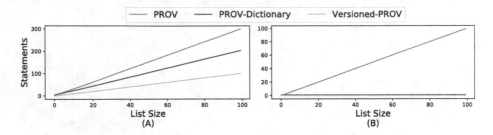

Fig. 7. Overhead functions for list definitions (A) and derivations by reference (B).

5   Related Work

Many approaches have been proposed to collect and represent provenance from scripts. Some tools export provenance from scripts to OPM [1,16], which is easily convertible to PROV. However, these tools work at coarse-grain and do not take mutable data structures into account. Other tools work at fine-grain but use non-interoperable mechanisms for storage and distribution [5,14,15]. Moreover, these approaches work only at the variable and statement dependency level and do not provide support for tracking the provenance of changes on data structures referred by multiple variables.

Michaelides et al. [7] collect fine-grained provenance from Blockly variables and export it to plain PROV. Plain PROV assumes that entities are immutable and uses *hadMember* statements to describe structures, but its usage is too verbose and imposes a high overhead in the storage of mutable data structures, as we present in Sect. 4.

PROV has been extended in many different ways [2,4,9], but most extensions focus only on representing domain-specific provenance and do not improve the support for data structures. The PROV-Dictionary extension [8] improves the PROV support for data structures by adding insertion and removal derivations. Such derivations reduce the storage overhead in comparison to PROV, but still produces a high overhead in comparison to Versioned-PROV due to the assumption of immutability.

6   Final Remarks

In this paper, we propose Versioned-PROV, a PROV extension that supports mutable data structures. Tools that collect fine-grained provenance from scripts can use Versioned-PROV to support the collection of provenance from complex data structures and variables that are implicitly modified due to the existence of other variables pointing to the same mutable data. Nevertheless, our extension is not restricted to scripts.

The proposed approach has some limitations. First, while our extension reduces the storage overhead for provenance collection from scripts, it introduces an extra overhead for querying due to the requirement of unfolding data structure versions based on checkpoints. Thus, users must consider this tradeoff according to their needs. Second, by using a dictionary-like structure to represent lists (i.e., indexes mapped to keys, and elements mapped to values), some operations still produce an overhead in the provenance storage. For instance, inserting an element at the beginning of a list will require updating all the other members of the list. Third, using an explicit checkpoint ordering imposes synchronization challenges for parallel provenance collection. Finally, the usage of optional attributes to extend PROV imposes a storage overhead in disk due to the attribute name repetition. However, this overhead may not occur depending on how it is stored. A normalized storage schema would remove the repetitions.

As future work, we intend to develop an efficient querying algorithm for Versioned-PROV. We also plan to adopt the proposed model in noWorkflow [12] to export its fine-grained provenance [14] and evaluate it in real scenarios. We foresee the elaboration of unfolding algorithms that converts Versioned-PROV into plain PROV to improve its interoperability and optimize analyses that require many queries. These algorithms could also run by demand, populating caches of unfolded data structures. Additionally, we plan to work on an extension of Versioned-PROV to improve the incremental membership definition of lists.

Finally, our companion website [13] contains all the source code used to generate images of this paper in addition to detailed descriptions of the mapping we applied in each approach, as well as a preliminary query implementation.

References

1. Angelino, E., Yamins, D., Seltzer, M.: StarFlow: a script-centric data analysis environment. In: McGuinness, D.L., Michaelis, J.R., Moreau, L. (eds.) IPAW 2010. LNCS, vol. 6378, pp. 236–250. Springer, Heidelberg (2010). https://doi.org/10.1007/978-3-642-17819-1_27
2. Costa, F., et al.: Capturing and querying workflow runtime provenance with ProV: a practical approach. In: Joint EDBT/ICDT Workshops. ACM, Genoa (2013)
3. Floyd, R.W.: Algorithm 97: shortest path. Commun. ACM. 5(6), 345 (1962)
4. Garijo, D., Gil, Y.: Augmenting PROV with plans in P-PLAN: scientific processes as linked data. In: LISC, Boston, USA (2012)
5. Lerner, B., et al.: Using introspection to collect provenance in R. Informatics 5(1), 12 (2018)
6. Moreau, L., Missier, P.: PROV-DM: The PROV Data Model (2012). http://www.w3.org/TR/prov-dm/
7. Michaelides, D.T., Parker, R., Charlton, C., Browne, W.J., Moreau, L.: Intermediate notation for provenance and workflow reproducibility. In: Mattoso, M., Glavic, B. (eds.) IPAW 2016. LNCS, vol. 9672, pp. 83–94. Springer, Cham (2016). https://doi.org/10.1007/978-3-319-40593-3_7
8. Missier, P., et al.: PROV-dictionary: modeling provenance for dictionary data structures. https://www.w3.org/TR/prov-dictionary/
9. Missier, P., et al.: D-PROV: extending the PROV provenance model with workflow structure. In: TaPP. USENIX, Lombard (2013)

10. Moreau, L., Freire, J., Futrelle, J., McGrath, R.E., Myers, J., Paulson, P.: The open provenance model: an overview. In: Freire, J., Koop, D., Moreau, L. (eds.) IPAW 2008. LNCS, vol. 5272, pp. 323–326. Springer, Heidelberg (2008). https://doi.org/10.1007/978-3-540-89965-5_31
11. Muniswamy-Reddy, K.K., et al.: Provenance-aware storage systems. In: USENIX Annual Technical Conference, pp. 43–56. USENIX, Boston (2006)
12. Murta, L., Braganholo, V., Chirigati, F., Koop, D., Freire, J.: noWorkflow: capturing and analyzing provenance of scripts. In: Ludäscher, B., Plale, B. (eds.) IPAW 2014. LNCS, vol. 8628, pp. 71–83. Springer, Cham (2015). https://doi.org/10.1007/978-3-319-16462-5_6
13. Pimentel, J.F., et al.: Versioned-PROV. https://dew-uff.github.io/versioned-prov/
14. Pimentel, J.F., Freire, J., Murta, L., Braganholo, V.: Fine-grained provenance collection over scripts through program slicing. In: Mattoso, M., Glavic, B. (eds.) IPAW 2016. LNCS, vol. 9672, pp. 199–203. Springer, Cham (2016). https://doi.org/10.1007/978-3-319-40593-3_21
15. Runnalls, A., Silles, C.: Provenance tracking in R. In: Groth, P., Frew, J. (eds.) IPAW 2012. LNCS, vol. 7525, pp. 237–239. Springer, Heidelberg (2012). https://doi.org/10.1007/978-3-642-34222-6_25
16. Tariq, D., et al.: Towards automated collection of application-level data provenance. In: TaPP. USENIX, Boston (2012)

Using the Provenance from Astronomical Workflows to Increase Processing Efficiency

Michael A. C. Johnson[1]([✉]), Luc Moreau[2], Adriane Chapman[1],
Poshak Gandhi[1], and Carlos Sáenz-Adán[3]

[1] University of Southampton, Southampton, Hampshire SO17 1BJ, UK
{Michael.Johnson,Adriane.Chapman,Poshak.Gandhi}@soton.ac.uk
[2] King's College London, London WC2B 4BG, UK
Luc.Moreau@kcl.ac.uk
[3] Department of Mathematics and Computer Science,
University of La Rioja, Logroño, Spain
carlos.saenz@unirioja.es

Abstract. Astronomy is increasingly becoming a data-driven science as the community builds larger instruments which are capable of gathering more data than previously possible. As the sizes of the datasets increase, it becomes even more important to make the most efficient use of the computational resources available. In this work, we highlight how provenance can be used to increase the computational efficiency of astronomical workflows. We describe a provenance-enabled image processing pipeline and motivate the generation of provenance with two relevant use cases. The first use case investigates the origin of an optical variation and the second is concerned with the objects used to calibrate the image. The provenance was then queried in order to evaluate the relative computational efficiency of use case evaluation, with and without the use of provenance. We find that recording the provenance of the pipeline increases the original processing time by $\sim$45%. However, we find that when evaluating the two identified use cases, the inclusion of provenance improves the efficiency of processing by $\sim$99% and $\sim$96% for Use Cases 1 and 2, respectively. Furthermore, we combine these results with the probability that Use Cases 1 and 2 will need to be evaluated and find a net decrease in computational processing efficiency of 13–44% when incorporating provenance generation within the workflow. However, we deduce that provenance has the potential to produce a net increase in this efficiency if more uses cases are to be considered.

1 Introduction

Provenance is a staple in the art communities as it is a record of the origin, ownership and custody of a work of art or artefact. In this context, it can be used to assess the authenticity and probe past possession, in order to value a work of art. The practice of provenance has also been adopted by the scientific

© Springer Nature Switzerland AG 2018
K. Belhajjame et al. (Eds.): IPAW 2018, LNCS 11017, pp. 101–112, 2018.
https://doi.org/10.1007/978-3-319-98379-0_8

community as reliability and reproducibility are two of its fundamental axioms. The use of provenance within science is becoming ever more important as the quantities of data and the number of people analysing each dataset increase.

Over the last few decades, the ability of the astronomer to collect and process data has increased dataset sizes from giga to tera to now peta-byte scale datasets. This is in part due to the creation of large scale survey telescopes such as the Sloan Digital Sky Survey (SDSS) [1], the Palomar Transient Factory [2] and, in future, the Large Synoptic Survey Telescope (LSST) [3]. As astronomy is increasingly becoming a data-driven science, many frameworks and tools have been designed to automate the generation of the accompanying provenance. Producing this detailed record of the provenance requires additional storage and introduces an initial runtime overhead to the execution time. However, it can also allow for a significant reduction in resources when analysing the final data products.

With the advent of new survey telescopes, such as LSST, which have extremely large datasets, it is becoming ever more crucial for the astronomer to make the most efficient use of the computational resources available. PROV-TEMPLATE [4] is a declarative approach to enable the generation of PROV compatible provenance and in this paper we investigate the implementation of PROV-templates as a means of producing the provenance of astronomical workflows. The aim is to quantitatively demonstrate the relative computational efficiency of astronomical image processing with and without the use of PROV-TEMPLATE generated provenance. In order to achieve this, firstly, PROV-TEMPLATES were used to generate the provenance of an astronomical image processing pipeline which was designed to measure the brightness variation of black hole binary systems. Secondly, within the context of this workflow, two use cases were identified for which provenance is vital for the astronomy community. Use Case 1 was to investigate the origin of an observed variation in a target astronomical object's brightness and in Use Case 2, a star was found to be incorrectly measured and it was investigated whether this star was used in the calibration process. These use cases were then evaluated with and without the use of the generated provenance and the relative resources required by each method were quantified. Finally, the total impact of provenance capture and usage was measured by comparing the computational resources required for implementation and use case evaluation with and without the use of provenance.

The contributions of this paper are: identifying two use cases for which provenance is vital for the astronomy community; a quantitative measurement of the impact of provenance capture and usage with these use cases and the application of PROV-Templates to a real world situation.

The structure of this paper is as follows, Sect. 2 outlines the astronomy application and identifies the use cases which will be evaluated. Section 3 describes the provenance generation method. Section 4 details the evaluation of the outlined use cases. Section 5 outlines the related work and finally, Sect. 6 discusses our findings.

2   Astronomy Application

The motivation of this paper is to investigate the potential for provenance to increase the efficiency of processing astronomical data, therefore we outline an astronomical dataset and image processing pipeline in this section. The astronomical images used throughout this were all taken of the low mass X-ray binary (LMXB), GS 1354-64 which consists of a star in orbit around a black hole. The pipeline identifies the objects in the images, measures the brightness of all objects and calibrates them to account for changing viewing conditions in order to find the variations in flux that GS 1354-64 exhibits over time. These optical variations can be used to determine properties of the system such as its orbital period, which can then be used, in-conjunction with spectral information, to infer the masses of the binary components. Currently, this is the only way we have to robustly measure the mass of stellar mass black holes and increasing the sample of known black hole masses enables us to better understand their properties. Survey telescopes are the ideal equipment in order to discover more systems as they are designed to systematically observe large swathes of the sky. As we are looking to discover new LMXBs, we do not know their position, although we may know areas of the sky where they are more likely to be. This means that large quantities of data must be analysed in order to find the objects of interest and it is essential to utilise any advantage in computational efficiency available which motivates our investigation into the use of provenance in this regard.

2.1   The Image Processing Pipeline

The image processing pipeline had two main functions: differential photometry and pattern recognition. As the measured brightness of the object in an image is dependent on conditions such as clouds, the image's proximity to the moon and light pollution, the images must be calibrated via differential photometry, whereby stars of known and constant brightness within the same image are used to adjust the measured brightness for differences in observing conditions. The pattern recognition was required in order to determine which source in the image corresponds to which astronomical object. The use cases are both concerned with differential photometry, therefore the explanation of the workflow will focus on this aspect.

The left hand side of Fig. 1 is a UML sequence diagram depicting a simplified version of the differential photometry in the image processing pipeline. The two lifelines of the UML diagram represent the script itself and the astronomical images. The first message, *performAperturePhotometry*, measures the brightness of all objects within the image. Then, *differentialPhotometry* compares the measured brightness of known objects (standard stars) to their true brightness in order to calculate the brightness correction needed for that particular image. The pipeline determined which stars should be used as standard stars for each image individually. Multiple standard stars were used in order to get a more consistent calibration as any individual star is more effected by things such as noise or systematic uncertainties. Bright stars were also chosen for the same

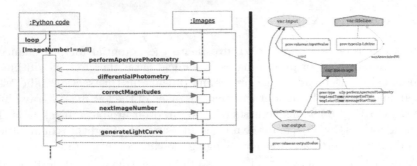

Fig. 1. The left hand side is a UML sequence diagram depicting a simplified version of the differential photometry process. The right-hand side is a PROV template generated from *performAperturePhotometry*.

reason. Once some candidate stars had been selected, they were cross-referenced with the SIMBAD astronomical database [5] to determine whether they were non-variable stars and if they were found to be so, then their true brightness was retrieved and compared to the measured value and the brightness correction for that image could be calculated. This process was repeated for each standard star in the image and the final correction was the averaged value. The brightness of the target object (in this case GS 1354-64) was then adjusted using this correction. This process was then repeated for all images. Finally, the corrected brightness of the object across all images was plotted against time to give the lightcurve, demonstrating the objects temporal optical variation.

2.2   Use Cases

In order to assess the usefulness of provenance for the astronomical community, the following use cases have been identified.

Use Case 1. *Variation Investigation* - An Astronomer, Alice, detects a change in luminosity in a star between two images taken on two different nights. Alice *determines whether the change was intrinsic to the object or a result of the image processing pipeline.*

First, this use case requires a record of the version of the pipeline that was used for the image processing. The change in brightness could also be the result of the standard stars used to correct the measurement, either different stars being selected for each image processing step.

If the image processing is found to be consistent between the observations, then the change in observed brightness can be deduced to be due to the object, however if there are inconsistencies then the images must be reprocessed to determine the true origin of the variation.

With no accompanying provenance, the processing would have to be repeated, ensuring the pipeline was identical in order to dispel any doubt in the origin of the variation.

Evaluation of Use Case 1 asserts absolute certainty that the origin of the optical variation was not due to the image processing pipeline. However, it is usually expected, for this application, that the origin of the variation is from the object. Therefore, it is likely that Use Case 1 would only be evaluated when the astronomer, Alice, detects an unexpected result, such as too much variation or no variation at all. An unexpected result from astronomical images is not uncommon, however, quantifying how often this will occur is difficult to determine as this kind of data is typically poorly documented within the astronomical community. Consequently, estimated probabilities of 1%, 10% and 30% were all investigated in order to assess the impact of evaluating Use Case 1 on the total computational resources required.

Use Case 2. *Calibration Propagation* - A star that was previously thought to be standard has been shown to demonstrate variability. Alice *determines which objects used this star for calibration and recalculates the photometry for them.* Standard stars are objects of known and constant luminosity that astronomers use to calibrate images. If a standard star that was used for calibration had a different brightness than what was accounted for, then the calibration could be incorrect and an incorrect calibration means that the measured brightness of the target object is wrong, invalidating the results.

Without the use of provenance, there are two possible solutions for this calibration propagation: firstly, with no knowledge of the standard stars used for calibration, all images which contain the previously standard star would have to be re-processed, ensuring that this star is not selected; secondly, the workflow could be re-run up until the standard stars are selected from each image, and with this information, only the images which use the previously standard star in the calibration would be repeated.

Conversely, when evaluating this use case with provenance, the provenance can be queried to return the list of standard stars used in the calibration process for each image. From this, only the images which contain the newly variable star have to be re-processed.

The invalidation of the use of a standard star could also be due to an incorrectly measured brightness as well as incorrectly determining the object to be variable. Determining how often Use Case 2 is likely to be evaluated is not trivial by any means as an object may be incorrectly measured or identified if: the object saturated the image; a cosmic ray interfered with the image; there were unaccounted for artefacts or systematics; the standard object exhibited sporadic variation or it transitioned into a variable object. Taking into account all of these scenarios, an estimated 1% probability that Use Case 2 would need to be evaluated was assumed. It should be noted that this number could be calculable if provenance use was more ubiquitous within the astronomy community.

3 Provenance in Astronomy Simulations

Whilst the aim of this paper is to demonstrate the use of provenance to reduce the overall processing cost, we must also address the initial overhead introduced by provenance capture. The PROV-TEMPLATE [4] approach was used to generate PROV-compatible provenance which described the workflow. Firstly, the full pipeline was modelled as a UML Sequence Diagram and later, UML2PROV [6] was used to generate *templates* that described the design of the provenance to be generated for each function. During the execution of the workflow, *bindings* were generated every time a function was called which contained the variable-value pairs (such as inputs or outputs) that were specific to that call of the function and had corresponding variables on the template for that function. On the right-hand side of Fig. 1 we can see a template generated from *performAperturePhotometry*. After completion of the workflow, these *bindings* were then expanded with their corresponding *templates* using the ProvToolbox[1] to yield the individual provenance files. These were then merged to produce the full provenance that described the system.

The image processing pipeline analysed a series of 10 images of LMXB GS 1354-64 taken by the Faulkes Telescope. All of the computation was repeated twenty times and the results in Fig. 2(a) represent the average and standard deviation of these execution times. One should note that the only relevant time increase for workflow execution time is the addition of *bindings* as the merging and expansion can both be done post pipeline. The size of the products of the workflow with and without provenance were also assessed and are shown in Table 1. The size of the inputs are also included to demonstrate that whilst the provenance files are large when compared to the outputs, they are still inconsequential on the scale of the full workflow.

All simulations were run on a Dell Latitude E7470 laptop with the following specifications: 8 GB of system memory; an Intel® Core™ i5-6200U CPU @ 2.30 GHz. The machine was running Ubuntu 16.04, kernel: 4.4.0-112-generic.

Table 1. The size of inputs consumed by and outputs produced by the image processing pipeline with and without provenance generation.

Method	Total input size	Total output size
Workflow only	21 MB	20 kB
Workflow with provenance	21 MB	546 kB

4   Evaluation

4.1   Use Case 1

The astronomical pipeline may not always perform a consistent analysis from image to image. It may have different parameters during the calibration such as which stars were used as standard stars. It may also use different library versions of the pipeline and the path that each data product made through

---

[1] https://lucmoreau.github.io/ProvToolbox/.

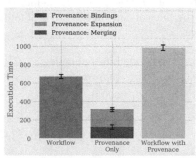
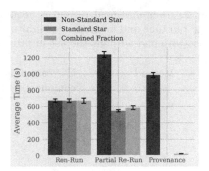

(a) Timing: Workflow Execution, with and without Provenance

(b) Timing: Analysis of Use Case 2

Fig. 2. (a) Average processing times for workflow execution, with and without provenance generation. (b) Computational resources required to evaluate Use Case 2, when implementing different solutions. Execution times vary depending on whether the newly variable star was used as a standard star in the calibration on not, so both times are shown. The combined fraction convolves these processing times with the probability that any star in the image was used as a standard star. Both sets of results are the average found over twenty simulations and the error bars represent their standard deviation.

the pipeline may not always be the same. Use Case 1 investigates an observed change in brightness from one image to another and tries to determine whether this variation was inherent to the object itself or whether its origin was due to inconsistencies in the image processing pipeline.

In order to evaluate Use Case 1 without provenance, the workflow must be re-run over the series of images where the variation was observed, with the pipeline versions and calibration settings made certain to be the same throughout. To evaluate Use Case 1 with the use of provenance, SPARQL queries were written to determine which versions of the pipeline and which standard stars were used for each image. The queries were <10 lines long and had a negligible run time (<1 s).

It was found that the same standard stars were used throughout the series of images and the versions of the pipeline used were the same throughout as well. Therefore, the observed variation could be deduced to not be due to the image processing and the data did not need to be reprocessed. This information resulted in a ~99% increase in computational efficiency over evaluating the use case without provenance. Table 2 shows the processing time necessary for evaluating each use case, as well as the length of the code required to do so.

4.2   Use Case 2

Use Case 2 was to determine whether a star that was recently determined to be variable was used in the image processing as a standard star and therefore invalidated the calibration for that image. Three ways of evaluating Use Case 2

Table 2. Computational resources required to evaluate Use Case 1, including the average run time and an order of magnitude of the lines of code needed to evaluate the use case with and without the use of provenance.

Method	Use case analysis computation time (s)	SD (s)	Lines of code (approximate)
Workflow only	671	22	500
With provenance	1	0	10

were investigated: firstly, the workflow was completely re-executed, ensuring that the variable star is not used in the calibration process; secondly the workflow was executed up until the selection of standard stars, this information was recorded and the images which contain the variable object were re-computed and finally, the provenance of the workflow was queried to determine which images should be re-processed.

For the first case, the time to evaluate Use Case 2 is the same as the original execution time as there is no information on which images did or did not use the variable object for calibration so all must be repeated. For the second scenario, the evaluation time is reduced when the variable star was found not to be used as a standard star as the workflow had to only be partially re-run. However, if it were found to be used as a standard star then the workflow must also be completely re-run with this star not being used in the calibration in addition to the partial run to find the standard stars used. The third evaluation queries the provenance in order to determine whether the newly variable star was used as a standard star. In summary, the first evaluation assumes no knowledge of the workflow and always completely re-runs. The second method determines information on the standard stars used by partially re-running the workflow then deciding whether it should all be re-run. The final method leverages provenance information in order to determine whether the workflow should be re-run.

If it was not used as a standard star, then there was only the computational cost of provenance querying required to evaluate the use case as the workflow does not need to be re-run. If it was used as a standard star, then the workflow must be re-run with the newly variable star not used during the calibration process. The SPARQL queries used to evaluate this use case were <10 lines long and had a negligible run time (<1 s), as before.

As the computational efficiency of two of the methods rely on whether the newly variable star was used as a standard star, the probability that any star in the image was used in the calibration as a standard star was calculated. This probability was convolved with the computation time required by each method of use case evaluation for if the star was used as a standard star and if it was not. This probability, P, was defined as $P = n/A$ where n is the number of standard stars per image and A is the average number of objects per image. For this example, 10 standard stars were used and the total number of objects in the image was $\sim$450, therefore, assuming all objects were treated equally, there was a ~2% chance that any star in the image was used as a standard star. By combining this probability with the two timings, we compute the average cost of use case evaluation if any given star in the image was found to be variable.

Figure 2(b) shows the results for evaluating Use Case 2 with the three possible solutions. The time represents the average execution time after repeating the simulation twenty times. The columns in Fig. 2(b) represent time taken when the object found to be variable was used as a standard star, when it was not used as a standard star and both these results combined with the probability that any star in the image was used as a standard star (the combined fraction).

We found that the computational processing cost of Use Case 2 evaluation if the star is found to be standard decreases by 21% with provenance when compared to partially re-running the workflow. However, we also found that the processing time increases in this respect with the use of provenance by 47% when compared to simply re-running the workflow. This is due to three reasons: firstly, the initial overhead of provenance production; secondly the relatively small cost of querying the provenance and finally, the workflow must be completely re-run in either case as the fact the star was used as a standard star invalidates the initial results. We also found that the cost of evaluation is greatly reduced if the star was not used as a standard star because here, the only computational cost is for querying the provenance which is negligible when compared to re-running the workflow, increasing the efficiency by ~99% when compared to either evaluation without the use of provenance. Finally, when we combine these efficiencies with the probability that the star will be used as a standard star, we found that with the use of provenance, the computational efficiency of evaluating Use Case 2 increases by a factor of 97% and 96% when compared to evaluating it by re-running and partially re-running the workflow, respectively.

5   Related Work

5.1   Provenance in Astronomy and e-Science

An early example of provenance within e-Science was outlined in Lanter et al. [7] where they designed lineage meta-data base system in order to document the sources of data in geographic information system (GIS) applications. This information then assisted in determining the quality of the data and the fitness of use for potential applications. Another example framework is [my]Grid [8], designed to meet the needs of *in silico* experiments in biology. [my]Grid prioritises semantic complexity over availability of computationally intensive resources to reflect the data centric nature of the bioinformatic experiments.

Examples of frameworks designed with the needs of the astronomy community in mind are Chimera [9] and Kepler [10]. One of the motivations for Chimera was SDSS, their data intensive needs and the requirement for scalability. Chimera therefore developed the virtual data system which allowed for on demand data generation, reducing the storage requirements.

Many scientists have adopted the use of scripting languages rather than working within scientific workflow systems due to their relative proficiency in them.

Fortunately for the modern astronomer, tools such as YesWorkflow [11] and NoWorkflow [12] have been developed to automate the generation of provenance from these scripts. Groth et al. [13] explored the use of provenance queries within astronomy. They identified relevant astronomy use cases for provenance which motivated the construction of a new provenance model which requires less storage than traditional provenance generation in anticipation for the large data production expected by LSST.

5.2 PROV-TEMPLATES

PROV-TEMPLATES facilitate the design and generation of provenance compatible with the PROV standard of the world wide web consortium [4]. PROV-TEMPLATE generated provenance has previously been employed by A Giesler et al. [14] to provide provenance tracking in scientific workflows.

One advantage of PROV-TEMPLATES over other methods of provenance generation is that only the bindings need be created during workflow execution and they can then be expanded later. This not only reduces the initial processing required at execution, but also can reduce the storage requirement as the bindings are typically only 40% of the size of the expanded provenance templates [4]. PROV-TEMPLATES also facilitate the generation of provenance without the need for writing code to do so, such as as the tools YesWorkflow [11] or NoWorkflow [12]. However, unlike these systems, PROV-TEMPLATES also allow for complex queries over the provenance that are possible in purpose built frameworks such as Chimera [9].

Table 3. Total computational processing cost of running the workflow with and without provenance. Including processing cost of use case analysis combined with the probability that the use case must be evaluated. Use Case 1 results are combined with the probability the use case would need to be evaluated 1%, 10% and 30% of the time.

	Workflow run time (s)	Use case 1 run time (s) (1%, 10%, 30%)	Use case 2 run time (s)	Total run time (s) (1%, 10%, 30%)
Workflow only	671	7, 67, 201	6	684, 744, 878
Workflow with provenance	987	<1	<1	988

6 Conclusions

We have found that recording the provenance of an image processing pipeline increases the initial processing cost by ~45%. However, we have also demonstrated that the use of provenance resulted in an increase in computational efficiency of 99% and 96% when evaluating Use Cases 1 and 2, respectively. We speculated that evaluation of Use Case 1 would occur from 1% to 30% of the time and Use Case 2 would likely need to be evaluated ~1% of the time. By combining the processing cost of provenance production, use case evaluation and the probability that the use cases will need to be evaluated, we compute the total net change in processing efficiency of the workflow by introducing provenance generation as a decrease in computational processing efficiency of 13–44%, depending on how often Use Case 1 needs to be evaluated. The full results are shown in Table 3.

We also found that when including provenance, the total size of artefacts produced by the workflow increased by a factor of ~6. Whilst these results do represent a large increase in data products, it should be noted that they are completely un-optimised for storage space savings. Also the provenance is fairly fine-grained and has the potential to evaluate many other use cases not investigated in this paper. This means that there is the possibility for a significant reduction in both the size of the final provenance and its intermediate products. Furthermore, the combined data products from provenance production and the workflow still represented <1% of the total data products consumed by the pipeline as the size of the input images dwarfs that of the data products.

These results pertain to the image processing pipeline used during this paper and it is likely to change from pipeline to pipeline. Having said this, other pipelines which are designed to achieve the same goals will likely be similar in operation and correlate with the results found in this paper. One interesting investigation would be the comparison between results obtained with the use of PROV standard provenance vs the home-grown provenance solutions developed by astronomers as part of their scripts.

One limitation of our approach was determining the probability that the use cases would need to be evaluated as we were only able to postulate estimated probabilities. The more often these use cases need to be evaluated, the more provenance positively impacts the computational efficiency of the workflow. The results therefore only serve as an estimation of the impact of provenance recording on the computational efficiency of astronomical workflows.

The results suggest that implementing provenance recording on astronomical workflows has a negative impact on the computational resources required. However, it has been clearly demonstrated that including provenance vastly reduces the evaluation time of the outlined use cases and identifying more use cases would therefore increase net computational efficiency of the workflow when using provenance.

In conclusion; can provenance be used to decrease the computational resources consumed by astronomical workflows? No, if the only use cases for provenance are the two outlined in this paper. However, there is the potential to do so with additional investigation into use cases for astronomical provenance.

References

1. York, D.G.: The Sloan digital sky survey: technical summary. Astron. J. **120**(3), 1579 (2000)
2. Law, N.M., et al.: The palomar transient factory: system overview, performance, and first results. Publ. Astron. Soc. Pac. **121**(886), 1395 (2009)
3. Anthony Tyson, J.: Large synoptic survey telescope: overview. In: Survey and Other Telescope Technologies and Discoveries, vol. 4836, p. 10–21. International Society for Optics and Photonics (2002)
4. Moreau, L., Batlajery, B., Huynh, T.D., Michaelides, D., Packer, H.: A templating system to generate provenance. IEEE Trans. Softw. Eng. **44**, 103–121 (2017)
5. Wenger, M., et al.: The SIMBAD astronomical database-the CDS reference database for astronomical objects. Astron. Astrophys. Suppl. Ser. **143**(1), 9–22 (2000)
6. Sáenz-Adán, C., Pérez, B., Huynh, T.D., Moreau, L.: UML2PROV: automating provenance capture in software engineering. In: Tjoa, A.M., Bellatreche, L., Biffl, S., van Leeuwen, J., Wiedermann, J. (eds.) SOFSEM 2018. LNCS, vol. 10706, pp. 667–681. Springer, Cham (2018). https://doi.org/10.1007/978-3-319-73117-9_47
7. Lanter, D.P.: Design of a lineage-based meta-data base for GIS. Cartograph. Geograph. Inf. Syst. **18**(4), 255–261 (1991)
8. Stevens, R.D., Robinson, A.J., Goble, C.A.: myGrid: personalised bioinformatics on the information grid. Bioinformatics **19**(suppl. 1), 302–304 (2003)
9. Foster, I., Vockler, J., Wilde, M., Zhao, Y.: Chimera: a virtual data system for representing, querying, and automating data derivation. In: Proceedings of 14th International Conference on Scientific and Statistical Database Management, pp. 37–46. IEEE (2002)
10. Ludäscher, B., et al.: Scientific workflow management and the Kepler system. Concurr. Comput.: Pract. Exp. **18**(10), 1039–1065 (2006)
11. McPhillips, T., et al.: YesWorkFlow: a user-oriented, language-independent tool for recovering workflow information from scripts. arXiv preprint arXiv:1502.02403 (2015)
12. Murta, L., Braganholo, V., Chirigati, F., Koop, D., Freire, J.: NoWorkFlow: capturing and analyzing provenance of scripts. In: Ludäscher, B., Plale, B. (eds.) IPAW 2014. LNCS, vol. 8628, pp. 71–83. Springer, Cham (2015). https://doi.org/10.1007/978-3-319-16462-5_6
13. Groth, P., Deelman, E., Juve, G., Mehta, G., Berriman, B.: Pipeline-centric provenance model. In: Proceedings of the 4th Workshop on Workflows in Support of Large-Scale Science, p. 4. ACM (2009)
14. Giesler, A., Czekala, M., Hagemeier, B., Grunzke, R.: UniProv: a flexible provenance tracking system for UNICORE. In: Di Napoli, E., Hermanns, M.-A., Iliev, H., Lintermann, A., Peyser, A. (eds.) JHPCS 2016. LNCS, vol. 10164, pp. 233–242. Springer, Cham (2017). https://doi.org/10.1007/978-3-319-53862-4_20

Scientific Workflows

Discovering Similar Workflows via Provenance Clustering: A Case Study

Abdussalam Alawini$^{(\boxtimes)}$, Leshang Chen, Susan Davidson, Stephen Fisher, and Junhyong Kim

University of Pennsylvania, Philadelphia, USA
{alawini,leshangc,susan}@cis.upenn.edu,
{safisher,junhyong}@sas.upenn.edu,
http://www.upenn.edu

Abstract. Several workflow management systems and scripting languages have adopted provenance tracking, yet many researchers choose to manually capture or instrument their processing scripts to write provenance information to files. The Next Generation Sequencing (NGS) project we are associated with is tracking provenance in such manner. The NGS project is a collaboration between multiple groups at different sites, where each group is collecting and processing samples using an agreed-upon workflow. The workflow contains many stages with varying degrees of complexity. Over time workflow stages are modified, but data samples are only comparable when processed with identical versions of the workflow. However, for various reasons (including the distributed nature of the collaboration) it is not always clear which samples have been processed with which version of the workflow. In this paper, we introduce new techniques for clustering provenance datasets and attempt to discover the ones that are likely to be generated by same workflow. Based on the clustering result, users can identify similar provenance and would be able to categorize them into different clusters for debugging and zoom-in/zoom-out viewing.

Keywords: Workflow provenance · Clustering
Document classification · Structural features · K-Means

1 Introduction

Workflow management systems and scripting languages are increasingly being instrumented to capture provenance, however many scientists choose not to use these tools. Instead, they manually capture or instrument their processing scripts to write a certain amount of provenance information to files (e.g. spreadsheets) and use this to enable verifiability and reproducibility. This is the case in the Next Generation Sequencing (NGS) project we are associated with, which is a collaboration between multiple groups at different sites. As sequencing samples

---

J. Kim—Evolutionary and Molecular Biology (Kim) Lab, University of Pennsylvania.

© Springer Nature Switzerland AG 2018
K. Belhajjame et al. (Eds.): IPAW 2018, LNCS 11017, pp. 115–127, 2018.
https://doi.org/10.1007/978-3-319-98379-0_9

are collected within a group, they are processed using an agreed-upon workflow. The workflow contains many stages with varying degrees of complexity. Over time workflow stages are modified, e.g. by updating software packages, updating reference libraries or simply changing parameter values. Data samples are only comparable when processed with identical versions of the workflow, however for various reasons (including the distributed nature of the collaboration) it is not always clear which samples have been processed with which version of the workflow. The goal of this work is to determine which samples were processed by which version of the workflow by clustering the collected provenance information.

In this paper, we introduce new techniques for clustering provenance datasets and attempt to discover the ones that are likely to be generated by same workflow. Based on the clustering result, users are able to identify similar provenance, and would be able to categorize them into different subsections for debugging and zoom-in/zoom-out viewing. Our approach takes as input a set of provenance datasets (modeled as PROV-DM graphs), computes abstracted provenance graphs, extracts textual and structural features from each graph, and uses these features to cluster provenance graphs into groups; each group indicates a similar workflow template. We have tested our approach using two datasets, a realistic gene-sequencing dataset and a synthetic dataset, as discussed in Sect. 4. To enable testing the clustering accuracy, our real dataset was manually labeled by human experts, and for our synthetic dataset we attached a label to each provenance graph that indicates the workflow that was used to generate them. In practice, we assume that no labels are attached.

The remainder of this paper is organized as follows. We introduce the motivation for this problem within next generation sequencing and discuss related work in Sect. 2. In Sect. 3, we introduce our provenance clustering framework and discuss our data model. In Sect. 4 we present our preliminary experimental results, and we conclude and discuss future work in Sect. 5.

2   Background

We start by introducing our running example and then discuss related work, in particular, techniques related to clustering workflow templates and their provenance.

2.1   Next Generation Gene Sequencing (NGS)

Sequencing is a technique used to decipher the nucleotide code in a strand of DNA or RNA. Next generation sequencing (NGS) is a high-throughput method of sequencing that has revolutionized genomic research over the past ten years. NGS experiments contain complex experimental procedures with extensive processing of the data after the actual sequencing event. Post-sequencing analysis workflows typically have many stages involving different programs, scripts, and reference libraries.

While the post-sequencing workflow is largely automated, due to the multitude of diverse programs and files used in the workflow there are many ways things can go wrong due to both human and computer errors. The programs and reference libraries used in the workflow are also under active development, and incorporating updates can be problematic. It is therefore critically important to be able to identify when either erroneous programs or reference libraries are used as these errors can have direct effects on downstream, high-level analyses. It is also important to be able to recover from unexpected or unidentified loss of provenance data. Hence it is necessary to be able to identify which pipeline was used to process a given sample which might be missing provenance data. Our provenance clustering approach can help with identifying workflow executions with erroneous or missing provenance as such provenance graphs would not be placed in the same cluster as those with correct and complete provenance information.

2.2 Related Work

There has been work on clustering workflow and provenance graphs using machine learning techniques such as K-Means and hierarchical clustering [4,11]. Because the accuracy of clustering relies heavily on the effectiveness of extracted features, it is crucial to identify an indicative set of features for workflows and provenance graphs. For workflow templates, clustering is more straightforward as module identifiers can be used to determine the identity of workflow modules and group workflows with similar modules. Santos et al. [11] developed two techniques for clustering workflow templates. In the first technique, they represent workflow graphs using one-hot encoding,[1] whereas in the second they use Maximum Common Induced Subgraphs.[2] Jung et al. [4] use both of these ideas in a two-phase clustering scheme. Since these papers treat workflow nodes as the smallest identifiable and labeled unit, their approaches can only be applied to workflows.

Another related line of work is process mining from log files. Lu et al. [5] studied detecting varying behaviors among executions of processes in the field of business analysis. There has been also work on subgraph mining. Garijo et al. [3] developed an approach that combines exact and inexact graph mining methods to identify the most common sub-graphs in a corpus of workflows.

Unlike workflow clustering, clustering provenance graphs imposes several challenges. Provenance graphs only capture workflow execution information, which makes it very difficult to infer information about the original workflow modules. Additionally, each workflow run may produce somewhat different provenance graphs due to different agents, timing or process id information. In [5], the minimum unit in each execution is labeled atomic event, while the label is not obtainable in our setting. Chen et al. [1] represented provenance

---

[1] One-hot encoding is a process in which categorical data is converted into a bit vector.
[2] An induced subgraph is a subset of nodes along with the edges connecting them in original graph.

graphs as temporal data, which are built from the execution order of the original workflow. They also introduce clustering methods that use temporal and connectivity information, such as the number of incoming edges of a particular type. However, most of their features were manually selected. Further, the features contain connectivity information, which can only be used for a specific application domain. Clustering provenance graphs requires a set of indicative and domain-agnostic features that allow for clustering provenances regardless of their application domain.

Graph edit distance (GED) has been studied in previous graph matching work [2,13]. GED is a metric used to quantify the distance between a pair of graphs by counting the minimum number of edge/node operations (insert, delete or update) required to transform one graph into the other. Computing the GED between two graphs is know to be NP-Hard [13]; it has also been shown to be hard to approximate (APX-Hard) [12]. Thus, in this paper, we use other similarity metrics as we discuss in the next section.

3   Clustering Workflow Provenance

In this section, we introduce our provenance clustering framework and data model.

3.1   Provenance Clustering Framework

As shown in Fig. 1, our provenance clustering framework consists of four processes: *Compute APG Graphs, Extract Textual Features, Extract Structural Features,* and *Cluster APG Graphs.* First, Compute APG Graphs builds Abstract Provenance Graphs (APGs) from each provenance graph. Then, Extract Textual and Structural Feature processes extract text and structural vectors, which will be used by the clustering algorithm. Next, Cluster APG Graphs uses these feature vectors to approximate similarity between APG graphs and cluster them accordingly. We discuss the details of our framework processes below.

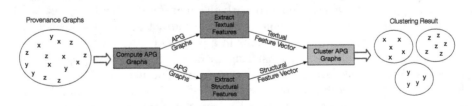

Fig. 1. Graph clustering framework

3.2   Data Model: Abstract Provenance Graphs

Provenance data is typically modeled as a graph $G = (V, E)$, where V denotes the set of workflow modules and E denotes the direction of data flow between modules. Specifically, we use the PROV-DM [7] as our data model, but the

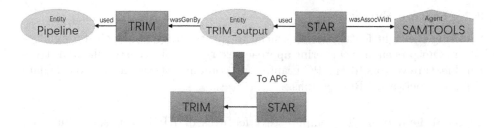

Fig. 2. Example of an PROV graph and its abstract activity graph

approach we propose is general and applicable to other formats. PROV graphs are very large and complex in structure. They store information about agents, entities and activities involved in a workflow execution. To improve clustering performance and accuracy, we summarize PROV graphs by removing certain types of provenance data, such as agents and entities, that are not useful for clustering provenance based on the workflow template.

In this paper, we introduce an approach for converting a PROV graph into an Abstract Provenance Graph[3]. $APG = (V_{APG}, E_{APG})$ is a graph where V_{APG} is a set of activity nodes and E_{APG} is a set of edges connecting them. We focus on analyzing activity nodes because they contain workflow modules (programs, scripts, software libraries, etc.) and execution information (e.g., function calls, execution parameters, software version, etc.) that we can use to reconstruct the modules of the original workflow template.

Because activity nodes in PROV graphs may not be directly connected, our technique also reconstructs connections between activities. For example, two activities could be connected via an entity node (i.e., one activity generated an entity, which was used by another activity). Thus, when constructing an APG graph, we connect two activities if the first activity is connected to an entity node via "GENERATED_BY" edge, and the second activity is connected to the same entity via "USED" edge. An example of a provenance graph and its APG is shown in Fig. 2. APG nodes also contain key-value properties containing provenance information of each activity. Listing 1 shows the properties of the "Trim" activity shown in Fig. 2.

```
1  {"name": "kimlab:_225f2b0c-e5bd-4a15-b606-5accc184b26f",
2   "attributes":
3   { "{.../provDefs/trim#}remove-N": "1",
4     "{.../provDefs/trim#}contaminants-file":
5         ".../provDefs/trim/contaminants.fa",
6     "...":"..." }
7  }
```

Listing 1. Properties of the "Trim" activity shown in Fig. 2

---

[3] Linking two activities with a common entity is now supported by PROV Constraint 33.

3.3 Feature Extraction

Selecting the right feature sets is crucial to the accuracy of any clustering algorithm. Our provenance clustering approach extracts indicative textual and structural feature vectors from APG graphs, and combines these features to calculate similarity between PROV graphs.

Textual Features. To compute text features of APG graphs, we build on ideas from textual cluster analysis (document clustering) techniques [10]. *Term Frequency and Inverse Document Frequency* (TF-IDF) is a widely used technique in information retrieval and text mining for weighting the importance of terms in a document [8]. We use TF-IDF to build a textual feature vector for each APG graph, as described below.

For each APG graph, we compute a feature vector as follows. First, we extract properties from each activity node. Second, we extract the key part of each key-value property (ignoring values as they change with each run). Third, for each APG graph, we generate a feature vector by computing TF-IDF over the extracted keys. TF-IDF can be computed by the following formula:

$$\text{TF-IDF}(g) = \text{TF}(g) * \text{IDF}(g) \tag{1}$$

$$\text{TF}_{t,g} = 1 + \log(c_{t,g}) \tag{2}$$

$$\text{IDF}_{t,g} = \log\left(\frac{|g|}{|g_t| + 1}\right) \tag{3}$$

Here, $c_{t,g}$ is the count of occurrence of word t in graph g. $|g_t|$ is the count of all graphs who contain word t, and $|g|$ is the total number of graphs in the dataset.

Table 1 shows an example of the feature vector extracted from the document shown in Listing 1:

Table 1. Text features extracted from example graph in Fig. 2

	kim	bio	upenn	provDef	trim	remove-N	contaminats-file	...
Graph1	0.2	0.2	0.2	0.2	0.2	0.1	0.1	...

Structural Features. In data mining, *spectral graph analysis* [2] is often used to analyze graph structure. Previous research [9] proposed clustering graphs by structural patterns, where they compute the distance of graphs by finding the sequence of edit operations, and costs are determined by the components of leading eigenvectors of adjacency matrix. The experimental results have shown that the algorithm is a good approximation of distance between graphs [6]. We use this method in extracting structural features from APG graphs.

First, we represent an APG graph $G_k = (V_k, E_k)$ by an adjacency matrix:

$$A_k(i,j) = \begin{cases} 1 & (i,j) \in E_k, \text{ or } (j,i) \in E_k \\ 0 & otherwise \end{cases} \tag{4}$$

where k refers to the k'th provenance graph. To ensure that feature values are real numbers, we convert the provenance graph to be undirected.

Then we calculate the eigenvalues of the adjacency matrix and place them in a vector by descending order.

$$B_k = \text{LeadingEigenvals}(A_k) = [\lambda_k^1, \ldots, \lambda_k^n]^T \tag{5}$$

Here n is the size of the adjacency matrix and λ_k^i is the eigenvalue. In spectral analysis, this vector stands for the major structural information (spectrum, and connectivity) of the provenance graph. Then, we compute Principle Component Analysis (PCA) to reduce the size of the feature space and get a regularized structural feature vector on a common vector space.

Here is an example of the structural feature extracted from an APG graph of 5 activity nodes linked in pipeline structure (Table 2).

Table 2. Structural features extracted from an example graph

	Largest eigenvalue	2nd largest eig	3rd largest eig
Graph1	1.73	1.0	0

Combining Features. There are cases where two provenance graphs have similar structure, but are generated from two different workflow templates, or visa versa. Thus, we need to combine text features and structural features to avoid clustering unrelated graphs together. To enable generalizability and customizability of our approach, we allow users to assign normalization weights as discussed below. The formula for combining textual and structural features is as follows:

$$\text{Text-Feature}(g) = \text{TFIDF}(g) = [f_{t_1,g}, \ldots, f_{t_d,g}]$$
$$\text{Structural-Feature}(g) = \text{LeadEigval}(g) = [x_{t_1,g}, \ldots, x_{t_m,g}]$$
$$\text{Combined-Feature}(g) = [\lambda * \text{TFIDF}, \quad \sqrt{1 - \lambda^2} * \text{LeadEigval}]$$

where λ is normalization factor used to determine feature importance. It is easy to see that if we only want to rely on textual feature, we can set $\lambda = 1$, ignoring structural features as their normalization factor will be set to zero in Combined-Feature. To enable combined textual and structural feature set, we can tune the value as $\lambda = \sqrt{\sum_j x_{t_j,g}^2 / (\sum_i f_{t_i,g}^2 + \sum_j x_{t_j,g}^2)}$ over a small subset of feature vectors g so that both features have approximately equal contribution to the objective function (squared distance) of K-Means (introduced later). Note that we also need to normalize the scale of the two kinds of features to make their average to be at the same level, in case that they are very different.

3.4   Measuring Graph Similarity

The similarity between two graphs is measured by the distance between their corresponding feature vectors. The closer the distance measure between a pair of feature vectors, the more similar their corresponding graphs are. Several similarity metrics can be used. If we naively treat the occurrence of each word independently, then the similarity between documents can be calculated based on *Euclidean Distance* between corresponding points. Another metric is the *Cosine-Similarity* metric, which can be used to compute the angle between a pair of document vectors. A third similarity metric is to compute the correlation between a pair of feature vectors. In Sect. 4, we report the results of clustering provenance graphs using these three similarity metrics.

Given a pair of feature vectors:

$$\text{Vector}(G) = \text{Features}(G) = [\text{feature}_1, \ldots, \text{feature}_m] \tag{6}$$

We can compute the similarity between a pair of APG graphs (G_1, G_2) as following, meaning that they are negatively correlated:

$$\text{Similarity}(G_1, G_2) \propto 1/\text{Distance}(\text{Vector}(G_1), \text{Vector}(G_2)) \tag{7}$$

3.5   Clustering Algorithm

There are several clustering algorithms, including K-Means, Hierarchical and Density-Based Spatial Clustering of Applications with Noise (DBSCAN). One of the most popular clustering approaches is the K-means algorithm. K-means groups an input set of data points into K clusters so it minimizes the intra cluster distance. K-Means algorithm aims at minimizing the following objective function (squared error function):

$$J = \sum_{n=1}^{N} \sum_{k=1}^{K} r_{nk} ||x_n - \mu_k||^2$$

where $||x_n - \mu_k||^2$ is the distance measure between a data point x_n and the cluster center μ_k. In our approach, we use K-Means with Euclidean, Cosine, and Correlation distance metrics, as we discuss in the next section.

4   Preliminary Experiments

In this section, we report the results of our preliminary evaluation on real and synthetic provenance datasets. We ran our experiments on a machine with a 3.2 GHz Intel i7 processor and 12 GB of RAM. We use Python machine learning library, scikit-learn, which includes packages for K-Means, TF-IDF, nltk.tokenize (word tokenizer), and NumPy (scientific computing library). We also use MAT-LAB to test K-Means over several distance metrics, as discussed below.

4.1 Provenance Datasets

Real Datasets. We compiled a dataset[4] from approximately 1,300 NGS experiments with extensive data provenance describing pre- and post-sequencing events. In particular, this dataset includes experimental samples processed by nine different variants of a post-sequencing workflow used for the primary analysis of NGS data. The analysis workflow includes six possible stages (i.e. Blast, FastQC, Trim, STAR, HTSeq, and Verse) with each sample being processed by three to five of the stages.

Synthetic Datasets. To test the performance of our graph clustering algorithm with varying and complex provenance graph structures, we generated a set of synthetic provenance graphs. We modified the structure of a random sample of the realistic datasets we described above by inserting or deleting activities, or adding subgraphs from other provenance graphs, generating about 866 provenance graphs with three different structures.

4.2 Analysis over Real Datasets

We first report on experimental results over real datasets. In the first experiment, we evaluated our clustering algorithm on combined textual and structural features using three distance metrics (Euclidean, cosine and correlation). We used the *elbow* method, a technique for determining the optimal number of clusters, by analyzing the change in the sum of squared intra-cluster distance error (squared error) as a function of the number of clusters. The optimal number of clusters should (1) minimize the squared error; and (2) reduce the number of clusters to avoid overfitting.

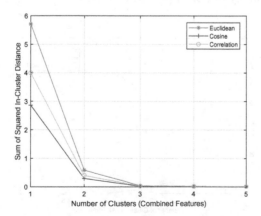

Fig. 3. Squared error of clustering over real datasets

---

[4] Our dataset is available for download at https://github.com/alawinia/provClustering.

Table 3. Matching of clusters when k = 3 using Euclidean distance

Actual cluster	In-cluster recall (%)	Data count
1	92.8	111
2	98.5	199
3	89.7	215

Figure 3 shows the result of this experiment. The Euclidean distance works best with our combined features as it assigns larger distance than the cosine or correlation metrics. We also see that the optimal number of clusters for our NGS dataset is 3, as three clusters reduced the error to almost zero. This results matches the golden standard of our real (labeled) datasets. We define the *in-cluster recall* to be the percentage of provenance graphs that are produced by the same workflow template and have been clustered together. Table 3 shows the recall of our clustering technique, which has a weighted average accuracy of 93.7%.

4.3   Analysis over Synthetic Datasets

We evaluated our clustering approach over the synthetic dataset using textual, structural and a combination of structural and textual features. Figure 4 plots the sum of intra-cluster squared distance of K-Means algorithm using Euclidean distance with varying number of clusters. The results shows that the optimal number of clusters are 3, 4 and 5 using structural, textual and combined features, respectively. Using combined textual and structural feature vectors, we were able to get the correct number of clusters in the synthetic dataset. Table 4 shows that the per-cluster accuracy of our approach is 96%.

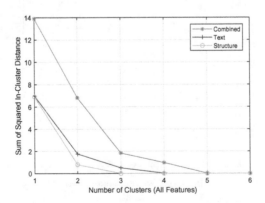

Fig. 4. In-cluster squared error over synthetic datasets

Table 4. Clustering at k = 5 using combined features and Euclidean distance

Cluster	In-cluster recall (%)	Data count
1	100	95
2	100	157
3	91.0	334
4	100	95
5	100	185

4.4   Running Time Analysis

We also test the running time of our provenance clustering approach under large workloads. For this experiment, we developed two synthetic provenance datasets. The first set has about 60 features and 120 words extracted from each graph in the dataset. The second set has about 120 features and 240 words. We evaluated the performance of feature extraction and clustering over different number of samples. The number of samples doubles at each test.

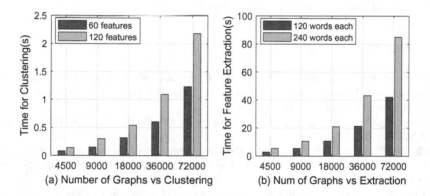

Fig. 5. (a) Time for clustering step vs. the number of graphs; (b) Time for feature extraction step vs. the number of graphs. Note that the number of input graphs increases exponentially, but the running time is linear.

Figure 5(a) shows the time analysis. We can see that clustering takes less than 2.5 s, which is very reasonable. Doubling the number of features (from 60 to 120) increases the processing time by about 1.75x. As a result, we can infer that our clustering approach is roughly linear in the size of the input.

Figure 5(b) shows that extracting text features takes more time than clustering. When extracting a large number of text features for a large graph dataset, feature extraction takes up to 85 s. However, since features are extracted on a per-graph-basis, we can run text feature extraction for different graphs in parallel. Meanwhile, extracting structural features is really fast, and the time is typically less than 10 s. The reason is that the structural information only consists of connectivity, and that various optimization techniques can be used to calculate eigenvalues.

5   Conclusion

This paper introduced a new approach for clustering workflow provenance, enabling effective management and utilization of large provenance datasets. Our approach uses text and structural feature sets extracted from summaries of the provenance graphs. We tested our approach on real and synthetic workloads; preliminary results show an accuracy of over 93% and a running time that is linear to the size of the input. The textual and structural information are domain-independent, and can be therefore used to cluster any type of provenance graph.

In future work, we plan to develop a visualization technique that uses our provenance clustering approach to enable workflow visualizations that can zoom-out to higher levels of abstraction. We will also explore clustering provenance graphs based on common subgraphs. To do so, we need to implement a fine-grained method for analyzing provenance graphs at the node- and edge-level. We will also explore adding features from entities (such as input and output parameters of workflow modules) and agents.

References

1. Chen, P., Plale, B., Aktas, M.S.: Temporal representation for mining scientific data provenance. Future Gener. Comput. Syst. **36**, 363–378 (2014). Special Section: Intelligent Big Data Processing
2. Gao, X., Xiao, B., Tao, D., Li, X.: A survey of graph edit distance. Pattern Anal. Appl. **13**(1), 113–129 (2010)
3. Garijo, D., et al.: FragFlow automated fragment detection in scientific workflows. In: 2014 IEEE 10th International Conference on e-Science, vol. 1, pp. 281–289, October 2014
4. Jung, J.-Y., Bae, J.: Workflow clustering method based on process similarity. In: Gavrilova, M.L., et al. (eds.) ICCSA 2006. LNCS, vol. 3981, pp. 379–389. Springer, Heidelberg (2006). https://doi.org/10.1007/11751588_40
5. Lu, X., Fahland, D., van den Biggelaar, F.J.H.M., van der Aalst, W.M.P.: Detecting deviating behaviors without models. In: Reichert, M., Reijers, H.A. (eds.) BPM 2015. LNBIP, vol. 256, pp. 126–139. Springer, Cham (2016). https://doi.org/10.1007/978-3-319-42887-1_11
6. Luo, B., Wilson, R.C., Hancock, E.R.: Spectral clustering of graphs. In: Hancock, E., Vento, M. (eds.) GbRPR 2003. LNCS, vol. 2726, pp. 190–201. Springer, Heidelberg (2003). https://doi.org/10.1007/3-540-45028-9_17
7. Moreau, L., Missier, P.: PROV-DM: The PROV Data Model, April 2013. http://www.w3.org/TR/2013/REC-prov-dm-20130430/
8. Robertson, S.: Understanding inverse document frequency: on theoretical arguments for IDF. J. Doc. **60**(5), 503–520 (2004)
9. Robles-Kelly, A., Hancock, E.R.: Graph edit distance from spectral seriation. IEEE Trans. Pattern Anal. Mach. Intell. **27**(3), 365–378 (2005)

10. Salton, G., Buckley, C.: Term-weighting approaches in automatic text retrieval. Inf. Process. Manag. **24**(5), 513–523 (1988)
11. Santos, E., Lins, L., Ahrens, J.P., Freire, J., Silva, C.T.: A first study on clustering collections of workflow graphs. In: Freire, J., Koop, D., Moreau, L. (eds.) IPAW 2008. LNCS, vol. 5272, pp. 160–173. Springer, Heidelberg (2008). https://doi.org/10.1007/978-3-540-89965-5_18
12. Selçuk, C.K., Sapino, M.L.: Data Management for Multimedia Retrieval, p. 114. Cambridge University Press, Cambridge (2010)
13. Zeng, Z., Tung, A.K.H., Wang, J., Feng, J., Zhou, L.: Comparing stars: on approximating graph edit distance. Proc. VLDB Endow. **2**(1), 25–36 (2009)

Validation and Inference of Schema-Level Workflow Data-Dependency Annotations

Shawn Bowers[1]([✉]), Timothy McPhillips[2], and Bertram Ludäscher[2]

[1] Department of Computer Science, Gonzaga University, Spokane, USA
bowers@gonzaga.edu
[2] School of Information Sciences, University of Illinois, Urbana-Champaign,
Champaign, USA
tmcphillips@absoluteflow.org, ludaesch@illinois.edu

Abstract. An advantage of scientific workflow systems is their ability to collect runtime provenance information as an execution trace. Traces include the computation steps invoked as part of the workflow run along with the corresponding data consumed and produced by each workflow step. The information captured by a trace is used to infer "lineage" relationships among data items, which can help answer provenance queries to find workflow inputs that were involved in producing specific workflow outputs. Determining lineage relationships, however, requires an understanding of the dependency patterns that exist between each workflow step's inputs and outputs, and this information is often under-specified or generally assumed by workflow systems. For instance, most approaches assume all outputs depend on all inputs, which can lead to lineage "false positives". In prior work, we defined annotations for specifying detailed dependency relationships between inputs and outputs of computation steps. These annotations are used to define corresponding rules for inferring fine-grained data dependencies from a trace. In this paper, we extend our previous work by considering the impact of dependency annotations on workflow specifications. In particular, we provide a reasoning framework to ensure the set of dependency annotations on a workflow specification is consistent. The framework can also infer a complete set of annotations given a partially annotated workflow. Finally, we describe an implementation of the reasoning framework using answer-set programming.

1 Introduction

Within most scientific workflow systems, a *workflow specification* (or *schema*) is modeled as a graph of nodes representing computational steps and edges representing the data and control flow between steps [5,10]. Each workflow step in a specification is typically treated as a "black box" by the workflow system. For example, steps are frequently configured to invoke external programs, execute scripts, or call web services, where the step exposes only the inputs needed and the corresponding outputs returned by the underlying calls. Once designed,

© Springer Nature Switzerland AG 2018
K. Belhajjame et al. (Eds.): IPAW 2018, LNCS 11017, pp. 128–141, 2018.
https://doi.org/10.1007/978-3-319-98379-0_10

workflow specifications serve as executable and potentially reusable (e.g., using different input data and parameter settings) scientific analyses. Because scientific workflow systems invoke and control the flow of data between steps during workflow execution, most systems provide support for recording (or logging) information about a workflow run. A *workflow trace* stores information associated with a run as an instance of a workflow specification [2,5]. In particular, traces are modeled as graphs with nodes representing the invocations of steps and edges representing the data passed between each step's execution. Traces are often used to infer the lineage of workflow data products. For instance, given a data product output by a run, many systems use the trace to determine the steps that were invoked as well as the input and intermediate data products that contributed to its generation [2,5].

However, because steps in a workflow specification are black boxes, workflow systems often "overestimate" the lineage relationships from a workflow trace [2]. For instance, many systems assume that all data input to a step is used to produce all outputs, when in fact only a portion of input data may produce any particular output [2,4]. Additionally, most systems consider only a single, often underspecified notion of dependency between a step's inputs and outputs, e.g., where data items are said to be "influenced by" or "contribute to" other data items [3]. Taken together, the lineage information inferred from workflow traces may result in lineage relationships that are not only unclear, but often misleading or even incorrect.

In prior work [2], we developed a set of declarative rules for specifying dependency patterns of individual computation steps. The inputs and outputs of a step are annotated with rules, which are then used to infer the specific input data used to produce an output for each invocation of a step within a trace. However, to be effective, this approach requires a complete set of annotations for every step within a workflow specification.

Contributions. We describe extensions to our prior work that supports partially annotated workflow specifications and employs reasoning techniques to validate and help infer a complete set of annotations. We consider different use cases related to annotating a workflow specification and provide a set of dependency types that can be used to help clarify the lineage relationships present within a workflow trace. Finally, we describe a prototype implementation of our approach (implemented using answer-set programming) that we plan to add to the YesWorkflow system [11] as future work.

Organization. In Sect. 2 we describe an abstract model of workflow specifications, give an overview of the dependency types we consider for annotations, and discuss use cases related to our framework. In Sect. 3 we describe the constraints associated with the dependency types as well as the corresponding inferences for reasoning over partially annotated workflow specifications. In Sect. 4 we present a prototype implementation of the reasoning approaches described in Sect. 3. Finally, in Sects. 5 and 6 we describe related and future work, respectively.

2   Workflow Dependency Annotations

This section describes an abstract model for workflow specifications used in the rest of the paper, an overview of the types of dependencies we consider for workflow annotations, and three example use cases related to annotation inference.

Workflow Specifications. We consider an abstract workflow model that conforms to YesWorkflow [11] and similar dataflow-oriented scientific workflow models [2,5]. A workflow $W = (P, D, E)$ consists of a set of *program blocks* P (workflow steps, i.e., computations), *data blocks* D (representing data items or data containers), and *input* and *output* edges $E \subseteq P \times L \times D \times \{\mathsf{in}, \mathsf{out}\}$ where L is a set of labels that uniquely identify edges within W. We use relations $\mathsf{in}(p_i, x_i, d_i)$ and $\mathsf{out}(p_j, x_j, d_j)$ to denote input and output edges, respectively, for $p_i, p_j \in P$, $x_i, x_j \in L$, and $d_i, d_j \in D$. Figure 1 shows an example workflow consisting of two program blocks (`normalize` and `filter`), five data blocks $(d_1, \ldots, d_5)$, four input edges (x_1, x_3, x_{range}, and x_{cutoff}), and two output edges (x_2 and x_4). Also shown in Fig. 1 are a set of initial dependency annotations (red, dashed) together with the corresponding inferred annotations (blue, dotted). The `normalize` block takes input data items d_1 and scales them to fit within the given range (consisting of a minimum and a maximum value). The output of `normalize` is then passed to `filter`, which outputs the data item if it is smaller than a given cutoff value d_4. In general, an input edge $\mathsf{in}(p_1, x_1, d_1)$ states that data items are input to the program block p_1 and an output edge $\mathsf{out}(p_1, x_2, d_2)$ states that data items are output by p_1. Data blocks allow for data items to be passed as input to multiple program blocks (e.g., to create workflow branches as in d_2 in Fig. 4). In contrast, data blocks typically receive only from a single writer, to avoid conflicts (e.g., $d_3 \neq d_4$ in Fig. 4).[1]

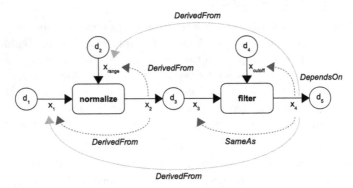

Fig. 1. Example workflow with program blocks `normalize` and `filter`, data blocks $d_1, \ldots, d_5$, and dataflow edges (solid, black) between nodes; user-declared dependency annotations (dashed, red edges); and inferred dependencies (dotted, blue edges), based on the given user annotations. (Color figure online)

---

[1] If data blocks denote containers (e.g., file folders or queues) multiple writers may be allowable.

Dependency Annotations. The set of dependency annotations $A \subseteq L \times L \times T$ for a workflow specification W associates different dependency types $t \in T$ to input and output edges of W. Dependency annotations are represented by a relation dep_rule(x_1, x_2, t) for input edges $x_1 \in L$, output edges $x_2 \in L$, and dependency types $t \in T$. The dashed, red arrows in Fig. 1 represent four explicit, user-supplied annotations: dep_rule$(x_1, x_2, \mathtt{DerivedFrom})$, dep_rule$(x_\mathtt{range}, x_2, \mathtt{DerivedFrom})$, dep_rule$(x_3, x_4, \mathtt{SameAs})$, and dep_rule $(x_\mathtt{cutoff}, x_4, \mathtt{DependsOn})$. In the example, we say that the output of normalize is *"derived from"* the input d_1 and the range d_2, and the output of filter *"depends on"* the cutoff d_4 and is the *"same (data item) as"* the input d_2. We note that annotations can be expressed over a single program block (e.g., the explicit annotations in Fig. 1) or can span multiple program blocks (e.g., the inferred annotations in Fig. 1).

Dependency Types. We consider a set of pairwise disjoint dependency types for specifying annotations. The *FlowsFrom* type simply represents the cases where an input data item was received and an output item was produced by a program-block invocation, but the output value is not determined by or computed from the input. A *FlowsFrom* annotation typically denotes that the input is simply a "trigger" to tell the program block to be invoked. The *DependsOn* type represents cases where a control dependence exists between the corresponding inputs and outputs (explained in more detail in Sect. 3). The *DerivedFrom* type represents cases where outputs are computed from inputs (again, described further in Sect. 3). The *ValueOf* type represents the cases where an output produces a new data item (with new object identifier) containing a copy of the input data item's value. Finally, the *SameAs* type represents the cases where the input data item was passed through to the output (i.e., the output is the same exact data item as the input data item).

Use Case 1: Inferring Dependency Annotations. Given a workflow specification that is partially annotated, we consider the case of inferring new annotations from a given set of user-supplied annotations. Figure 1 gives a simple example where each program block is annotated (dashed, red arrows) and the corresponding annotations that are implied by the given annotations are also shown (blue arrows). In this example, each individual workflow step is annotated by a user, and the goal is to infer the annotations that span multiple steps. In general, understanding the dependency relationships that span workflow steps as a result of the composition of program blocks is useful for verifying the intent and/or construction of the workflow (e.g., to ensure that certain workflow outputs are actually derived from certain workflow inputs). Having a complete set of annotations is also useful when answering queries at the trace level, e.g., to determine the inputs that specific outputs were derived from (as opposed to the inputs that were simply copied from the input or were used for basic control flow).

Use Case 2: Constraining Dependency Annotations. In this case, higher-level annotations that span multiple program blocks (e.g., between workflow

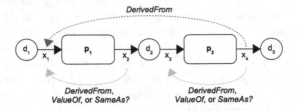

Fig. 2. Example workflow with initial user annotation (dashed, red) from the output x_4 to the input x_1. Which of the undeclared dependency options (dotted, blue) are correct? (Color figure online)

inputs and outputs) are used to help guide annotation choices for the rest of the workflow specification. As a simple example, we may know that the output is (or should be) derived from the input as shown in Fig. 2 by the dashed red annotation. Specifying this annotation first limits the choices for the lower-level annotations (in this case of program blocks). The corresponding choices are shown by the dotted blue annotations in Fig. 2. In this case, different combinations of annotations over the two program blocks are compatible (consistent) with the initial (dashed red) annotation of Fig. 2.

Use Case 3: Validating Dependency Relationships. Finally, we consider the case where there is a mix of (potentially partial) higher-level (i.e., indirect) and lower-level (i.e., direct) annotations of a workflow specification that a workflow designer wants to ensure are compatible (consistent). Figure 3 is one such example where the workflow specification consists of a subworkflow (named `generate_sample` as shown on the bottom of the figure). Each subworkflow step

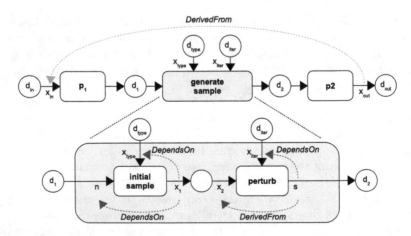

Fig. 3. Workflow specification consisting of an annotated subworkflow (dashed red, bottom) and an inconsistent higher-level annotation assertion (dashed purple, top) that spans workflow steps. (Color figure online)

is annotated (in red) and the containing workflow (shown on the top of the figure) has a higher-level annotation asserting that the output should be derived from the input. However, the given annotations are incompatible (i.e., inconsistent) since the composition of the two subworkflow steps introduce an implied *DependsOn* relationship between the input and output of generate sample. Thus, based on the workflow specification, d_{in} and d_{out} cannot participate in a *DerivedFrom* relationship (as shown at the top in purple).

The reasoning framework we describe in the rest of this paper is designed to handle each of these three cases. In particular, we assume that a workflow specification is either fully or partially annotated, from which the reasoning framework (i) ensures consistency of the given annotations (e.g., as in Fig. 3); (ii) infers all specific implied annotations (e.g., as in Fig. 1); and (iii) provides the allowable annotation options when there are multiple possible implied annotations (e.g., as in Fig. 2).

3   Reasoning over Dependency Types

This section describes our reasoning framework for dependency type validation and inference. We first give a more detailed description of the annotation types and then describe the annotation composition rules and constraints used within our framework.

3.1   Dependency Types

In the following, we assume a simple program block p with input edge $in(p, x_1, d_1)$ and output edge $out(p, x_2, d_2)$ as shown below.

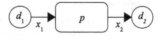

Let D_1 be the set of allowable values (the *domain*) of p with respect to the input edge x_1 and D_2 be the set of possible output values (the *range*) with respect to the output edge x_2. We write $p : D_1 \to D_2$ to denote the *signature* of p with respect to x_1 and x_2. We assume data items are passed to and from program blocks as objects o with unique identifiers $id(o)$ and corresponding values $val(o)$. For a domain D and a sequence of data items $\bar{o}$, we write $val(\bar{o}) \subseteq D$ if for every data item $o_i \in \bar{o}$, $val(o_i) \in D$. Given the program block signature $p : D_1 \to D_2$, an *invocation* $p(\bar{o}_1) = \bar{o}_2$ states that p read a sequence of data items $\bar{o}_1$ on x_1 such that $val(\bar{o}_1) \subseteq D_1$, and wrote a (possibly empty) sequence of data items $\bar{o}_2$ on x_2 such that $val(\bar{o}_2) \subseteq D_2$.[2] Program blocks are not required to be deterministic, and so different invocations over the same input may produce different output.

---

[2] The use of sequences of data items allows for more complex program blocks such as filters and aggregators as well as workflow computation models supporting implicit iteration [1,2].

The *image* $p[\bar{o}_1]$ of $\bar{o}_1$ under p is the set of all possible output sequences produced by invocations of p receiving $\bar{o}_1$. Note that if p has multiple input edges, the same notion of image still applies since we are interested in the relationship between a single input and output edge (although additional constraints are imposed in some cases as described below).

Following the traditional convention used in programming language implementation [3,7], we use the ideas of "control" and "data" dependence between statements when defining the dependency types below. For example, consider the following statements (adapted from [7]).

```
S1: C = A * B
S2: E = C * D + 1
S3: if (E > 0) then
S4:    H = F + G
```

Statement S2 is said to have a *data dependence* on S1 since the value of E depends on the value of C. A data dependence is also referred to as a *"read-after-write"* dependence since C is read as part of S2 to compute a value to write to E. Note that data dependence relationships can either be direct or indirect. For instance, in the example above, E directly depends on C (via S2) but indirectly depends on A (via S1 and S2). Below, we write $\mathtt{raw\_dep}(p, x_1, x_2)$ to denote that within a program block p, output edge x_2 has either a direct or indirect read-after-write dependence on input edge x_1. Similarly, statement S4 is said to have a *control dependence* on statement S3 since the execution of statement S4 (and hence, the value of H) depends on the execution of S3 (specifically, the value of E). However, note that H's value is not computed from E's value (which would imply a data dependence). A control dependence can also be either direct or indirect. We assume that if an x_2 is indirectly control dependent on x_1 then either: (i) x_2 is control dependent on another variable that is either directly or indirectly control or data dependent on x_1; or (ii) x_2 is data dependent on a variable that is either directly or indirectly control dependent on x_1. Below, we write $\mathtt{ctl\_dep}(p, x_1, x_2)$ to denote that x_2 has either a direct or indirect control dependence on x_1. We define the dependency types below in terms of the constraints they impose between possible inputs and outputs of program-block invocations as well as their corresponding control and data dependences.

FlowsFrom. A *FlowsFrom* annotation implies that x_2 does not have a control or data dependence on x_1, which is expressed by the constraint:

$$\neg\,\mathtt{ctl\_dep}(p, x_1, x_2)\ \wedge\ \neg\,\mathtt{raw\_dep}(p, x_1, x_2).$$

FlowsFrom simply suggests that the input was present when p was executed, e.g., the input was used as a "trigger" to invoke a program block p.

DependsOn. A *DependsOn* annotation implies that x_2 has a control dependence, but not a data dependence on x_1, which is expressed by the constraint:

$$\mathtt{ctl\_dep}(p, x_1, x_2)\ \wedge\ \neg\,\mathtt{raw\_dep}(p, x_1, x_2).$$

DerivedFrom. A *DerivedFrom* annotation implies that x_2 has a data dependence on x_1, but that not all outputs have the same value(s) as their corresponding inputs (which would suggest a *ValueOf* or *SameAs* relationship):

$$\texttt{raw\_dep}(p, x_1, x_2) \;\wedge\; (\exists \bar{o}_2 \in p[\bar{o}_1]: val(\bar{o}_2) \not\subseteq val(\bar{o}_1)).$$

As explained further below, we consider *DerivedFrom* to be a "stronger" dependency relationship than *DependsOn*. Thus, while it is possible for x_2 to have both a control and data dependence on x_1, it would be represented as *DerivedFrom* within our framework.

ValueOf. A *ValueOf* annotation implies that the values of data items received on x_1 are output on x_2 (e.g., by copying inputs to new outputs). Unlike with *SameAs*, *ValueOf* assumes new data items are created as a result, and so the identifiers for the input and output data items differ:

$$(\forall \bar{o}_2 \in p[\bar{o}_1]: val(\bar{o}_2) \subseteq val(\bar{o}_1)) \;\wedge\; (\exists \bar{o}_2 \in p[\bar{o}_1]: id(\bar{o}_2) \not\subseteq id(\bar{o}_1)).$$

We use $id(\bar{o})$ to denote the set of identifiers of the sequence of data items $\bar{o}$. Note that *ValueOf* implies a data dependence from x_2 to x_1 since data items must be read from input x_1 and then written into data items that are output to x_2.

SameAs. A *SameAs* annotation differs from *ValueOf* by requiring all outputs to be the same as data items from the inputs:

$$\forall \bar{o}_2 \in p[\bar{o}_1]: o \in \bar{o}_2 \rightarrow o \in \bar{o}_1.$$

Here, $o \in \bar{o}$ holds if the object o is a member of the sequence $\bar{o}$. A *SameAs* relationship also implies a data dependence from x_2 to x_1 since the input data items must be read from x_1 and then written to x_2.

3.2   Composing Dependency Annotations

Annotation inference within a workflow specification is largely based on understanding how annotations "propagate" under compositions (or "sequences") of workflow steps. Here we assume two connected program blocks $p_1 : D_1 \rightarrow D_2$ and $p_2 : D_2 \rightarrow D_3$:

When p_1 and p_2 are connected by a data block as above, we write $p_1 \circ p_2$ to denote the connection. We also define the ordering $\prec$ to represent the intuitive "dependency strength" of annotation types. In particular, if $t_i \prec t_j$ then we say t_i is a "weaker" dependency type than t_j (or similarly, that t_j is a "stronger" dependency type than t_i). The dependency types are ordered according to dependency strength as follows.

$$FlowsFrom \;\prec\; DependsOn \;\prec\; DerivedFrom \;\prec\; ValueOf \;\prec\; SameAs$$

For instance, a *DependsOn* relationship suggests a "weaker" dependency than a *DerivedFrom* relationship. The definitions of the annotation types with the ordering above imply the following annotation composition rules for a sequence of program blocks $p_1 \circ p_2$, with $\texttt{in}(p_1, x_1, d_1)$, $\texttt{out}(p_1, x_2, d_2)$, $\texttt{in}(p_2, x_3, d_2)$, and $\texttt{out}(p_2, x_4, d_3)$ as defined above, and $\preceq$ denoting weaker or of equal strength (and where all variables are assumed below to be universally quantified).

$$\texttt{dep\_rule}(x_1, x_2, t_i) \wedge \texttt{dep\_rule}(x_3, x_4, t_j) \wedge t_i \preceq t_j \leftrightarrow \texttt{dep\_rule}(x_1, x_4, t_i)$$
$$\texttt{dep\_rule}(x_1, x_2, t_j) \wedge \texttt{dep\_rule}(x_3, x_4, t_i) \wedge t_i \preceq t_j \leftrightarrow \texttt{dep\_rule}(x_1, x_4, t_i)$$

These rules can also be applied to indirect annotations (spanning multiple blocks) as well, which is further described in Sect. 4. As an example of propagation, in Fig. 1, `normalize` has a *DerivedFrom* annotation and `filter` has a *SameAs* annotation. Since *DerivedFrom* is "weaker" than *SameAs*, the composite annotation is *DerivedFrom*. Similarly, in Fig. 2 the composite annotation is *DerivedFrom*, which implies that p_1 and p_2 have either *DerivedFrom* annotations or "stronger" types (i.e., *ValueOf* or *SameAs*), since *DerivedFrom* must be the "weaker" annotation. Additionally (and not shown in Fig. 2), note that at least one of p_1 or p_2 must have a *DerivedFrom* annotation to satisfy the composition rules above. The example in Fig. 3, while slightly more complex, follows the same idea in that along the path from x_{out} to x_{in}, the `generate_sample` subworkflow implies a *DependsOn* annotation, and since *DependsOn* is strictly weaker than *DerivedFrom*, the higher-level *DerivedFrom* annotation violates (is inconsistent with) the composition rules.

According to the composition rules, weaker annotations propagate through program-block compositions, which is due to the nature of the dependencies established by the weaker annotation. For instance, if x_2 *FlowsFrom* x_1, then d_2 (via x_2) does not have a control or data dependence on d_1 (via x_1). Thus, since the value of d_1 does not participate in the computation of d_2, d_1 also does not participate in the computation of the values that have a control or data dependence on d_2. A similar situation exists when p_2 has a *FlowsFrom* annotation. Determining indirect control dependences (i.e., when looking at sequences of statements involved in control and data dependences) was described in the beginning of this section, and follows from the idea that control dependence can be indirectly established through other control and/or data dependences. The same ideas apply to copying the values of data items. If d_2 is a (value) copy of d_1 with potentially different data item identifiers as d_1 (i.e., x_2 has a *ValueOf* relationship with x_1), but d_2 is passed through to d_3 (i.e., x_4 has a *SameAs* relationship with x_3), then d_3 will also have the same value but a different identifier as d_1 (since d_2 and d_3 are the same data item). The same situation occurs when the two annotations are flipped, i.e., p_1 has a *SameAs* relationship and p_2 has a *ValueOf* relationship. Finally, when p_1 and p_2 have the same exact annotation, the same annotation is also propagated, which follows from similar arguments as those above.

3.3   Additional Annotation Constraints

We also consider an additional "global" constraint on the dependency annotations of a workflow specification related to inferring annotations when there
are two or more paths of program-block compositions within a workflow specification. Consider the example annotated workflow specification of Fig. 4, which
shows two paths (i.e., sequences of program block compositions) between x_1 and
x_9. While the top path (through p_2) implies a *FlowsFrom* relationship from x_9
to x_1 (since *FlowsFrom* is the weakest type along the path), the bottom path
implies a stronger *DerivedFrom* relationship from x_9 to x_1. Since we allow at
most one dependency type between an input and an output, we use the annotation inferred from the path with the strongest type.

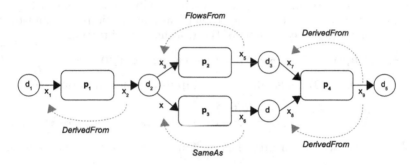

Fig. 4. Example workflow specification with multiple paths between the input and
output.

4   Prototype Implementation

This section describes a prototype implementation of our annotation reasoning
framework using the Potassco[3] suite of answer-set programming (ASP) tools.
Potassco implements ASP using a syntax similar to Datalog with additional support for nonmonotonic reasoning based on the answer set semantics [8]. Potassco
programs are often written using a generate-and-test algorithmic approach where
the result of a program is a set of minimal models, or "*answer sets*", that satisfy the rules and constraints defined within the program. Our implementation
follows this same approach by:

(i) "guessing" dependency annotations for each input-output pair in a workflow specification without a corresponding user-supplied annotation (the
generate step);

(ii) ensuring that each of the input-output pair annotations satisfy the program-
block annotation compositions described in the previous section (the test
step); and

---

[3] See: https://potassco.org/.

(iii) ensuring that annotations satisfy the additional constraints described in the previous section, i.e., ensuring the "strongest" indirect annotations are used between inputs and outputs with multiple paths of program blocks between them (the test step).

In the generate-and-test approach, conceptually all possible models are created—which in our case means that all possible combinations of input-output pair combinations along a dataflow path are considered—and only those models (answer sets) that satisfy the given constraints are returned. Our prototype implementation uses the answer sets for a workflow specification and then (i) outputs all annotations that are contained in each answer set (i.e., the annotations that are "entailed" by the program); and then (ii) outputs the annotation choices (i.e., the union of annotations across answer sets) for the annotations that are not entailed (e.g., as is the case with the blue annotations in Fig. 2).

Our prototype uses a "choice rule" to generate annotations for input-output pairs not already annotated as part of the workflow specification:

```
{dep_rule(I,O,R) : dep_type(R)} = 1 :- up_stream(I,O).
```

Where up_stream(I,O) finds all potential input-output annotation pairs:

```
up_stream(I,O) :- in(I,P,_), out(O,P,_).
up_stream(I,O) :- in(I,P1,_), out(O1,P1,D1), in(I2,P2,D1), up_stream(I2,O).
```

The following constraint ensures that all annotations satisfy the composition rules:

```
:- dep_rule(I,O,R), not valid_dep_path(I,O,R).
```

In ASP the head of the (constraint) rule above is assumed to be false. Thus, if the body is satisfied the constraint fails. To satisfy the constraint, the body must not be true. So, in the constraint above, either there does not exist a dependency between the input I and output O, or the dependency forms a valid dependency path. The relation valid_dep_path(I,O,R) is true if there is a valid annotation with type R between the input I and output O as defined below.

```
valid_dep_path(I,O,R) :- in(I,P,_), out(O,P,_), dep_rule(I,O,R).
valid_dep_path(I,O,R) :- in(I,P,_), out(O1,P,_), O != O1,
                         dep_rule(I,O1,R1), connected(O1,I1), I != I1,
                         valid_dep_path(I1,O,R2), compose(R1,R2,R).
```

The connected(O,I) relation is true if the output O shares a data block with the input I (implying two program blocks share a dataflow connection from O1 to I1):

```
connected(O,I) :- out(O,_,D), in(I,_,D).
```

The compose(R1,R2,R) relation implements the basic dependency composition rules defined in the previous section:

```
compose(R1,R2,R1) :- weaker(R1,R2).
compose(R1,R2,R2) :- weaker(R2,R1).
```

The weaker(R1,R2) relation encodes the "strength" of dependency ordering over types (i.e., the $\preceq$ relation; see Sect. 3). Thus, weaker(R1,R2) is true for types R1 and R2 iff R1 $\preceq$ R2. The two compose rules select the weaker relation of R1 and R2. If R1 is weaker than R2, then the first compose rule selects R1, and if R2 is weaker than R1, then the second compose rule selects R2. Finally, the first rule of valid_dep_path considers the case where the path is a single program block, and the second rule considers the case where a path consists of multiple program blocks. For the the second valid_dep_path rule, we require O and O1 as well as I and I1 to be different values, respectively, for the case where I and O form a simple cycle. Without the inequalities, checking valid_dep_path for I and O would require valid_dep_path for I and O to be already known (from the body of the rule). We note that workflow cycles, however, are supported by the rules. The following constraint ensures that annotations are the "strongest" along multiple program-block paths.

```
:- dep_rule(I,O,R), valid_dep_path(I,O,R1), R != R1, weaker(R,R1).
```

The constraint ensures there is not a stronger type between the input I and output O than the one given (guessed or inferred) by the annotation dep_rule(I,O,R).

5   Related Work

We focus on the PROV model, data provenance, and other workflow-based approaches:

The PROV model [12] defines a general *wasInfluencedBy* relationship with *wasDerivedFrom* as the main lineage relationship between entities. PROV also defines subtypes of *wasDerivedFrom*, including *wasRevisionOf*, *wasQuotedFrom*, and *hadPrimarySource*. Although *DependsOn* and *DerivedFrom* are similar to *wasInfluencedBy* and *wasDerivedFrom*, because our approach is designed for computation via workflows, we adopt the more specific notions of dependency (i.e., control and data dependence) from [3]. Our approach is also similar to PROV-O [14], which models provenance at the schema level. We also consider compositions of dependency annotation types, which are not considered within PROV-O.

Cui and Widom [4] define three types of transformations for ETL workflows— dispatchers, aggregators, and black-boxes—and for each a set of techniques for inferring data-level lineage. They also define a number of specialized (i.e., a hierarchy of) transformation types for computing data lineage. While our approach also provides dependency types for transformations (in our case, program blocks), the focus in [4] is to compute data-level workflow lineage (the input items that contributed to output items), and does not consider the differences between dependency, derivation, and so on. The approach used in LabelFlow [1] is also similar to that in [4], in which different types of workflow steps are considered and used for data annotation propagation (i.e., arbitrary metadata attribute-value pair "labels"). Like [4], LabelFlow focuses on workflow execution by inferring data-level labels for intermediate and final workflow data products.

Cheney *et al.* [3] employ dependency analysis techniques (program slicing), which are focused on calculating data dependencies to infer "dependency provenance" for a query language based on the nested relational calculus. Unlike other approaches for inferring lineage from queries, [3] employs dependency analysis to formalize the notion of lineage relationships. Huq *et al.* [9] describe a tool to compute data-level lineage for workflows defined as Python scripts using Program Dependence Graphs (PDGs) [7]. However, control dependencies are converted to data dependencies to simplify lineage relationships for scientists. PDGs are closely aligned with program slicing techniques, and offer a formal interpretation of dependency also adopted by our model.

In [6], data dependencies are inferred from scripts and are then connected to YesWorkflow specifications; a prototype linking YesWorkflow models and noWorkflow traces has been described in [13]. Our approach differs from, but complements these approaches by explicitly supporting lineage assertions for both control and data dependency information (among other types of dependencies) for workflow specifications and enables validation and inference procedures over lineage annotations.

6   Conclusion and Future Work

This paper defines provenance dependency types for modeling lineage constraints within scientific workflow specifications along with a reasoning framework that can validate dependency annotations and infer a complete set of annotations for workflow specifications, including the allowable choices (*possible worlds*) when multiple annotation types are possible. We plan to extend YesWorkflow [11], which uses annotations to declare workflow specifications for executable scripts, with dependency annotations and the reasoning framework described here. We also plan to develop support for annotating subworkflows within YesWorkflow. While the dependency types described here cover a wide range of cases, additional types may be needed for some workflows. For instance, although not described in this paper, we have recently developed extensions for supporting a *NotFlowsFrom* dependency type, which is needed in some subworkflows to capture cases where subworkflow inputs are not connected (i.e., not "up-stream") from subworkflow outputs. Adding *NotFlowsFrom* required only minimal changes to the rules presented in Sect. 4. Finally, we also intend to explore using static dependency annotations in YesWorkflow models to infer trace-level (runtime) data lineage relationships, thus combining our prior work in [2] with the reasoning framework presented here.

Acknowledgements. Work supported in part through NSF award SMA-1637155.

References

1. Alper, P., Belhajjame, K., Curcin, V., Goble, C.: LabelFlow framework for annotating workflow provenance. Informatics **11**(5), 11 (2018)
2. Bowers, S., McPhillips, T., Ludäscher, B.: Declarative rules for inferring fine-grained data provenance from scientific workflow execution traces. In: Groth, P., Frew, J. (eds.) IPAW 2012. LNCS, vol. 7525, pp. 82–96. Springer, Heidelberg (2012). https://doi.org/10.1007/978-3-642-34222-6_7
3. Cheney, J., Ahmed, A., Acar, U.A.: Provenance as dependency analysis. Math. Struct. Comput. Sci. **21**(6), 1301–1337 (2011)
4. Cui, Y., Widom, J.: Lineage tracing for general data warehouse transformations. VLDB J. **12**(1), 41–58 (2003)
5. Davidson, S.B., Freire, J.: Provenance and scientific workflows: challenges and opportunities. In: SIGMOD (2008)
6. Dey, S.C., Belhajjame, K., Koop, D., Raul, M., Ludäscher, B.: Linking prospective and retrospective provenance in scripts. In: TaPP (2015)
7. Ferrante, J., Ottenstein, K.J., Warren, J.D.: The program dependence graph and its use in optimization. ACM Trans. Program. Lang. Syst. **9**(3), 319–349 (1987)
8. Gelfond, M., Kahl, Y.: Knowledge Representation, Reasoning, and the Design of Intelligent Agents: The Answer-Set Programming Approach. Cambridge University Press, Cambridge (2014)
9. Huq, M.R., Apers, P.M.G., Wombacher, A.: ProvenanceCurious: a tool to infer data provenance from scripts. In: EDBT, pp. 765–768 (2013)
10. Ludäscher, B., Bowers, S., McPhillips, T.: Scientific workflows. In: Liu, L., Özsu, M. (eds.) Encyclopedia of Database Systems, pp. 2507–2511. Springer, Heidelberg (2009). https://doi.org/10.1007/978-1-4899-7993-3
11. McPhillips, T., et al.: YesWorkflow: a user-oriented, language-independent tool for recovering workflow information from scripts. Intl. J. Digit. Curation **10**(1), 298–313 (2015)
12. Moreau, L., Missier, P.: PROV-DM: The PROV Data Model. W3C recommendation, W3C, April 2013. http://www.w3.org/TR/2013/REC-prov-dm-20130430/
13. Pimentel, J.F., et al.: Yin & Yang: demonstrating complementary provenance from noworkflow & yesworkflow. In: Mattoso, M., Glavic, B. (eds.) Provenance and Annotation of Data and Processes, IPAW 2016. LNCS, vol. 9672, pp. 161–165. Springer, Heidelberg (2016). https://doi.org/10.1007/978-3-319-40593-3_13
14. Sahoo, S., Lebo, T., McGuinness, D.: PROV-O: The PROV Ontology. W3C recommendation, W3C, April 2013. http://www.w3.org/TR/2013/REC-prov-o-20130430/

Applications

Belief Propagation Through Provenance Graphs

Belfrit Victor Batlajery[1]([✉]), Mark Weal[1], Adriane Chapman[1],
and Luc Moreau[2]

[1] University of Southampton, Southampton, UK
{b.v.batlajery,m.weal,adriane.chapman}@soton.ac.uk
[2] King's College London, London, UK
luc.moreau@kcl.ac.uk

Abstract. Provenance of food describes food, the processes in food transformation, and the food operators from the source to consumption; modelling the history food. In processing food, the risk of contamination increases if food is treated inappropriately. Therefore, identifying critical processes and applying suitable prevention actions are necessary to measure the risk; known as due diligence. To achieve due diligence, food provenance can be used to analyse the risk of contamination in order to find the best place to sample food. Indeed, it supports building rationale over food-related activities because it describes the details about food during its lifetime. However, many food risk models only rely on simulation with little notion of provenance of food. Incorporating the risk model with food provenance through our framework, *prFrame*, is our first contribution. *prFrame* uses Belief Propagation (BP) over the provenance graph for automatically measuring the risk of contamination. As BP works efficiently in a factor graph, our next contribution is the conversion of the provenance graph into the factor graph. Finally, an evaluation of the accuracy of the inference by BP is our last contribution.

1 Introduction

Provenance of food is well understood by both business and the public. Notions of *Appellation d'Origine Contrôllée* are regulatory labels indicating that some food products can be trusted to originate from a given region, thus vouching for the authenticity and quality of the products. Likewise, organic labels encompass more or less stringent guarantees that adequate processes have been followed in the production of food products. The provenance model PROV (`PROV-DM`) complemented by domain-specific ontologies [1,2] have been used to describe processes of the food supply chain, enabling such descriptions to be shared and queries over them to be answered. These capabilities allow confidence in food products and processes to increase. For instance, the requirement for food operators to identify suppliers one level up and customers one level down can easily be addressed using provenance-based modelling of the food supply chain [3].

Regulations demand that food operators undertake due diligence [4]. While this term is not formally defined in law, it is usually understood to include

© Springer Nature Switzerland AG 2018
K. Belhajjame et al. (Eds.): IPAW 2018, LNCS 11017, pp. 145–157, 2018.
https://doi.org/10.1007/978-3-319-98379-0_11

identifying all the food safety critical stages of food production, storage and distribution, then identifying suitable control measures to adequately prevent the risk of food safety failures and putting in place appropriate management control procedures to ensure they effectively happen [4, 5].

Our claim in this paper is that provenance models such as PROV can be the basis for food operators to develop a rationale for control procedures. Indeed, our discussions with them show that food samples are analysed to check contamination levels as part of a due diligence process to manage risk. However, such samplings are costly in terms of resources, and a rationale needs to be developed on how best to sample food supply chains. Regulators and food operators are constantly on the lookout for better ways to measure, track, and analyse risk in the food supply chain. In this paper, we discuss two techniques, adapted to operate over provenance graphs, which result in a powerful tool to reason, estimate, and understand risk of contamination across the food supply chain, over which we have partial knowledge of level of contamination.

First, PROV provenance can be used to model the food supply chain in the Modular Process Risk Model (MPRM), which is a tool for Quantitative Microbial Risk Assessment (QMRA) [6]. MPRM uses Monte-Carlo (MC) simulation, which is a computer-based technique allowing variation of randomly distributed inputs to be propagated through mathematical models [7], to generate bacterial concentration with the aim to understand the distribution of bacteria in the food supply chain. This approach relies on the directed nature of provenance graphs, and propagate bacterial concentration along edges of these graphs, according to evidenced formulae of micro-organisms transmissions. However, MPRM does not support any actual knowledge of contamination level as it relies on distributions of bacterial concentration, derived from past studies.

Second, in this context, Belief Propagation (BP) is a technique that takes observations of contamination levels in the food supply chain to calculate the marginal distribution for each unobserved node, conditional on these observed nodes [8]. BP, initially defined by Pearl, has been showed to operate on trees, but also to provide useful approximations for graphs. It requires a notion of Factor Graph (a bipartite graph containing nodes for variables and factors), which we demonstrate can be easily derived from provenance graphs.

The aim of this paper is to introduce a *prFrame*, as a framework to estimate risk of contamination in a food supply chain described by provenance, which allows for observations (by directly sampled contamination levels) to be taken into account, as well as estimates to be inferred for unobserved part of the chain. We demonstrate the effectiveness of the methodology within this framework lies when new evidence (i.e. sampling report) can easily be incorporated to more accurately estimate the actual risk.

The concrete contributions of the paper are as follows:

1. A Monte-Carlo based simulation technique to derive contamination levels of provenance-based descriptions of a food supply chain.
2. A transformation of food supply chain provenance graphs into factor graphs to enable sum-product algorithm as a variant of Belief Propagation.

3. An evaluation framework, allowing contamination levels to be systematically hidden in a provenance described supply chain (effectively creating unobserved nodes) to generate estimations of contamination levels through Belief Propagation.

Following this introduction, background to support our work is given in Sect. 2. We present our case study and our approach with *prFrame* in Sects. 3 and 4 subsequently. Section 5 shows how our approach can be applied and Sect. 6 concludes the paper and suggests potential future work.

2   Background

In this section, some theoretical concepts are presented. In general, we have two intersected concepts, namely provenance to describe what happened to food and BP to infer the risk of contamination over the provenance graph.

2.1   Provenance

The World Wide Web Consortium (W3C) defines provenance as *a record that describes the people, institutions, entities, and activities involved in producing, influencing, or delivering a piece of data or a thing in the world* [9]. It contains the description of data and the processes involved during the data lifetime, such as how something is derived, who is responsible for certain actions, what the consequences and the risks of an activity are, etc. As provenance describes the lifetime of something, it can provide a crucial information for investigation.

The Provenance Data Model (PROV-DM) and Provenance Ontology (PROV-O) [9,10] enable the modelling of something in provenance.

As PROV-O is designed to be domain agnostic, it often gets extended in specific domains. For instance, Markovic et al. extend the PROV-O to monitor food safety by documenting constraints that may be associated with an HACCP plan [2] and Batlajery et al. provide *prFood* ontology to capture and model food and risk along the food supply chain [1]. Another works by Ali and Moreau [11], Packer et al. [12], and Markovic et al. [13] also extend PROV-O for their specific purposes.

2.2   Belief Propagation

BP is an approach to perform inference based on message passing algorithm. Here, we focus on sum-product, as an algorithm in the BP family.

Theory of Belief Propagation. In Probabilistic Graphical Model (PGM), probability theory and graph theory are utilised to capture the knowledge in graph-based representations [14]. Probability is about measuring uncertainty of an occurrence in the world, which refers to the degree of confidence that an event will occur [15]. For example, the probability $P(X)$ of an event X quantifies the degree of confidence that X will occur. With $P(X) = 1$, we are certain that one of the outcomes in X occurs and $P(X) = 0$ indicates that all outcomes in X are impossible. Other probability values between 0 and 1 represent options that lie between them. Probability can be expressed in 2 fundamental rules, sum rule and product rule, which become the basic calculations of sum-product algorithm.

$$(a) \textbf{ sum rule} \quad P(X) = \sum_Y P(X,Y) \qquad (b) \textbf{ product rule} \quad P(X,Y) = P(Y|X)P(X) \quad (1)$$

In Eq. 1, $P(X)$ is referred to as marginal distribution over the distribution of random node X and is simply verbalized as the probability distribution of X. In many cases, the questions often involve the values of several random nodes or a Joint Probability Distribution (JPD), written as $P(X,Y)$. Similarly, a Conditional Probability Distribution (CPD) can be verbalized as the probability of Y given X or $P(Y|X)$ that specifies the belief in Y under the assumption that X is known (observed) with certainty [16]. Entering an evidence to update our belief about the probability is often mentioned as propagation and its mechanism with BP is described in the following paragraph.

Mechanics Behind Belief Propagation. BP relies on an iterative message passing algorithm inherently from bayesian procedure to perform an inference efficiently. This technique explores the conditional independence relationship over a Factor Graph. A factor graph is a bipartite graph that expresses the global function into a product of local functions [17]. This graph consists of 2 types of nodes, namely a variable node for each node in the network and a factor node for each factor $f(x)$ in the joint distribution between nodes.

The message passing algorithm allows the nodes to communicate their local state by sending messages over the edges [14, 18, 19]. By local, we mean that a given node updates the outgoing messages on the basis of incoming ones from the previous iterations. In general, the messages are passed around and get updated until a stable belief state is reached (convergence). However, depending on the type of graph, some may not reach the convergence due to circular reasoning. In the context of food provenance, the circular process exists in the event of splitting and joining food. Thus, having the provenance of food with a tree-based structured, such as the sequential linear chain from the source to consumption, can guarantee the convergence. Although convergence is not guaranteed, BP has been found to have outstanding empirical success in loopy graphs too [14].

3   Food Supply Chain as a Use Case

This section presents a case study where a notion of provenance is needed in the food domain in order to achieve due diligence. The study involves a food risk model for the food domain and its modelling by provenance.

3.1 Food Provenance and Food Regulations

In order to achieve due diligence, food regulations (e.g. ISO 9000, Food Safety Act (FSA) 1990, HACCP, etc.) are created for assuring food that people consume is safe [4,20]. By identifying what, where, when, who, and how food is handled, regulators and food operators can have an overview of potential contamination and have more comprehensive way of understanding the risk.

Definition 1. *Food Provenance is a record that describes a food product and its ingredients; the processes involved in food transformation; and food operators who are responsible for those processes in the food supply chain.*

In modelling food provenance into the standardized provenance format, we use PROV because of its capability to capture and describe the entities, activities, and agents that may have influenced the piece of data about food. The modelling is performed by codifying a food stage (e.g. *Prepared, Cooked,* etc.) as *prov:Entity,* a food process (e.g. *preparing, cooking,* etc.) as *prov:Activity,* and a food operator as *prov:Agent.* Figure 1 shows an excerpt of food provenance.

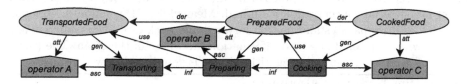

Fig. 1. An excerpt of provenance graph of the food supply chain.

Figure 1 describes the provenance of food, which conveys its history and the information about risk of contamination. To model the risk, the *prFood* ontology [1] is used to capture the necessary data for risk calculation, such as bacterial concentration, contamination level, risk factor, etc as attributes of entities.

Definition 2. *Bacterial Concentration is the total bacteria in food.*

Definition 3. *Contamination Level is a range of values to categorize bacterial concentration.*

Definition 4. *Risk Factor is any aspect that contributes to the risk of contamination, such as improper storage, time and temperature abuse of food, etc. [21].*

3.2 Modular Process Risk Model (MPRM)

MPRM is a process-driven framework to estimate the risk of food contamination based on how food is handled [6]. This framework splits the food supply chain into smaller modules and the transmission of bacteria is calculated based on the well-known formulae with the MC simulation. The simulation selects a random value from the distribution of a risk factor to generate bacterial concentration after each food process, and it will be the input for the next process.

MPRM supports 6 basic processes that can affect the bacterial concentration after the food process. They are Growth, Inactivation, Partitioning, Mixing, Removal, and Cross Contamination. Growth and inactivation are two basic microbial processes, which are strongly depending on the characteristic of bacteria investigated and the surrounded environmental condition. Partitioning, mixing, removal, and cross-contamination are 4 handling processes. Partitioning occurs when a major unit of food is split up into several minor units, while mixing describes the opposite process. Removal is a process where some units are removed and cross-contamination describes the transmission of bacteria between objects.

4 The prFrame Framework

This section discusses *prFrame*, our proposed framework that incorporates Provenance, Risk Model, and PGM to achieve due diligence. With multiple food risk models that use a MC simulation, the input-output interaction of bacterial concentration only works in one direction (forward, from source to destination), making predicting the contamination level before a food process difficult, given the bacterial concentration after that process. In addition, its capability to incorporate an actual bacterial concentration is limited. Meanwhile, BP is a non-directional approach as it propagates information forward and backward. Thus, inferencing is easier with additional observed information anywhere in the chain. The pseudocode of *prFrame* is shown in Algorithm 1 and is described below.

Algorithm 1. prFrame Algorithm

Input : pG: Provenance Graph
Output: $infBin$: Inferred Bacterial Level
1 var $bConc$: Bacterial Concentration ;
2 var $preBin$: Predicted Bacterial Level ;
3 $\langle bConc, preBin \rangle \leftarrow \underline{monteCarlo}(pG)$;
4 ;
5 var $preBin$: Predicted Bacterial Level ;
6 var $binMtx$: Bin Matrix ;
7 $binMtx \leftarrow \underline{computeBinMtx}(preBin)$;
8 ;
9 var $binMtx$: Bin Matrix ;
10 var $jpdMtx$: JPD Matrix ;
11 var $cpdMtx$: CPD Matrix ;
12 $\langle jpdMtx, cpdMtx \rangle \leftarrow \underline{computeCpd}(binMtx)$
;

13 ;
14 var pG: Provenance Graph ;
15 var $cpdMtx$: CPD Matrix ;
16 var $pGcpd$: Provenance Graph with CPD;
17 $pGcpd \leftarrow \underline{attachCpd}(pG, cpdMtx)$;
18 ;
19 var $pGcpd$: Provenance Graph with CPD;
20 var fG: Factor Graph ;
21 $fG \leftarrow \underline{convertPG}(pGcpd)$;
22 ;
23 var fG: Factor Graph ;
24 var e: Observed nodes ;
25 var i: Inferred nodes ;
26 var $infBin$: Inferred Bacterial Level ;
27 $infBin \leftarrow \underline{beliefPro}(fG, e, i)$;

4.1 Food Risk Model with Monte-Carlo Simulation

Our framework begins with a given provenance graph that describes food. The provenance graph is expected to hold data about risk factors as parameters to simulate the flow of food based on MPRM. An MPRM basic process in a food process depends on the activities described and the assumption hold in that food process. For example, it is assumed that the number of microbes increases during the transporting process; hence, the growth model becomes the basic process for transporting. Changing or adding a basic process will affect the formula to predict the number of microbes, which is not the scope of this paper. We refers the readers to [21] for the details of risk factors and their distributions in each food process as well as the formula for each MPRM basic process.

The simulation is needed as we do not know the exact risk factors, such as time and temperature in processing food, leading us to only have partial information about contamination levels. With this reason, we estimate bacterial concentration by conducting MC simulation, which takes into account all the possible values of risk factors in form of a distribution, to predict contamination level along the provenance network. The MC simulation is performed the same as in [21], which generates predicted bacterial concentration after each food process.

Each generated bacterial concentration is categorized into the contamination level. The aim for categorization is that it is easier to compare the actual data with the categorical data (contamination level) rather than with the continuous data (bacterial concentration) in order to infer the updated risk of contamination. Thus, each contamination level counts food that have bacterial concentration within its defined range (Algorithm 1 *line 3*). In the end, a *Bin matrix* is constructed to capture all possible combinations between contamination levels before (upwards) and after (downwards). The column and row of the matrix represent the levels upward and downward consecutively (Algorithm 1 *line 7*). For example, Fig. 2 shows that there are a total 24 food products in the transporting process (Transported Food) and storing process (Stored Food). Four of them had microbial level 1 after transporting and level 2 after storing.

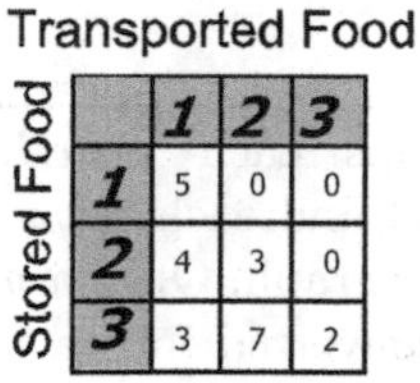

Fig. 2. An example of a bin matrix. A blue square represents the level of contamination. (Color figure online)

4.2 Belief Propagation in the Provenance Network

A Joint Probability Distribution (JPD) is captured in a *JPD matrix* by dividing each value in the Bin matrix with the total number in Bin matrix (total food used that have undergone the food process). Subsequently, a CPD matrix is derived by dividing each value of the JPD matrix with its corresponding row as the row represents the level downward the food process (Algorithm 1 *line 12*). A complete bin matrix, jpd matrix, and cpd matrix are presented in online appendix (https://goo.gl/hXvici). Next, the CPD matrix is added as an attribute in the provenance graph (Algorithm 1 *line 17*) and the conversion into a factor graph is performed (Algorithm 1 *line 21*).

In a factor graph, a factor can be described as a function that takes arguments from the random nodes and return a value for every possible combinations over those random nodes. A CPD is used as a factor, which holds the notion of conditional probability for every *prov:Entity* that is linked with a *prov:Activity* via both *prov:usage* (*use*) and *prov:wasGeneratedBy* (*gen*), in the present of a *prov:wasDerivedFrom* (*der*) that identifies the origin and the result of the food process for a CPD matrix. Algorithm 2 shows the pseudocode of the conversion.

Algorithm 2. function factorGraph(*pGcpd*)

    Input : *pGcpd*: Provenance Graph with CPD
    Output: *fG*: Factor Graph
1 var n_x: Variable node ;
2 var f_x: Factor node ;
3 var $unEdge_x$: Undirected Edge ;
4 var *o*: Object ;
5 **foreach** $o \in pGcpd$ **do**
6   **if** *type(o)=prov:Entity AND type(o)=prFood:FoodStage* **then**
7 | $n_x \leftarrow$ <u>convertEntity</u>(*o*) ;
8   **end**
9   **if** *type(o)=prov:Activity AND type(o)=prFood:FoodProcessing* **then**
10 | $f_x \leftarrow$ <u>convertActivity</u>(*o*) ;
11   **end**
12   **if** *type(o)=prov:usage OR type(o)=prov:wasGeneratedBy* **then**
13 | $unEdge_x \leftarrow$ <u>convertEdge</u>(*o*) ;
14   **end**
15 **end**
16 **return** *Factor Graph (fG)*

Overall, the conversion maps each *prov:Entity* into a variable node $(\mathbf{n_1}, \ldots, \mathbf{n_x})$ (Algorithm 2 *line 6*) and each *prov:Activity* into a factor node $\mathbf{f_x}$ (Algorithm 2 *line 9*) in the factor graph. Only a *prov:Activity* that has the type *prFood:FoodProcessing* will be converted into a factor node, and a *prov:Entity* of type *prFood:FoodStage* will be converted to a variable node. The factor node $\mathbf{f_x}$ holds the notion of CPD, which is a factor to determine the probability of each variable nodes that are connected to it $(\mathbf{n_1}, \ldots, \mathbf{n_x})$. In the conversion, we ignore *prov:Agent* to make the graph as simple as possible. Figure 3 shows an example of the conversion.

In Fig. 3, in order to link the factor nodes with the variable nodes, we identify *prov:wasGeneratedBy* (*gen*) and *prov:usage* (*use*) and convert them into undirected edges (Algorithm 2 *line 12*) provided a corresponding *prov:wasDerivedFrom* (*der*) exists (as its notion has been encapsulated in the CPD matrix). For example, the probability of $\mathbf{n_x}$ given $\mathbf{n_{x-1}}$ has implied the derivation between $\mathbf{n_x}$ and $\mathbf{n_{x-1}}$. Finally, the sum-product algorithm that utilizes bayesian rules is applied to calculate the likelihood of a certain event (Algorithm 1 *line 27*). The figures of initial provenance graph and factor graph are available in on-line appendix.

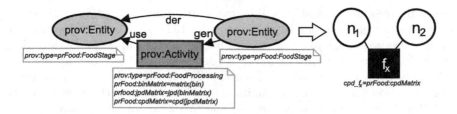

Fig. 3. A conversion from provenance graph into factor graph.

4.3   Methodology to Infer Risk of Contamination

As a framework, *prFrame* is intended to automatically infer the risk of food contamination. It incorporates the general food risk model that uses MC simulation, MPRM, with the inference technique, BP. BP infers the actual contamination level by propagating belief based on the previous knowledge and the actual data (i.e. sampling result). Our methodology compares the inference of contamination level by BP (*InfBin*: Inferred Bacterial Level) with the prediction by the MC simulation (*prBin*: Predicted Bacterial Level).

The aim in this methodology is to understand the accuracy of inference across the food provenance network by capturing exhaustively experiments, where nodes values are hidden and observed systematically, in order to evaluate the performance of BP. To define an accuracy of inference, consider a bacterial concentration in level 1 that was predicted by the MC simulation. There are three possible inferences by BP. The first inference reveals with 100% probability that the prediction is in level 1. The second inference reveals with 97.6% probability that the prediction is in level 1 and 2.4% probability in level 2. The third inference reveals with 90% probability that the prediction is in level 1 and 5% probability is in both level 0 and level 2. Here, the most accurate inference is the first inference, followed by the second and the third inferences.

5   Evaluation of the Methodology

The complete list of chains for our first and second setup is shown in the on-line appendix. To keep the calculation and propagation simple, we use an example of a fixed linear network that represents the food chain as configured in [21]. It is also possible to define more complicated network as provenance of food can be non-linear network. However, the use of linear chain in this paper is guaranteed to reach a convergence in inferring with BP for further measurement of accuracy. The defined network comprises 6 food stages, namely *Initial*(**I**), *Retailed*(**R**), *Transported*(**T**), *Stored*(**S**), *Prepared*(**P**), and *Cooked*(**C**). We then predict bacterial concentration and contamination level by performing MC simulation with 50,000 iterations to represent the travelling of food products through this chain and results in 10,502 food being contaminated.

Each bacterial concentration will be categorized into a fixed determined *bin* that represents contamination level. We consider 13 levels of bacteria because the number is precise enough to categorize the bacterial concentration. While adding more levels produces more precise result, it comes with higher computational. We also introduce an *inferred node*, an *unobserved node* that its probabilities are in our investigation when performing an inference. Finally, we perform an inference with BP and compare the results against the prediction of MC simulation.

5.1   The Effect of the Distance and Position Between Nodes

Our first setup intends to measure accuracy of inference based on the distance between an *observed node* and an *inferred node*. We set node **I** as an *observed node* and the remaining nodes will be inferred. Figure 4(a) shows that the accuracy decreases as we infer the further nodes. Inferencing nodes **R** and **T** is always correct as all of the inferences suggest the same level as predicted by MC simulation. The inference becomes less accurate with total 10,432 correct inferences (99.33%) in node **S**. In other words, it can be verbalized as there are 99.33% contaminated food with 88%–100% probability of being correct. Finally, there are 97.86% and 88.87% correct inferences in node **P** and node **C** consecutively. In addition, inferring node **C** by observing node **I**, **R**, **T**, **S**, and **P** for our second setup also suggest the same result.

In regards to the position of nodes, we condition some nodes (solid-filled-node) and let BP does the inference in node **S** as a *inferred node* (dashed-unfilled-node) as shown in several chains (ch.) in the on-line appendix. In Fig. 4(b), inferencing node **S** with upward *observed nodes* (nodes **I**, **R**, and **T**) gives the same result (ch.3a, ch.3b, and ch.3c). Among 10,502 inferences, only 159 inferences (1.51%) are with 100% probability of being correct. In fact, more upward *observed nodes* produces the same result too (ch.3e). The inference becomes more accurate if the *inferred node* is set in between the *observed nodes* (ch.3f, ch.3g, and ch.3h) with 1.75% correct inferences. However, the result is less accurate if we observe nodes **I** and **C** (ch.3i) with only 1.51% correct inferences. The opposite result is shown in ch.3d and ch.3j, where a downward node is observed with the remaining nodes unobserved. This scenario shows the deterioration of the accuracy with 0.66% and 0.0% correct inferences consecutively.

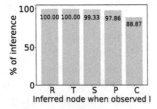

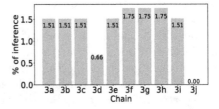

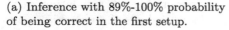

(a) Inference with 89%-100% probability of being correct in the first setup.

(b) Inference with 100% probability of being correct in third setup.

Fig. 4. The effect of distance and location of nodes in the accuracy of inferring.

5.2   Analysis of the Result

From our evaluation, we conclude that the closer the distance between *observed node* and *inferred node* is, the more accurate the inference will be. This can be proved through the first and second setup. Moreover, the highest accuracy of inference is achieved when the *inferred node* is placed between the *observed nodes*. This is obvious as the upward and downward nodes can infer the middle one with more certainty. In fact, the accuracy is similar when we add more *observed nodes*, indicating that the only important nodes are one node upward and one node downward the *inferred node*. Although *inferred node* is located in between *observed nodes*, the accuracy decreases if there is *unobserved node* in between those *observed nodes*, which provokes the uncertainty.

Our evaluation also reveals that observing several nodes prior the inferred one will not improve the accuracy if the nodes downward the *inferred node* remain unobserved. Again, it means that adding more nodes prior the *inferred node* does not affect the inference as long as the downward nodes remaining unobserved. The same result derived if the *observed nodes* are located downward the *inferred node* with remain nodes unobserved. However, the inference is more accurate when observing upward nodes than the downward nodes of the *inferred node*.

6   Conclusion and Future Work

We have presented our work on using BP as an inference technique over the provenance network through *prFrame* to infer the probability of a node, given a condition of the others. We conclude that *prFrame* successfully combines BP with the provenance network and our evaluation produces inferences with high accuracy between 89% and 100% of being correct. In the food context, it can be translated as the contaminated food are inferred with 89% to 100% chance of being correct. We believe that more reliable results can be achieved with more data captured in provenance, such as risk factors or sampling data. From an implementation point of view, *prFrame* can accommodate the existence food risk models in order to help food authority achieve due diligence in food.

In a case when a sampling report is used as the actual information, an inference can be performed after the fact that food has travelled to several places as opposed to real time, because sampling analysis can take several days. In this situation, provenance or the past description of food is an important information to explain the reason behind the sampling result and assess the risk to identified the next potential places to sampling food on the basis of the sampling report.

In the paper, we limit our work in a linear network only, while provenance networks are mostly non-linear networks. In fact, many food chains in reality are not a linear chain, such as tree structure. Our investigation reveals that as long as the chain does not have cycle in it, the inference becomes converged. However, even though the food chain have a cycle and the state belief cannot be achieved, an approximate inference with BP has been proven as a good estimation as well.

Finally, in performing the inference, we did not take into account the type of activity of food process to assess the accuracy of inference. We believe that a deeper investigation is required in order to systematically characterise BP-band in inference in provenance trace.

References

1. Batlajery, B.V., Weal, M., Chapman, A., Moreau, L. prFood: ontology principles for provenance and risk in the food domain. IEEE, December 2017
2. Markovic, M., Edwards, P., Kollingbaum, M., Rowe, A.: Modelling provenance of sensor data for food safety compliance checking. In: Mattoso, M., Glavic, B. (eds.) IPAW 2016. LNCS, vol. 9672, pp. 134–145. Springer, Cham (2016). https://doi.org/10.1007/978-3-319-40593-3_11
3. Thakur, M., Hurburgh, C.R.: Framework for implementing traceability system in the bulk grain supply chain. J. Food Eng. **95**(4), 617–626 (2009)
4. Food Standards Agency: Food Law Code of Practice (England)-April 2015. Report, Food Standards Agency, April 2015
5. Eves, A., Dervisi, P.: Experiences of the implementation and operation of hazard analysis critical control points in the food service sector. Int. J. Hosp. Manag. **24**(1), 319 (2005)
6. Nauta, M.J.: A modular process risk model structure for quantitative microbiological risk assessment and its application in an exposure assessment of Bacillus cereus in a REPFED. RIVM Rapport 149106007 (2001)
7. Duarte, A.S.R.: The interpretation of quantitative microbial data: meeting the demands of quantitative microbiological risk assessment. Ph.D. thesis, National Food Institute, Technical University of Denmark (2013)
8. Pearl, J.: Reverend Bayes on inference engines: a distributed hierarchical approach. In: AAAI 1982. AAAI Press (1982)
9. Moreau, L., Groth, P., Cheney, J., Lebo, T., Miles, S.: The rationale of PROV. Web Semant.: Sci. Serv. Agents World Wide Web **35**(4), 235–257 (2015)
10. Moreau, L., Missier, P.: PROV-DM: the PROV Data Model, W3C Recommendation REC-prov-dm-20130430, World Wide Web Consortium, April 2013
11. Moreau, L., Ali, M.: A provenance-based policy control framework for cloud services, May 2014
12. Packer, H.S., Drăgan, L., Moreau, L.: An auditable reputation service for collective adaptive systems. In: Miorandi, D., Maltese, V., Rovatsos, M., Nijholt, A., Stewart, J. (eds.) Social Collective Intelligence. CSS, pp. 159–184. Springer, Cham (2014). https://doi.org/10.1007/978-3-319-08681-1_8
13. Markovic, M., Edwards, P., Corsar, D.: SC-PROV: a provenance vocabulary for social computation. In: Ludäscher, B., Plale, B. (eds.) IPAW 2014. LNCS, vol. 8628, pp. 285–287. Springer, Cham (2015). https://doi.org/10.1007/978-3-319-16462-5_35
14. Koller, D., Friedman, N.: Probabilistic Graphical Models: Principles and Techniques. MIT Press, Cambridge (2009)
15. Cohen, M.H.: The unknown and the unknowable-managing sustained uncertainty. West. J. Nurs. Res. **15**(1), 77–96 (1993)
16. Pearl, J.: Causality: Models, Reasoning and Inference, 2nd edn. Cambridge University Press, New York (2009)

17. Frey, B.J., Kschischang, F.R., Loeliger, H.A., Wiberg, N.: Factor graphs and algorithms. In: Proceedings of the Annual Allerton Conference on Communication Control and Computing, vol. 35, pp. 666–680. University of Illinois (1997)
18. Bishop, C.M.: Pattern Recognition and Machine Learning. Information Science and Statistics. Springer, Secaucus (2006)
19. Kschischang, F.R., Frey, B.J., Loeliger, H.A.: Factor graphs and the sum-product algorithm. IEEE Trans. Inf. Theor. **47**(2), 498–519 (2006)
20. Holleran, E., Bredahl, M.E., Zaibet, L.: Private incentives for adopting food safety and quality assurance. Food Policy **24**, 669–683 (1999)
21. World Health Organization: Risk Assessments of Salmonella in Eggs and Broiler Chickens, vol. 2. Food & Agriculture Organization, Geneva (2002)

Using Provenance to Efficiently Propagate SPARQL Updates on RDF Source Graphs

Iman Naja$^{(\boxtimes)}$ and Nicholas Gibbins

Electronics and Computer Science, University of Southampton, Southampton, UK
{i.naja,nmg}@ecs.soton.ac.uk

Abstract. To promote sharing on the Semantic Web, information is published in machine-readable structured graphs expressed in RDF or OWL. This allows information consumers to create graphs using other source graphs. Information, however, is dynamic and when a source graph changes, graphs based on it need to be updated as well to preserve their integrity. To avoid regenerating a graph after one of its source graphs changes, since that approach can be expensive, we rely on its provenance to reduce the resources needed to reflect changes to its source graph. Accordingly, we expand the W3C PROV standard and present RGPROV, a vocabulary for RDF graph creation and update. RGPROV allows us to understand the dependencies a graph has on its source graphs and facilitates the propagation of the SPARQL updates applied to those source graphs through it. Additionally, we present a model that implements a modified DRed algorithm which makes use of RGPROV to enable partial modifications to be made on the RDF graph, thus reflecting the SPARQL updates on the source graph efficiently, without having to keep track of the provenance of each triple. Hence, only SPARQL updates are communicated, the need for complete re-derivation is done away with, and provenance is kept at the graph level making it better scalable.

Keywords: Provenance · PROV · RDF · SPARQL update

1 Introduction

The Semantic Web promotes the publishing, understanding, discovery, integration, and re-use of information, with recent years seeing a boost in the publication, inter-linkage, and consumption of large amounts of public datasets. Knowledge is presented in machine-understandable formats, namely RDF [1] and OWL [2] graphs, which provide well-defined meanings and support rules for reasoning, and is queried and updated using SPARQL [3]. Graphs may be manually created or automatically formed by combining information from other graphs, and automated reasoning may be performed on them.

However, this is not without challenge, as knowledge is neither static nor complete and its expansion and change is inevitable. Thus, in systems having

© Springer Nature Switzerland AG 2018
K. Belhajjame et al. (Eds.): IPAW 2018, LNCS 11017, pp. 158–170, 2018.
https://doi.org/10.1007/978-3-319-98379-0_12

graphs which relied on other source graphs when created, changes to those source graphs need to be incorporated and reflected so as to keep such graphs up-to-date. Typically, systems recreate those graphs from scratch and reason anew on them. This may be expensive, and sometimes impractical to re-obtain the data used and to re-reason with it. Alternatively, a system may contain its own reasoner which takes responsibility for re-reasoning, like in [4].

Another challenge arises in the fact that the Semantic Web is an open environment where 'anyone can say anything about anything'. This begets the need for means to appraise the trustworthiness, reliability, and reputation of data in graphs to be consumed; and such assessments are intrinsically linked to knowing their provenance. Provenance describes the history of a datum or thing, and which activities, entities, and people were involved in how they came to be [5]. It has proven to be useful in numerous domains, as developers, researchers, and users have been utilising it to establish trust, understanding, transparency, attribution and accountability for outputs of intelligent systems. Moreover, the recent community-driven work to achieve an open provenance vision resulted in the PROV data model [6], a W3C recommendation.

While PROV facilitates interoperable provenance modelling, it is generic; a more specialised vocabulary better serves to track and express the provenance specific to RDF graphs, relating their creation and detailing and facilitating their modification. Accordingly, we expand PROV and present RGPROV, a vocabulary which models the classes and properties involved in an RDF graph's creation and update. It allows the specific capture of the provenance of an RDF graph created using other graphs and understanding its dependencies on them. It also expedites the propagation of SPARQL updates applied to its source graphs without wide scale insertions or deletions and then complete re-derivation, thus promoting the capture of the provenance of the update precisely and efficiently, without resorting to tracking the provenance of individual triples.

The contributions of this paper are fourfold. (*i*) Our main contribution is the RGPROV vocabulary, a specialisation of PROV-O which models the classes and properties involved in an RDF graph's creation and the SPARQL updates applied on it. (*ii*) A partial re-derivation algorithm, based on DRed [7], which makes use of RGPROV to propagate all or some of the SPARQL updates applied on source graphs. (*iii*) A model which implements both RGPROV and the partial re-derivation algorithm and (*iv*) A quantitative evaluation of our model demonstrating that less resources are needed to achieve the same results.

Outline: Sect. 2 presents related work. Section 3 provides the running example used throughout. Section 4 presents RGPROV. Section 5 describes our model and presents the partial re-derivation algorithms. Section 6 describes the implementation of our system and presents the results. Finally, Sect. 7 presents our conclusions and future work.

2   Related Work

The Delete and Rederive (DRed) algorithm [7] deletes the base data and all the data that was derived from it, then re-inserts the subset of the derived data that can be re-derived using other still present base data. RDFox [4] initially materialises queries and its reasoner implements an incremental maintenance algorithm based on DRed, but without making use of provenance. Elseways, [9] presents an initial model, where they aim to have versioned data and functions which would use provenance to detect changes between data versions, select processes that require re-computation, and decide between complete or partial re-computation. [10] extends their work on provenance semirings in [11] to support update exchange, schema mapping, and trust evaluation and to also extend the DRed algorithm. When a deletion occurs, they utilise provenance to flag and delete tuples which are no longer derivable. Similarly, [12] extends [13]'s work and utilises colours to represent triple sources, although they consider inferred quadruples independent of their sources. Before a quadruple is deleted, all the quadruples that can be inferred from it are inserted first. Then, all the quadruples that would entail it are deleted along with the quadruple itself. Further, [14] extends both [11,13]'s work by also using quadruples. Their quadruples' fourth elements are named graphs and quadruples' provenance is maintained in separate tuples with an id element linking to them. They, however, do not consider deletions; their algorithm describes how to insert quadruples and record their provenance. The aforementioned works track provenance on the triple level, an approach we avoided because of scalability concerns since tracking each triple's provenance using PROV would result in a graph having the size of its provenance graph substantially larger than it[1]. Instead, using RGPROV we track provenance on the graph level. [15] presents work similar to ours that tracks dynamic provenance of collections using a specialisation of PROV, upd, which allows them to capture SPARQL queries and updates performed on raw data in a dataset. Their work only considers updates and ignores the other operations that may affect a graph or its provenance, namely fetching, set theoretic operations, and re-entailment.

3   Running Example

We assume there are four systems A, B, C, and D, as shown in Fig. 1, each having ownership of some RDF graphs and maintaining their provenance. We focus on system C and explain our notations whilst identifying activities performed on graphs. A graph $G_{X,n}$ belongs to system X, differentiated from other graphs by the subset n, and $P_{X,n}$ is its provenance graph.

(1) _Graph retrieval:_ the activity of fetching a graph and its provenance from an external system and saving their copies internally. When copied to system C, $G_{X,n}$'s name becomes $G_{copy(X,n)}$ in C. Similarly $P_{X,n}$'s name becomes $P_{copy(X,n)}$. To reflect the activity of copying, $P_{copy(X,n)}$ is updated and becomes $P^*_{copy(X,n)}$.

---

[1] If each triple's provenance consists of only `triple prov:wasDerivedFrom sourceTriple`, a graph's provenance graph would be a little larger than it. Even adding provenance information about only the activity and agent that produced a triple would result in the graph's provenance graph being at minimum triple its size.

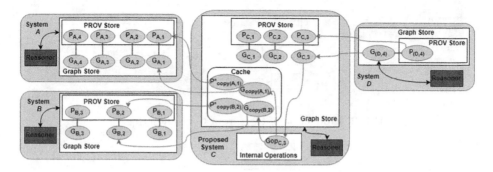

Fig. 1. Example of distributed graph usage.

(2) *Set theoretic operations:* An intermediary graph $Gop_{C,m}$ is produced by applying one of Union, Merging, Intersection, and Difference. We currently ignore blank nodes, and subsequently Merging.

(3) *Entailment:* In C, the entailed graph $G_{C,m}$ is produced from $Gop_{C,m}$ by running it through a reasoner. Entailment operations depend on which entailment regime is implemented, namely: RDF, RDFS, Datatype, OWL 2 RDF-Based Semantics, OWL 2 Direct Semantics, or RIF. We use RDFS Entailment [8] in our system.

An example of $G_{C,3}$'s production is shown in Fig. 2. Throughout the identified activities, C produces and updates the provenance $P_{C,3}$ of $G_{C,3}$. Note that the aforementioned list of operations to create a graph is not exhaustive; other operations, including the use of join, CONSTRUCT, OPTIONAL, etc., are beyond the scope of this paper and may be addressed in some future work.

(4) *SPARQL updates:* If a system, say B, performs a SPARQL update $Up_{op(B,2)}$ on $G_{B,2}$ resulting in it becoming the new graph $G_{B',2}$, then C should know about this update and subsequently needs to update $G_{C,3}$, or whichever parts of it should be affected, thus resulting in the more accurate and up-to-date $G_{C',3}$. SPARQL updates are Insert, Delete, Delete/Insert, Load, and Clear. We only focus on Insert and Delete as the latter three can be seen as combinations or special cases of the former. The standard approach is to retrieve a copy of $G_{B',2}$ and $G_{A,1}$ - if not internally stored, reapply Gop on them, and re-entailing to produce $G_{C',3}$. This becomes impractical in large systems for two reasons: (1) it is computationally expensive to re-entail a sizeable graph from scratch whenever there is an update, and (2) it requires additional storage, communication overhead, or both since the source graphs either need to be stored or re-fetched whenever a change occurs. Thus, we identify the need for a more efficient way to reflect updates and produce $G_{C',3}$. Our approach considers both the set theoretic operation which created $Gop_{C,3}$ and the nature of $Up_{op(B,2)}$. This allows us to retrieve only the update $Up_{B,2}$ applied to $G_{B,2}$ instead of retrieving all of $G_{B',2}$ and to identify whether $G_{copy(A,1)}$ is required, whether all or part of $Up_{B,2}$ needs to be propagated, and which parts of $G_{C,3}$ need to be re-derived.

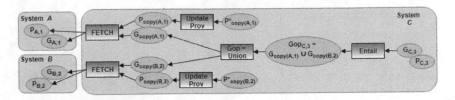

Fig. 2. Production of $G_{C,3}$ from $G_{A,1}$ and $G_{B,2}$.

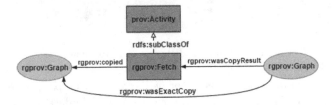

Fig. 3. RGPROV components for graph retrieval.

4   The RGPROV Vocabulary

RGPROV extends PROV-O and has the namespace prefix rgprov. Although we only use it for RDF graphs, we intend it to be used for OWL graphs as well.

In accordance with PROV, we recognize that RDF and PROV graphs are entities. To differentiate them from other types of entities, we introduce the class *Graph*, a subclass of prov:Entity, that contains only entities which are graphs. The actions that retrieve, produce, or update a Graph are activities, initiated by agents. We extend these concepts and any necessary properties as follows.

Vocabulary for Graph Retrieval: We require stricter terms than prov:hadPrimarySource and prov:wasQuotedFrom to represent copying a graph as-is from its sources. Based on the description in Sect. 3, we show them in Fig. 3. We see no need to create additional vocabulary for provenance production and updating because provenance graphs are members of Graph, hence RGPROV's terms can be adequately applied to them.

Vocabulary for Graph Operations: We introduce the class *GraphOperation*, a subclass of prov:Activity, that encompasses operations performed on a graph.

Vocabulary for Set theoretic Operations: Because there is a need to keep track of which graph operation produced a graph, we introduce terms for set theoretic operations, based on the description in Sect. 3, and show them in Fig. 4.

Vocabulary for Entailment Operations: To describe entailment operations, we introduce the following, based on the description in Sect. 3, and depict a selection of them in Fig. 5:

(1) *Entailment*, a subclass of GraphOperation, with subclasses representing particular entailment regimes.

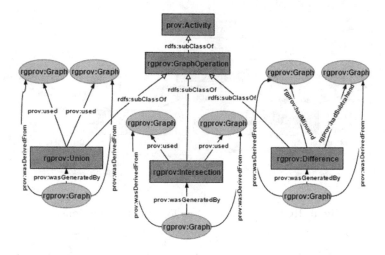

Fig. 4. RGPROV components for set theoretic graph operations.

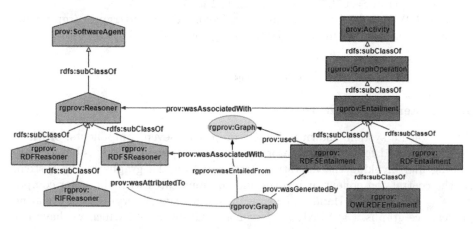

Fig. 5. Some RGPROV components for entailment operations.

(2) *Reasoner*, a subclass of prov:SoftwareAgent that represent a reasoner, with subclasses representing reasoners performing particular entailment regimes.

(3) *wasEntailedFrom*, a subproperty of prov:wasDerivedFrom, has domain Graph, has range Graph.

Vocabulary for Updates: First, we introduce *UpdateGraph*, a subclass of Graph that represents the graphs whose triples are to be inserted or deleted. We argue for this because a graph that is stored in and being used by a system should be differentiated from one whose entire purpose is containing triples to be inserted or deleted in the former type of graph. Additionally, since we differentiate the types of updates performed on a graph, we require stricter terms than prov:Revision

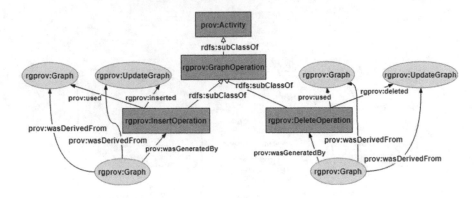

Fig. 6. RGPROV components for update operations.

and prov:wasRevisionOf. Thus we introduces terms for graph updates based on the description in Sect. 3, and show them in Fig. 6.

RGPROV is published on https://archive.org/download/rgprov/rgprov.owl and https://archive.org/download/rgprov/rgprovTurtle.owl.

5   The Model and Algorithms

5.1   System Architecture

We designed a system, shown in Fig. 7, comprising seven components, of which we implemented four. (1) Operator, the main component, responsible for controlling and invoking the operations performed on the graphs in the system. As the central component, it invokes and communicates with the other components. (2) Provenance Handler, responsible for creating, querying, and updating provenance graphs. (3) SPARQL Server and Graph Store, which we have not implemented but used the third party Jena Fuseki Server[2]. (4) Reasoner, which we have also not implemented but used the third party Jena[3]. Jena is responsible for performing the set theoretic and entailment operations on all graphs. (5) Update Producer, handles any updates applied on graph $G_{C,3}$ for any outside system that uses it. (6) Cache, used to store copies of retrieved graphs or updates and any other temporary graphs as needed. Finally, (7) REST client, handles the communications between the different systems. We have not implemented it, as it does not pertain to the demonstrating the application of the RGPROV vocabulary nor does it affect the evaluation of the system. Components have been implemented in Java.

Note that unless they have been marked as inferred triples, all triples in the source graphs are treated as ground triples in the system. Then, after it is

---

[2] Fuseki2 is available on https://jena.apache.org/documentation/fuseki2/.

[3] All Jena binary distributions are available on http://archive.apache.org/dist/jena/binaries/.

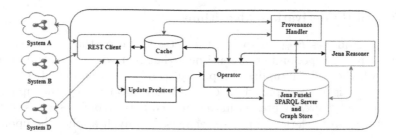

Fig. 7. System design.

produced, graph $G_{C,3}$ is split into and stored as two graphs. The first consists of the ground triples and the second consists of the inferred triples produced by our systems' reasoner. This separation proves beneficial when re-deriving to minimise over-deletions and re-insertions.

5.2   Update Propagation per Set Theoretic Operations

We now analyse how the combination of the set theoretic operation and the kind of update influence what part of the triples in the update graph $U_{PB,2}$ inserted into or deleted from $G_{B,2}$ are to be propagated into graph $G_{C,3}$ and how. Note that inserting triples which already exist in a graph has no effect, nor does deleting triples which do not exist.

Union $G_{C,3} = G_{copy(A,1)} \cup G_{copy(B,2)}$.
Insert: equivalent to inserting into $G_{C,3}$ the triples in $U_{PB,2}$. $G_{copy(A,1)}$ is not needed and the only new entity needed is $U_{PB,2}$.
Delete: equivalent to deleting from $G_{C,3}$ the triples in $U_{PB,2} \setminus G_{copy(A,1)}$. $G_{copy(A,1)}$ is needed along with $U_{PB,2}$.
Intersection $G_{C,3} = G_{copy(A,1)} \cap G_{copy(B,2)}$.
Insert: equivalent to inserting into $G_{C,3}$ the triples in $U_{PB,2} \cap G_{copy(A,1)}$. $G_{copy(A,1)}$ is needed along with $U_{PB,2}$.
Delete: equivalent to deleting from $G_{C,3}$ the triples in $U_{PB,2}$. $G_{copy(A,1)}$ is not needed and the only new entity needed is $U_{PB,2}$.
Difference Case 1 $G_{C,3} = G_{copy(A,1)} \setminus G_{copy(B,2)}$.
Insert: equivalent to deleting from $G_{C,3}$ the triples in $U_{PB,2}$. $G_{copy(A,1)}$ is not needed and the only new entity needed is $U_{PB,2}$.
Delete: equivalent to inserting into $G_{C,3}$ the triples in $U_{PB,2} \cap G_{copy(A,1)}$. $G_{copy(A,1)}$ is needed along with $U_{PB,2}$.
Difference Case 2 $G_{C,3} = G_{copy(B,2)} \setminus G_{copy(A,1)}$.
Insert: equivalent to inserting into $G_{C,3}$ the triples in $U_{PB,2} \setminus G_{copy(A,1)}$. $G_{copy(A,1)}$ is needed along with $U_{PB,2}$.
Delete: equivalent to deleting from $G_{C,3}$ the triples in $U_{PB,2}$. $G_{copy(A,1)}$ is not needed and the only new entity needed is $U_{PB,2}$.

5.3   Partial Re-derivation Algorithms

The Operator queries $P_{C,3}$ for the set theoretic operation that produced $G_{C,3}$, checks the update type, and cross-references that pair with the list in Sect. 5.2 to decide whether all the update graph $Up_{copy(B,2)}$ or a subset of it, namely $Subs_{Up_{copy(B,2)}}$, is to be applied to $G_{C,3}$. Before propagating the update, it removes the triples already present in the inferred portion of $G_{C,3}$, so as to avoid over-insertions/over-deletions and re-insertions. Finally, it applies the update as follows.

If the update is an insert, the Operator creates an Insert statement and sends it to Fuseki to be loaded into $G_{C,3}$. It then requests the graphs resulting from the Describe of those triples. The SPARQL Describe of a triple 'describes' it by returning a graph containing all those triples that are connected to it, i.e., all the triples which have as a subject any of the IRIs of the described triple's subject, predicate, or object. The union of the triples to be inserted and their descriptions constitute the entirety of information that is needed for re-derivation. This union is then forwarded to the reasoner, Jena, for inference. When the entailed graph resulting from reasoning on this union is returned, the Operator creates another Insert statement containing those inferred triples to be added by Fuseki thus resulting in $G_{C',3}$. The aforementioned is shown in Algorithm 1.

Algorithm 1. Apply Insert Update

Function: *describe* : *graph* x *triple* → *graph*
Function: *entail* : *graph* → *graph*

procedure APPLYINSERTUPDATE(*graph, triplesTBI*)
    described ← ϕ
    graph ← *graph* ∪ *triplesTBI*
    for each *triple* in *triplesTBI* **do**
        described ← *described* ∪ *describe(graph, triple)*
    graph ← *graph* ∪ *entail(described)*

If the update is a delete, then the Operator first gets, from Fuseki, the graphs resulting from the Describe of the triples to be deleted. It then loops over each triple to be deleted and examines its predicate. If the predicate is an rdf:type or has super-properties (i.e. it is a sub-property of another property), then it adds, to the list of the triples to be deleted, the triples with the same subject and any objects that relate it to the predicate. This is in accordance with the RDFS entailment rules described in [8]. Next, the Operator sends a Delete statement containing the updated list of triples to Fuseki, so that the latter deletes them from $G_{C,3}$, thus resulting in $Gop_{C',3}$. Afterwards, the Operator requests the Describe of all the subjects and objects that were in the deleted triples and sends the union of the resulting graphs to Jena for reasoning. When the entailed graph resulting from reasoning on the union is returned, the Operator sends

---

Algorithm 2. Apply Delete Update

Function: *describe* : *graph* x *triple* → *graph*
Function: *entail* : *graph* → *graph*

procedure APPLYDELETEUPDATE(*graph, triplesTBD*)
   described ← ϕ
   for each *triple* in *triplesTBD* **do**
      described ← *described* ∪ *describe(graph, tripleTBD)*
   for each *triple* in *triplesTBD* **do**
      subject = triple.Subj
      t ← $\{t \in described | t.Subj = triple.Subj \land t.Prop = t.Prop\}$
      for each $t2$ in t **do**
         if $t2.Prop = rdf : type$ **then**
            superClasses ← $\{tsOAsS.Obj | tsOAsS \in described$
                $\land tsOAsS.Subj = t2.Obj \land tsOAsS.Prop = rdfs : subClassOf\}$
            for each *superClass* in *superClasses* **do**
               infTriple ← $\langle t2.Subj, rdf : type, superClass\rangle$
               triplesTBD ← *triplesTBD* ∪ *infTriple*
         else
            superProps ← $\{tp.Obj | tp \in described \land tp.Subj = t2.Prop$
                     $\land tp.Prop = rdfs : subPropertyOf\}$
            for each *superProp* in *superProps* **do**
               infTriple ← $\langle t2.Subj, superProp, t2.Obj\rangle$
               triplesTBD ← *triplesTBD* ∪ *infTriple*
   graph ← *graph* \ *triplesTBD*
   ▷ Re-derive and insert inferred triples.
   subjsAndObjs ← $\{iri | iri \in triplesTBD.Subjects \cup triplesTBD.Objects\}$
   for each *iri* in *subjsAndObjs* **do**
      described2 ← *described2* ∪ *describe(graph, iri)*
   graph ← *graph* ∪ *entail(described2)*

---

an Insert statement containing the inferred triples to Fuseki which inserts them thus producing $G_{C',3}$. The aforementioned is shown in Algorithm 2[4].

6   Results

To test our system, we created a small RDF-Schema to represent fictional characters and places, with both $G_{A,1}$ and $G_{B,2}$ making use of it. There are 12 classes and 35 properties. In addition to this schema, both graphs $G_{A,1}$ and $G_{B,2}$ contain instances of fictional characters and places. Graph $G_{A,1}$ contains 275 triples, while graph $G_{B,2}$ contains 265 triples. 15 triples are inserted into $G_{B,2}$ and then 4 triples are deleted from it. Table 1 displays the sizes of the produced graphs.

The evaluation criteria intends to verify that there is less overhead, in terms of the number of triples being processed, when performing the following:

---

[4] Due to space restrictions, the preceding description and subsequent algorithm only focus on **rdfs 5**, **7**, **9**, and **11**. Expanding them to cover the rest is straightforward.

Table 1. Size of $G_{C,3}$ initially, after Insert, and after Delete.

ST\sizes	Initial	Entailed	After Insert	Entailed	After Delete	Entailed
Union	355	865	369	913	366	905
Intersection	185	336	186	341	185	338
Difference 1	90	109	89	108	90	108
Difference 2	71	75	94	98	91	95

1. **Communication:** retrieving the update is less overhead than retrieving both source graphs.
2. **Execution:** propagating the update results in less triples processed during: (a) the set theoretic operation, and (b) re-derivation.

Experimental Results. There is indeed less overhead in applying our approach as detailed below.

(a) Communication. When the update is an Insert, the size of update will always be less than the size of the whole graph. Hence, there is less communication overhead. However, when the update is a Delete, the overhead of communicating the update is acceptable unless more than half of the triples in the graph are to be deleted, because the size of the update is greater than the size of the new source graph, and it may be more preferable to retrieve $G_{B',2}$ rather than $Up_{B,2}$. As shown in the analysis of the update propagation in Sect. 5.2, in the cases of intersection and the second difference, there is no need for $G_{copy(A,1)}$, but retrieving $G_{B',2}$ will force the re-retrieval of $G_{A,1}$ - if it is not stored in the system - plus the generation of $G_{C',3}$ from scratch. Combined, this would cause more overhead depending on the availability and the comparative size of $G_{A,1}$. Hence, retrieving $G_{B',2}$ would be more preferable. In the cases of union and the first difference where $G_{copy(A,1)}$ is needed, it may be more beneficial to retrieve $G_{B',2}$ instead of $Up_{B,2}$. So, it boils down to a case-by-case bases and can be alleviated by requesting the size of the update from system B and depends on if the other source graph is needed as well.

(b) Execution:

    i. Set theoretic operations: We were not able to use Jena to count the triples processed in set theoretic operations. However, from our analysis in Sect. 5.2, we see that there are less triples to be checked because we are at most using the whole update and one source graph and not the entirety of both source graphs.

    ii. Re-derivation: Inserting or deleting part of the update and then re-deriving by only taking into account the affected triples and those related to them reduces the number of triples processed by the reasoner in our experimental example by: 53% and 77% for the Union, 78% and 83% for the Intersection, 67% and 68% for the Difference 1, and 48% and 64% for the Difference 2. We point out that these gains may fluctuate depending on the triples chosen for insertion and deletion.

7   Conclusion and Future Work

We examined where provenance of graphs on the Semantic Web should be tracked, from their initial creation and through their modification, and based on this we introduced a specialisation of the PROV ontology, RGPROV. Then, we looked into how an update on a source graph needs to be propagated in a graph which is based on it and applied RGPROV to do so efficiently. Finally, we showed that our approach reduces overhead, in terms of number of processed triples, when compared to re-creating a graph from scratch by implementing a system which utilises algorithms to partially re-derive graphs.

There are a few directions worth exploring that extend our work. First, we aim to test our approach using benchmark data like LUBM[5] and UOBM[6]. Second, our system and re-derivation algorithms can be extended to support OWL graphs as well as RDF graphs by including OWL 2 entailment rules in the deletion and re-entailment phases. Finally, they may be extended to deal with source graphs which use different entailment regimes.

References

1. Schreiber, G., Raimond, Y.: RDF 1.1 primer. W3C note, W3C, June 2014. http:// www.w3.org/TR/2014/NOTE-rdf11-primer-20140225/
2. Krötzsch, M., Patel-Schneider, P., Hitzler, P., Parsia, B., Rudolph, S.: OWL 2 web ontology language primer (second edition). Technical report, W3C, December 2012. http://www.w3.org/TR/2012/REC-owl2-primer-20121211/
3. SPARQL 1.1 overview. W3C recommendation, W3C, March 2013. http://www. w3.org/TR/2013/REC-sparql11-overview-20130321/
4. Motik, B., Nenov, Y., Piro, R., Horrocks, I.: Incremental update of datalog materialisation: the backward/forward algorithm. In: Proceedings of the 29th AAAI Conference on Artificial Intelligence, pp. 1560–1568. AAAI Press (2015)
5. Moreau, L., Groth, P.: PROV-overview. W3C note, W3C, April 2013. http://www. w3.org/TR/2013/NOTE-prov-overview-20130430/
6. Lebo, T., Sahoo, S., McGuinness, D.: PROV-o: the PROV ontology. W3C recommendation, April 2013. http://www.w3.org/TR/2013/REC-prov-o-20130430/
7. Gupta, A., Mumick, I.S., Subrahmanian, V.S.: Maintaining views incrementally. ACM SIGMOD Rec. **22**(2), 157–166 (1993)
8. Hayes, P., Patel-Schneider, P.: RDF 1.1 semantics. W3C recommendation, W3C, February 2014. http://www.w3.org/TR/2014/REC-rdf11-mt-20140225/
9. Missier, P., Cala, J., Wijaya, E.: The data, they are a-changin'. In: 8th USENIX Workshop on the Theory and Practice of Provenance (TaPP 2016). USENIX Association, Washington, D.C. (2016)
10. Green, T.J., Karvounarakis, G., Ives, Z.G., Tannen, V.: Update exchange with mappings and provenance. In: Proceedings of the 33rd International Conference on Very Large Data Bases, Vienna, Austria, pp. 675–686 (2007)
11. Green, T.J., Karvounarakis, G., Tannen, V.: Provenance semirings. In: Proceedings of the 26th ACM SIGMOD-SIGACT-SIGART Symposium on Principles of Database Systems, Beijing, China, pp. 31–40. ACM (2007)

---

[5] http://swat.cse.lehigh.edu/projects/lubm/.

[6] https://www.cs.ox.ac.uk/isg/tools/UOBMGenerator/.

12. Flouris, G., Fundulaki, I., Pediaditis, P., Theoharis, Y., Christophides, V.: Coloring RDF triples to capture provenance. In: Bernstein, A., et al. (eds.) ISWC 2009. LNCS, vol. 5823, pp. 196–212. Springer, Heidelberg (2009). https://doi.org/10.1007/978-3-642-04930-9_13

13. Buneman, P., Cheney, J., Vansummeren, S.: On the expressiveness of implicit provenance in query and update languages. ACM Trans. Database Syst. **33**(4), 1–47 (2008)

14. Avgoustaki, A., Flouris, G., Fundulaki, I., Plexousakis, D.: Provenance management for evolving RDF datasets. In: Sack, H., Blomqvist, E., d'Aquin, M., Ghidini, C., Ponzetto, S.P., Lange, C. (eds.) ESWC 2016. LNCS, vol. 9678, pp. 575–592. Springer, Cham (2016). https://doi.org/10.1007/978-3-319-34129-3_35

15. Halpin, H., Cheney, J.: Dynamic provenance for SPARQL updates. In: Mika, P., et al. (eds.) ISWC 2014. LNCS, vol. 8796, pp. 425–440. Springer, Cham (2014). https://doi.org/10.1007/978-3-319-11964-9_27

System Demonstrations

Implementing Data Provenance in Health Data Analytics Software

Shen Xu[1], Elliot Fairweather[1], Toby Rogers[2], and Vasa Curcin[1(✉)]

[1] King's College London, London, UK
{shen.xu, elliot.fairweather, vasa.curcin}@kcl.ac.uk
[2] Imosphere Ltd, Nottingham, UK
Toby.Rogers@imosphere.co.uk

Abstract. Data provenance is a technique that describes the history of digital objects. In health applications, it can be used to deliver auditability and transparency, leading to increased trust in software. When implementing provenance in end-user scenarios, on top of standard provenance requirements, it is important to properly contextualize the provenance features within the domain and ensure their usability. We have developed a novel user interface, embedded into Imolytics data analysis tool and based on our Provenance Template technology, to help the end-user consume provenance information. In this demonstration, we shall demonstrate how the interface can be used to examine the audit trail of analysis results to spot when the two analytical methods start producing different results. In addition to the novel provenance UI, this is the first implementation of standard-based data provenance in a commercial data analytics software tool.

Keywords: Data provenance · System demo

1 Introduction

Atmolytics is a data analytics tool aimed at health and social care that focuses on simplifying the data insight process by providing users with a set of generic apps that can be customized into powerful interactive reports. The reports operate on cohorts – patient data sets that are created from various databases integrated into Atmolytics internal data warehouse. This model has proven effective for a range of use cases, from genetical studies and cancer centres to primary care repositories for epidemiological studies. In the Atmolytics architecture, an enterprise service bus is used to receive data tasks before they are distributed over several farms for processing. Programmatic calls within Atmolytics are invoking a RESTful API upon the provenance server. The provenance services correspond to standard actions in the system and are implemented using abstract *provenance templates* which get instantiated during API service calls with concrete data and persisted into the provenance data store [1]. Provenance capturing is triggered by a controller in Atmolytics – a Targeted Activity. After a new graph segment, denoting a specific Atmolytics component, is created, it is linked into the overall provenance graph by grafting the new nodes onto the existing structure.

The architecture of the Provenance Template Server is shown in Fig. 1. At the core of the system is the model component. Provenance documents are represented as

K. Belhajjame et al. (Eds.): IPAW 2018, LNCS 11017, pp. 173–176, 2018.
https://doi.org/10.1007/978-3-319-98379-0_13

graphs in which vertices and edges are typed and annotated with key-value pairs. The graph itself may also have key-value properties. Serialisation and deserialisation to PROV data formats is accomplished using the parsers provided by ProvToolbox library. Substitutions also form part of the model and parsers to both a proposed PROV-N format and JSON are given in the implementation. The template instantiation algorithm by which new fragment documents are generated from templates and substitutions is also defined within the model component.

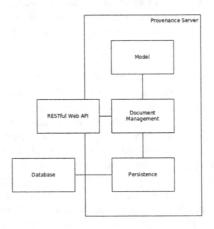

Fig. 1. Provenance template server architecture

Storage of data in the system is abstracted by a persistence component to enable the use of different database technologies. Here, a Neo4j graph database is used but a relational database, SPARQL-enabled or alternative graph database could be used either instead or concurrently. The metadata of documents is stored and updated separately to the graph data itself to facilitate indexing and other administrative operations upon the documents stored [3].

The system is accessed via the document management component. This controls and executes operations such as the creation of new target documents, namespace management, the registering of templates, and the generation and merging of new fragment documents. Fragment generation is achieved through interaction with the model component. Operations requiring the import, export or update of document data and metadata are supported via the persistence component.

Access to the document management interface is provided via a RESTful web service. Documents and substitutions are passed to and from the server encoded as JSON and analysis is conducted by running Cypher queries over the underlying Neo4j database. The specifics of a higher-level query interface for the system, agnostic to a particular storage solution, is an area of ongoing research.

2   Use Case

Atmolytics system is based on the use of patient cohorts for data analysis, which are updated over time to reflect new additions to the data set. These cohorts can be created either as dynamic queries or as static patient lists generated through set operations. A common problem users are facing is to confuse the two and then later noticing that the latter does not get automatically updated when new patients are added to the cohort [2]. In our demonstration, we shall demonstrate how provenance data captured in Atmolytics can be used to trace the origin of this problem.

Taking as an example an investigation of female hypertensive heart disease (Fig. 2), a cohort could be created in two ways: (1) by creating a query for a group of female patients with added criteria for presence of hypertensive heart disease, (2) by creating a group of female patients and another group of hypertensive heart disease patients, and then applying the subgroup function to create a static list which is the intersection of the two groups. The results of the two approaches will initially be identical, however over time, the cohort sizes might change.

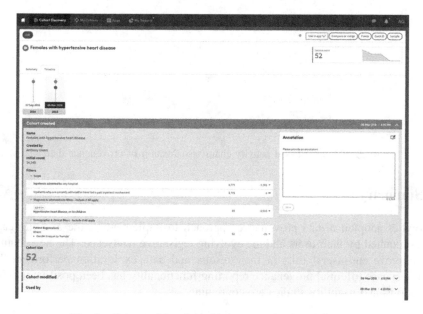

Fig. 2. Cohort of females with hypertensive heart disease

To that goal, the demonstration will show:

a. The Atmolytics use case of diverging cohorts
b. How provenance is captured through the Provenance Template Server
c. How provenance data is visualized in Atmolytics
d. How this visualization is used to address the use case.

Figure 3 shows the temporal provenance view, visualizing relevant events on a timeline, but also allowing free text to be shown alongside the provenance information. This facilitates the justification of activities while reviewing the origin of results or patient cohorts. Following user feedback, the interface highlights the changes between activities, e.g. cohort updates, change of base cohort size etc. The events history provenance reporting will also be demonstrated on a separate data example.

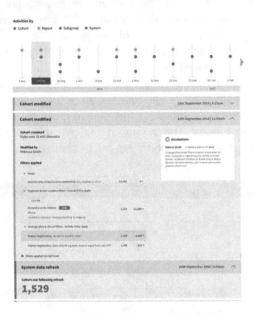

Fig. 3. Timeline-based activity chain visualization of provenance data

3 Summary

Atmolytics adopted a data provenance approach to implementing the auditing capabilities required by their users and the evolving legislative landscape. The new features help improve end-users' trust in their results and data exploration performed. The users' response to initial provenance reporting functionality has been positive in initial evaluations, and usability studies are continuing.

References

1. Curcin, V., et al.: Templates as a method for implementing data provenance in decision support systems. J. Biomed. Inform. **65**, 1–21 (2017)
2. Xu, S., et al.: Application of data provenance in healthcare analytics software: information visualisation of user activities. In: Proceedings in AIMA Informatics Summits (2018)
3. Xu, S., et al.: Capturing provenance of visual analytics in social care needs. In: Informatics for Health 2017, Manchester, p. 2 (2016)

Quine: A Temporal Graph System for Provenance Storage and Analysis

Ryan Wright[(⊠)]

Galois, Inc., Portland, OR 97214, USA
rrwright@gmail.com

Abstract. This demonstration introduces "Quine", a prototype graph database and processing system designed for provenance analysis with capabilities that include: fine-grained graph versioning to support querying historical data after it has changed, standing queries to execute callbacks as data matching arbitrary queries is streamed in, and queries through time to express arbitrary causal ordering on past data. The system uses a novel combination of schema-less data storage and strongly-typed query language to enable well-typed analyses of types unexpected when the database was initialized. The system is designed to handle very large data with support for partitioning the graph to run across any number of hosts/shards across a network.

Keywords: Provenance · Graph database · Graph query language
Distributed systems

1 Introduction

Provenance data in its richest form can be represented as a connected property graph. Property graphs are ideal for representing the highly connected structure of provenance data as given by various established and experimental tracing tools. However, existing tools for working with graph data are not designed to favor provenance analysis. This demonstration introduces "Quine", a distributed graph database and processing system meant to address the following infrastructure and usability challenges faced when analyzing provenance data.

1.1 Highly Connected Temporal Data

Representing the state of a computer system at one point in time leads to highly connected representations. In a running computer system, provenance data likely includes information about the process tree hierarchy, the filesystem hierarchy, network connections or perhaps network topology, the flow of data from one source to another, or the graph of control flow among executing programs. Data elements among each of these topics can be highly related to many elements from other topics.

Graph databases are a natural choice for representing the highly connected nature of this kind of data. However, existing graph databases require modeling that data as a single graph, so that current and historical states are mixed together uniformly and

K. Belhajjame et al. (Eds.): IPAW 2018, LNCS 11017, pp. 177–180, 2018.
https://doi.org/10.1007/978-3-319-98379-0_14

distinguishable only by timestamps or other property-level data. This makes the database very large in terms of node/edge count.

Quine is implemented as a property graph which maintains the current state of each data item (nodes, edges, properties) as the derived result of its entire history. This history is stored in a manner that allows efficiently querying back in time for previous states, monitoring changes in state, or querying with other temporal constraints such as causal ordering.

1.2   Queries on Complex Structures over Time

Existing graph query languages allow expression of terms at the level of nodes, edges, and properties. Writing queries soon becomes akin to writing complex programs where the query author must maintain a mental model of the graph schema or face incomplete (or incorrect) query results. The complexity is compounded when the graph data is meant to represent events and changes over time—as is common among provenance data. When the history of data provenance is spread across a single graph, the query-writer must weave temporal constraints into each hop and each value test as a query is evaluated across the graph.

Quine is designed to represent time and change in graph data in a more manageable way. The runtime for Quine manages the history of every value as they change. The query language for Quine is meant to allow expressing queries at a level of abstraction higher than primitive node/property/edge queries. Graph patterns are expressed as classes and objects in a high-level programming language which offers type-safety at the query level, so that a query author has immediate feedback when the query they are assembling does not match the graph structure they are expecting. As a result, very complex queries can be expressed as the composition of smaller parts and can be evaluated on current and historical data, at one point in time or many.

1.3   Evolving Schema

Database schemas enforce types on singular values at data write-time, and aid query writing at read-time, but this help comes at the cost of flexibility. NoSQL and other "schema-less" databases provide speed and flexibility in the storage runtime, but little help in understanding the shape of the data when writing queries.

Quine tries to balance this tradeoff by putting the schema and corresponding constraints in the query language. Query instances first choose which schema to use, then issue type-checked queries corresponding to that schema. This approach is similar in spirit to the approach taken with GraphQL [1], however Quine does not require the client and server to share schemas—or keep them in sync.

As analysis evolves, the schema can change as well. One kind of evolution can occur by creating more meaningful/complex query terms by composition of existing terms. Another evolution is the creation/discovery of a useful schema entirely disjoint from the schema used to write the data initially. With either evolution, queries using that schema will be type-checked before a query to the backend is issued.

1.4   Scalability for Large Datasets

Provenance datasets such as those produced by DARPA's Transparent Computing program are quite large, even though they are from one single system. Interesting provenance questions spanning a large number of systems will be encumbered by the size and processing constraints of such large data. These large datasets will need to be processed by distributed systems designed for distributing a graph across many machines. Existing commercial and open source solutions struggle in this area. Neo4j scales across machines with read-only replicas that cannot support a high writing load. JanusGraph (née TitanDB) relies on the distributed capabilities of its backing store and ends up constrained by the administrative overhead and many round-trips between the graph layer and the backing store [2, 3].

Quine was designed as a genuinely distributed graph. This system is partitioned into graph shards even when run on a single system. One holistic view of the graph is transparently queryable even when those shards are served from many different hosts across a network. This allows the computational burden of reading *and writing* a large graph to be distributed across many machines, opening the possibility of supporting the large provenance datasets we hope to see in the near future.

2   Demonstration Topics

Streaming Ingest of Provenance Data. Provenance data from the DARPA Transparent Computing program will be loaded in a streaming fashion and used as the basis of the other demonstrations (see below). This data includes benign and malicious activity from multiple host machines and operating systems.

Statically-Typed Query Language. A language for ingesting data will be demonstrated. The query language is an eDSL embedded in Scala as the host language. Defining a language is done by defining classes in Scala.

Visualizing Data. A visualization of the ingested data will be demonstrated to give an intuition for how provenance data is represented in the system.

Query the Current State. The query language for Quine is realized as an embedded DSL in the strongly-typed host language, Scala. Expressions of complex patterns in the graph are aided by compile-time errors (i.e. before the query is issued to the database) to give early user feedback when large and complex queries violate the chosen schema. These kinds of queries aid provenance analysis by answering: Is the system *currently* in a state such that ___?

Query Historical Data. Quine maintains all historical data for all data in the graph, making it possible to query past states of the graph as they existed at any arbitrary point in history. Complex queries spanning large sections of the graph can be issued for many different times simultaneously. These kinds of queries aid provenance analysis by answering: Was the system *previously* in a state such that ___?

Query Through Time[1]. In addition to searching a single point in the past, Quine aims to provide the capability to efficiently query all points in the past to find whether a certain query predicate holds. These kinds of queries aid provenance analysis by answering: Was the system *ever* in a state such that ___?

Standing Queries. Quine allows queries to be expressed as "standing queries" which execute a provided callback for each result found. A standing query will match existing data and all cases where new additions or transformations of data result in a match. These kinds of queries aid provenance analysis by answering: Did the system *just* transition to a state such that ___?—if so, execute the desired action in real-time.

Graph Sharding (see footnote 1). Quine is built from the ground up as a distributed system. One of the primary design goals for Quine is to support running a distributed database across an arbitrary number of host machines on a network.

3   Conclusion

Research Contributions. Quine represents a management system contribution to the domain of provenance research: a graph database with first-class representations of time and changes over time. In addition, this system represents significant research progress in the areas of graph query languages and distributed graph databases.

Acknowledgments. Portions of this research have been supported by DARPA under contract number FA8650-15-C-7557. Opinions or conclusions expressed in this material are those of the author and do not necessarily reflect the views of DARPA.

References

1. Facebook, Inc.: GraphQL. Working Draft, October 2016. http://facebook.github.io/graphql. Accessed 3 June 2018
2. Holzschuher, F., Peinl, R.: Performance of graph query languages: comparison of cypher, gremlin and native access in Neo4j. In: Proceedings of the Joint EDBT/ICDT 2013 Workshops, pp. 195–204. ACM (2013)
3. Pacaci, A., Zhou, A., Lin, J., Özsu, M.T.: Do we need specialized graph databases?: benchmarking real-time social networking applications. In: Proceedings of the Fifth International Workshop on Graph Data-Management Experiences and Systems, p. 12. ACM (2017)

---

[1] Demonstration of this feature depends on some functionality which is not complete at the time of this writing. This feature will either be demonstrated or explained as "future directions" depending on progress made before the conference.

Joint IPAW/TaPP Poster Session

Capturing Provenance for Runtime Data Analysis in Computational Science and Engineering Applications

Vítor Silva[1]([✉]), Renan Souza[1,2], Jose Camata[1,3], Daniel de Oliveira[4], Patrick Valduriez[5], Alvaro L. G. A. Coutinho[1], and Marta Mattoso[1]

[1] COPPE/Federal University of Rio de Janeiro, Rio de Janeiro, Brazil
silva@cos.ufrj.br
[2] IBM Research, Rio de Janeiro, Brazil
[3] Federal University of Juiz de Fora, Juiz de Fora, Brazil
[4] Fluminense Federal University, Niterói, Brazil
[5] Inria and LIRMM, Montpellier, France

Abstract. Capturing provenance data for runtime analysis has several challenges in high performance computational science engineering applications. The main issues are avoiding significant overhead in data capture, loading and runtime query support; and coupling provenance capture mechanisms with applications built with highly efficient numerical libraries, and visualization frameworks targeted to high performance environments. This work presents DfA-prov, an approach to capture provenance data and domain data aiming at high performance applications.

Keywords: Provenance · User steering
Computational Science and Engineering · HPC

1 Introduction

Computational Science and Engineering (CSE) applications are based on computational models that solve problems typically requiring High Performance Computing (HPC) [1]. CSE applications are not tied to a particular domain. They can be found in biology, chemistry, geology, several engineering areas, etc. They have the exploratory nature of scientific applications but have to deal with large-scale executions, which last for a long time even when using HPC. The software ecosystem for developing these applications involves much more than writing scripts or invoking a chain of legacy scientific codes. Computational scientists develop their simulation codes based on complex mathematical modeling that results in invoking components of CSE frameworks and libraries. For example, components are invoked to provide for: (i) support for PDE discretization methods like libMesh, FEniCS, MOOSE, deal.II, GREENS, OpenFOAM; (ii) algorithms for solving numerical problems with parallel computations, like PETSc, LAPACK, SLEPc; (iii) runtime visualizations, like ParaView Catalyst, VisIt, SENSEI; (iv) parallel graph partitioning, like ParMetis, Scotch; and (v) I/O data management like ADIOS.

© Springer Nature Switzerland AG 2018
K. Belhajjame et al. (Eds.): IPAW 2018, LNCS 11017, pp. 183–187, 2018.
https://doi.org/10.1007/978-3-319-98379-0_15

As a result, a typical CSE software code works like a script, in the sense that to code the underlying mathematical modeling it requires invoking functions, components, or APIs from these libraries or frameworks. Figure 1 shows a fragment of the FEniCS Python code for solving the Cahn-Hilliard equation, a mathematical model from material science. The Cahn-Hilliard equation leads to a prototype of a transient nonlinear multi-physics code. Several parameters have to be set to invoke these highly efficient components, which are very difficult to preset and need monitoring for runtime fine-tuning. The Interoperable Design of Extreme-scale Application Software (IDEAS) [2] is a family of projects, involving several institutions in the US, concerned with the complexity of developing software for CSE applications. IDEAS aims at "enabling a fundamentally different attitude to creating and supporting CSE applications" with desirable features like provenance and reproducibility [3]. In fact, provenance data can help in registering parameter choices. Associating them to results can improve both fine-tuning and data analyses at runtime.

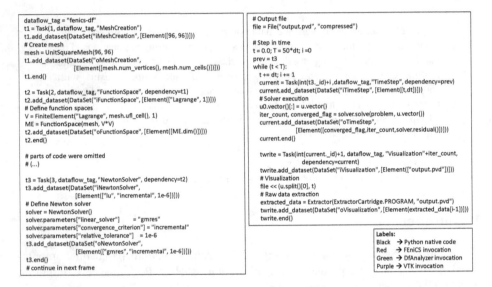

Fig. 1. FEniCS Python script for the Cahn-Hilliard equation adapted from [4].

Despite the several solutions available for making applications provenance-aware [5–7], capturing provenance data in CSE applications is still an open issue. The challenges are mainly related to performance and provenance granularity. Stamatogiannakis *et al.* [5] evaluated tradeoffs in provenance capture mechanisms. They consider that solutions that are easy to deploy collect provenance in a very fine grain and present a significant overhead, while solutions that are based on function calls present low overhead and granularity is controlled by the code instrumentation. The disadvantage of inserting function calls is the need to have access to the code. This is not an issue in CSE applications as very often the code to be instrumented (Fig. 1) is written by the computational scientist, who can assist in inserting the calls.

In CSE applications, the mechanism for provenance capture has to be deployed in an HPC environment and preferably manage provenance data, asynchronously, in computing nodes separate from the application. This separation avoids resource competition, particularly in the memory hierarchy data space. Since CSE data are very large, provenance capture cannot be in fine grain. Capturing provenance at the operating system or file level is not an option. CSE applications, like the one in Fig. 1, are written in languages, like Python and C/C++, which are mapped to the CSE software ecosystem, therefore solutions that are language specific are a limitation. HPC Scientific Workflow Management Systems (SWMS) would be a natural solution for CSE. However, conflicts among the parallel execution control of the workflow engine and the CSE libraries prevent using SWMS in CSE software.

This work presents DfA-prov, an approach that follows the PrIMe methodology [8] to make CSE applications provenance-aware and to provide runtime data analysis. DfA-prov is language agnostic and does not present the limitations of capture mechanisms that compete with the computing nodes that execute the CSE application. DfA-prov adopts DfAnalyzer [9] as provenance-aware components to be invoked by the CSE applications. It works in the same way computational scientists invoke the CSE and visualization libraries. Provenance data is captured by directly accessing input data and parameters of the CSE function calls using *in-situ* and *in-transit* approaches. To address the limitation of having coarse-grain provenance, DfA-prov provides function calls that access raw data from files. In a previous work [10], we used DfAnalyzer tightly coupled to a CSE application observing negligible overhead (less than 1%) in its provenance capture, while providing rich data analytics at runtime. These results encouraged us to propose DfA-prov as a standalone library with a corresponding methodology to help on the adoption of provenance capture in CSE applications.

2 DfA-prov Making CSE Applications Provenance-Aware

DfA-prov follows the PrIMe methodology [8] to address CSE challenges for provenance capture. After applying the methodology, DfA-prov generates a provenance database, W3C PROV-compliant, enriched with domain data to be queried at runtime or after the CSE application execution. DfA-prov is based on two main components from DfAnalyzer, the provenance data capture and the raw data extractor.

PrIMe defines three phases. The first phase is an analysis step that identifies questions related to provenance for data analysis. More specifically, Phase 1 identifies data items and data transformations (or processing steps), all to be modeled using a data representation. Phase 2 iteratively analyzes the application structure to identify actors and interactions that provide the data items and data transformations to be registered as provenance data. Phase 3 aims at adapting the application to capture provenance data. We adapted these phases to match CSE application requirements.

DfA-prov requires a collaboration between the CSE application developer (named as user) and a PROV specialist, as expected in Phase 1. The user identifies data items to be tracked and how it relates to other data items along its lineage. The PROV specialist models the data transformation chain using W3C PROV-DM activities and entities with extensions for the domain data items, particularly data that need to be extracted from raw data files. The result of this phase is a UML class diagram. The UML classes are then mapped to a relational provenance database. The participation of the user in this data modeling helps on query formulations. In addition, it selectively chooses only application data of interest to be registered, providing a coarse-grain with relevant provenance data and selected raw data. In Fig. 1, examples are: solver convergence, number of iterations, and residual norms.

Provenance library calls are inserted in the CSE application as shown in Fig. 1 as *input, output, task* and *output* followed by an *extracted data* call. Similarly to PROV-Template [6], DfA-prov has a set of RESTful services (and libraries on C++, Python, and Java) to help plugging the calls into the CSE applications. The invoked provenance components capture data asynchronously during the CSE application execution. They get the data and send all insert/update requests to a columnar database system that runs in computing nodes different than the CSE application. As new phases within DfA-prov, users configure CSE applications coupled to provenance-aware components to specify input parameter values and the HPC environment. Then, they submit provenance monitoring queries like *what is the average error estimate calculated in all iterations so far*. Users can submit provenance queries using graphical interfaces or SQL queries based on a dataflow abstraction. Finally, the monitoring helps parameter fine tunings on the CSE application as evidenced in [10]. Real life applications are much more complex than the script in Fig. 1, involving monitoring at runtime on an HPC machine quantities of interest over time, metadata to visualization snapshots, nonlinear systems solves, mesh adaptation parameters etc. These issues can be seen in [10] for a particular CSE application, with examples in [11].

3   Conclusions

DfA-prov is an approach for making CSE applications provenance-aware and providing runtime data analytics. DfA-prov is based on application analysis, provenance data modeling, and provenance-aware components to be invoked by the applications. In addition to well-known advantages of collecting provenance in CSE applications, such as reproducibility and reliability, runtime provenance augments online data analytical potential and is especially useful for CSE simulations in large-scale. Visualization tools (*e.g.*, ParaView Catalyst) have been coupled to DfA-prov calls to complement domain data analyses. Based on runtime data analyses, the user may dynamically adapt dataflow elements.

Acknowledgments. We thank Vinícius Campos for his help in DfA-prov development. The research has received funding from CAPES, CNPq, FAPERJ and Inria (SciDISC projects), the European Commission (HPC4E H2020 project), and the Brazilian Ministry of Science, Technology, 290 Innovation and Communications. It has been performed (for P. Valduriez) in the context of the Computational Biology Institute.

References

1. Rüde, U., Willcox, K., McInnes, L.C., Sterck, H.D., Biros, G., et al.: Research and Education in Computational Science and Engineering. CoRR. abs/1610.02608 (2016)
2. IDEAS productivity. https://ideas-productivity.org
3. Bernholdt, D., Dubey, A., Heroux, M., Klinvex, A., McInnes, L.C.: Improving reproducibility through better software practices. In: SIAM Conference on CSE, Atlanta, GA (2017)
4. Alnæs, M., Blechta, J., Hake, J., Johansson, A., Kehlet, B., et al.: Archive of Numerical Software: The FEniCS Project Version 1.5. University Library Heidelberg (2015)
5. Stamatogiannakis, M., et al.: Trade-offs in automatic provenance capture. In: Mattoso, M., Glavic, B. (eds.) IPAW 2016. LNCS, vol. 9672, pp. 29–41. Springer, Cham (2016). https://doi.org/10.1007/978-3-319-40593-3_3
6. Moreau, L., Batlajery, B.V., Huynh, T.D., Michaelides, D., Packer, H.: A templating system to generate provenance. IEEE Trans. Softw. Eng. 44, 103–121 (2018)
7. Pimentel, J.F., Murta, L., Braganholo, V., Freire, J.: noWorkflow: a tool for collecting, analyzing, and managing provenance from python scripts. PVLDB 10, 1841–1844 (2017)
8. Miles, S., Groth, P., Munroe, S., Moreau, L.: PrIMe: a methodology for developing provenance-aware applications. ACM Trans. Softw. Eng. Methodol. 20, 1–42 (2011)
9. Silva, V., De Oliveira, D., Valduriez, P., Mattoso, M.: DfAnalyzer: runtime dataflow analysis of scientific applications using provenance. In: PVLDB, Rio de Janeiro, Brazil (2018)
10. Camata, J.J., Silva, V., Valduriez, P., Mattoso, M., Coutinho, A.L.G.A.: In situ visualization and data analysis for turbidity currents simulation. Comput. Geosci. 110, 23–31 (2018)
11. DfAnalyzer tool demonstration. https://github.com/vssousa/dfanalyzer-spark

UniProv - Provenance Management for UNICORE Workflows in HPC Environments

André Giesler$^{(\boxtimes)}$ ⓘ, Myriam Czekala ⓘ, and Björn Hagemeier ⓘ

Juelich Supercomputing Centre, Forschungszentrum Juelich GmbH,
Juelich, Germany
{a.giesler,m.czekala,b.hagemeier}@fz-juelich.de

Abstract. The goal of comprehensive provenance tracking in the scientific environment should be the inclusion of the entire life cycle of data management. Thus, the data collection process begins with the registration of lab-generated or sensor-generated data, continues to organize and manage data in the storage repositories, processing analysis and simulation data on clusters and HPC systems, and finally referencing and verifying computational results in scientific publications. In the associated provenance tracking life cycle, UniProv initially concentrates on the processing and simulation of data in scientific workflows used in particular on supercomputers in the HPC environment. In this context, UniProv aims to create the core of a provenance management framework that can be extended in order to integrate different sources of the scientific provenance cycle. Here UniProv should facilitate the creation, the standardized formalization, the storage and the retrieval of Provenance Information.

Keywords: Provenance · Scientific workflows · Interoperability
PROV-O · Neo4j · UNICORE

1 Introduction

Scientific workflows are an integral part of using High-performance Computing (HPC) systems in data centers. Some users rely on workflows that consist of a sequence of logically concatenated programs and scripts between which intermediate results are transferred and processed. Another group of users applies Workflow Management Systems (WfMS) to enable complex, coherent simulations and calculations. These tools provide a higher level of abstraction in terms of predefined structures, the channeling of well-defined input and output data, standardization of analysis methods and monitoring of all tasks within a workflow. The latter allows a continuous automated provenance tracking of scientific workflows by capturing information from the processing logic of the WfMS.

© Springer Nature Switzerland AG 2018
K. Belhajjame et al. (Eds.): IPAW 2018, LNCS 11017, pp. 188–191, 2018.
https://doi.org/10.1007/978-3-319-98379-0_16

2   Interoperable Provenance Framework for UNICORE

The UNICORE[1] federation software suite includes a generic WfMS [1], which is currently being used increasingly in the field of neuroscience [2]. UNICORE does not provide proprietary provenance management. It is thus the initial goal of the UniProv framework to process provenance information in UNICORE-based workflows to allow UNICORE users to track their submitted workflows. For this purpose, UniProv was initially integrated into the existing UNICORE service architecture. Based on the UNICORE implementation UniProv is to be converted later to an autonomous framework, to which further provenance providers can be attached. In this context, UniProv pursues the following concept:

- Monitoring and extracting provenance information from UNICORE Job and Workflow management services
- Processing of collected provenance information into an interoperable provenance model according to W3C-PROV[2]
- Storing the provenance graph in a Neo4j graph database and allowing arbitrary queries on the data

UniProv takes an interoperable approach in two respects: firstly, the potential processing of the resulting provenance data should be enabled in other standard compliant provenance services. Secondly, the later integration of such provenance providers should be facilitated, which are capable of generating standard compliant provenance data. For this reason, all provenance data is modeled based on the recognized W3C-PROV standard. UniProv uses the PROV-O ontology to express generated provenance information in compatibility with PROV. Furthermore, PROV acts as a reference model to create application-specific ontologies for UniProv.

For instance, the general complexity of scientific workflows and processing WfMS cannot be mapped sufficiently with the capabilities of the generic PROV standard. For this reason, UniProv integrates the ProvONE ontology developed in the context of the DataONE[3] project and used in the context of the Pbase workflow provenance repository [3]. The advantage of ProvONE lies in its variable specification of the cyclical sequences of workflow logic, so that it can be very well modeled on UNICORE based workflows. UniProv benefits from the conceptual decoupling of workflow provenance into a prospective, a retrospective and a data-specific provenance view. In terms of UNICORE-based workflows, this has the advantage that the static workflow definition persisted in an XML file as well as the runtime information captured from the UNICORE workflow engine can now be mapped in a common provenance graph. Additionally, the appropriate data flow of the workflow trace can be mapped and added accordingly.

However, even the ProvONE ontology is not sufficient to map the entire resources, elements and structures of a UNICORE workflow running on an HPC machine. To

---

[1] https://www.unicore.eu/.

[2] https://www.w3.org/TR/prov-overview/.

[3] https://www.dataone.org/.

achieve this, ProvONE[4] was specialized in the form of the UniPROV[5] ontology. It introduces the vocabulary that UNICORE uses for specifying structures such as workflow loops, groupings, or synchronizations. For example, in ProvONE, the logical dependency of two consecutive computational jobs in a workflow definition is described by the class `Controller`. In UNICORE, the class `Transition` inheriting from `Controller` describes the transition from one job to the next, and contains an additional condition describing that a job will not be executed until the associated condition is met. In addition, the UniProv ontology provides the ability to include annotations from users in the provenance graph. The UniProv ontology was serialized in the OWL2 format such as PROV-O and the ProvONE ontology. All three ontologies form the vocabulary of the UniProv framework to map UNICORE based workflows. Using the Apache Jena RDF and Ontology API, Java interfaces were generated from the ontologies so that compliant provenance data can be modeled in the UniProv framework when processing UNICORE workflows.

3 Capturing and Storing Provenance Data

For extracting and processing provenance information from UNICORE, loggers have been implemented and integrated into the UniProv framework. The Job Logger hooks into the respective job management service of a UNICORE installation on a supercomputer and tracks the status of running computation jobs, the respective program code, defined environment variables, the job properties (number of cores per node, RAM, walltime, etc.), the use of imported files, and the generation of result data. In addition, UNICORE job monitoring provides runtime information about the status of the submitted job, hostnames, or the runtime of jobs.

The UNICORE workflow engine controls the logical sequence and synchronization of interdependent jobs as well as the flow of data within a workflow. This information is captured by the UniProv Workflow Logger, which is triggered by status messages from the workflow engine. It then traverses all nodes and edges of the workflow graph to capture current runtime information. Once a single job of the workflow is successfully completed, the provenance information is prepared by the Job Logger of the corresponding UNICORE instance, sent to the Workflow Logger, and added to the internal UniProv workflow model. In this process, the WfModelOntProcessor module processes the workflow model to the overall provenance graph by using the Apache Jena RDF and Ontology API to generate ontology compliant provenance data. The provenance graph is serialized by default in Turtle RDF, but can easily be managed to a different syntax like XML or JSON.

UniProv supports the storage of provenance data in repositories based on a Neo4j graph database, which was inspired by the scientific work in [4, 5]. Such a database model allows a natural mapping of graph structures as modeled for workflow provenance data in UniProv. One advantage of Neo4j is the support of highly connected data

---

[4] https://purl.dataone.org/provone/2015/01/15/ontology#.

[5] https://datapub.fz-juelich.de/uniprov.

as given in provenance graphs, particular as application-specific provenance data is often subject to evolutionary changes. In this context, the schema-less character of a graph database allows more flexibility than for example a relational database where schema redesigning can be a time-consuming process. In Neo4j, it is possible to add new data or relationships based on revised ontologies on the fly. On the other hand, the connected graph structures of provenance data, especially of workflow provenance, can cause complex nested queries along the nodes and edges of a graph. A graph database such as Neo4j allows easy traversing of the data due to its graph-oriented Cypher query language, while complex JOINs would be expected for traversal queries in a relational database.

Since UniProv generates provenance output in PROV-based Turtle RDF syntax for interoperability reasons, the created provenance graph must be migrated into the Labeled Property Graph (LPG) model of Neo4j. For that reason, the UniProv framework has been supplemented by the Neosemantics module representing an extension point of Neo4j that is used to import existing RDF provenance data into the graph database without the loss of its graph nature. The UniProv Neosemantics extension can be installed in any Neo4j 3.x database as a plugin.

As future work, we intend to support Persistent Identification[6] (PID) of data in UniProv in order to provide a more consistent data flow tracking. We plan to support and integrate other WfMS in UniProv such as Snakemake[7], which is also a tool frequently used in the domain of neuroscience.

Acknowledgements. The authors wish to thank all people and institutions involved in LSDMA. We also thank the German Helmholtz Association for funding.

References

1. Demuth, B., et al.: The UNICORE rich client: facilitating the automated execution of scientific workflows. In: 2010 IEEE Sixth International Conference on e-Science (e-Science), Brisbane, Australia, pp. 238–245 (2010)
2. Amunts, K., Bücker, O., Axer, M.: Towards a multiscale, high-resolution model of the human brain. In: Grandinetti, L., Lippert, T., Petkov, N. (eds.) BrainComp 2013. LNCS, vol. 8603, pp. 3–14. Springer, Cham (2014). https://doi.org/10.1007/978-3-319-12084-3_1
3. Cuevas, V., Kianmajd, P., Ludäscher, B., et al.: The PBase scientific workflow provenance repository. Int. J. Digit. Curation 9(2), 28–38 (2014)
4. Brauer, P.C., Fittkau, F., Hasselbring, W.: The aspect-oriented architecture of the CAPS framework for capturing, analyzing and archiving provenance data. In: Ludäscher, B., Plale, B. (eds.) IPAW 2014. LNCS, vol. 8628, pp. 223–225. Springer, Cham (2015). https://doi.org/10.1007/978-3-319-16462-5_19
5. Heinis, T., Chapman, A.: Provenance storage. In: Liu, L., Ozsu, M.T. (eds.) Encyclopedia of Database Systems. Springer, New York (2017). https://doi.org/10.1007/978-1-4899-7993-3

---

[6] https://eudat.eu/services/userdoc/pids-in-eudat.
[7] https://snakemake.readthedocs.io/en/stable/.

Towards a PROV Ontology for Simulation Models

Andreas Ruscheinski[(✉)], Dragana Gjorgevikj, Marcus Dombrowsky,
Kai Budde, and Adelinde M. Uhrmacher

Institute of Computer Science, University of Rostock,
Albert-Einstein-Str. 22, 18059 Rostock, Germany
andreas.ruscheinski@uni-rostock.de

Abstract. Simulation models and data are the primary products of simulation studies. Although the provenance of simulation data and the support of single simulation experiments have received a lot of attention, this
is not the case for simulation models. The question of how a simulation
model has been generated requires to integrate diverse simulation experiments and entities at different levels of abstractions within and across
entire simulation studies. Based on a concrete simulation model, we will
use the PROV Data Model (PROV-DM) and illuminate the benefits of
the PROV-DM approach to identify and relate entities and activities
that contributed to the generation of a simulation model, thereby taking
first steps in defining a PROV-DM ontology for simulation models.

Keywords: Simulation model · Provenance · Simulation study

1 Introduction

Provenance provides "information about entities, activities, and people involved
in producing a piece of data or thing, which can be used to form assessments
about its quality, reliability, or trustworthiness" [2]. Applying provenance to
outcomes of modeling and simulation studies, such as output data and the
simulation model, requires to identify central activities and products and to
put those into relation. Existing standards like SBML [3] or the ODD protocol [1] document *what has been developed* rather than *how it has been developed*.
The provenance of simulation data and the execution of individual simulation
experiments, be this single runs, parameter scans, or simulation-based optimization, have been the subjects of major research efforts. Accordingly, different
approaches like scripts, domain-specific languages, and scientific workflows, e.g.,
Taverna [8] and Kepler [4], support the execution and replication of individual
simulation experiments. Thereby, simulation models are part of the simulation
data's provenance rather than being its primary subject. The development of

The research was funded by the DFG (German Research Foundation) UH 66/18
"GrEASE" and by DFG CRC 1270 "Elaine".

© Springer Nature Switzerland AG 2018
K. Belhajjame et al. (Eds.): IPAW 2018, LNCS 11017, pp. 192–195, 2018.
https://doi.org/10.1007/978-3-319-98379-0_17

a simulation model involves collecting and analyzing diverse data sources and executing various simulation experiments interleaved with the refinement, composition, or extension of the simulation model. As the generation of a simulation model is a highly intricate process, the accessibility of entities and diverse activities that contributed to its generation is as important as the accessibility of the simulation model itself. To capture the provenance of simulation models within and beyond individual simulation studies, we will exploit the PROV Data Model (PROV-DM) [2]. In combination with simulation experiments as first class entities and a multi-level approach, (nearly) the full tale behind a simulation model and its development can be revealed.

2 Exploiting PROV-DM for Simulation Model Development

The potential of PROV-DM in describing the provenance of a simulation model shall be illuminated based on a concrete biochemical model. The Wnt/β-catenin signaling is involved in central cellular processes, such as differentiation, proliferation, and migration of cells. As a central signaling pathway, significant efforts have been dedicated to understand the mechanisms of the pathway by developing a variety of simulation models. In [7], we presented a preliminary provenance model to relate a Wnt/β-catenin simulation model to earlier simulation models and data. This provenance model has been refined, as seen in Fig. 1, and transferred to PROV-DM. The connections of the five models (M1–M3') to other entities and activities are described in the following part.

Data, Hypotheses and Model Development: Data artifacts are used as input (*W3* - LRP6 initial values - in *A8*), for calibration (*W4* - nuclear β-catenin - in *A9*), and for validation (*D1* - cross validation with data produced with model *M1* - in *A11*). Assigning roles to the *used* relationship between activities and data artifacts facilitates assessing the diverse data sources and how they were used in generating simulation models.

Roles between activities and simulation models, such as *used* for adaptation (*M1* - for a different cell type - *A2*), extension, or *used* for composition (*M2* - by a membrane model - *A4*, *M3* - by a ROS model - *A6*), allow to assess the relationships between simulation models and to reuse entities and activities for a simulation model's progeny [6].

Simulation Experiments: During the development of a simulation model, diverse simulation experiments, such as parameter scans, sensitivity analysis, simulation-based optimization, or statistical model-checking, are executed, alternating with phases of simulation model refinement, extension, or composition. Simulation experiments are part of a simulation model's generating process: directly, e.g., in terms of simulation-based optimization or parameter fitting (*E3*), or indirectly, by providing insights into the simulation model's behavior based on which the simulation model can be refined, extended, composed, or found to be valid (*E1, E2*). In addition, specifications of simulation experiments

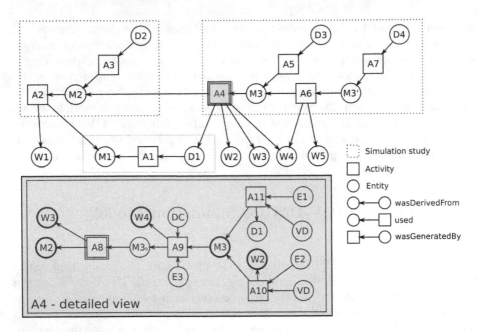

Fig. 1. Provenance model at multiple levels (in gray: detailed view of *A4*). The letters refer to: *W* - wet-lab data, *D* - model validation data, *M* - simulation model, *A* - activity like simulation experiment, *DC* - data calibration result, *VD* - model validation result, *E* - simulation experiments.

form important entities of a simulation model's provenance in their own right. They give substance to the generation process of a simulation model [7] and allow reusing simulation experiments across simulation models for consistency checks [6].

Activities at Different Levels: Similarly, as complex simulation models require to integrate description levels at multiple levels of abstractions, the "requirement of providing details at different levels of abstraction or from different viewpoints is (also) common in provenance systems" [5]. As the development of a simulation model is an intricate process, we cannot expect activities such as *A2, A4* or *A6* to be monolithic. For example, developing the simulation model *M3* relied on diverse simulation experiments which become visible by a more refined account (view) of activity *A4*. First, based on *M2* and wet-lab data, a model ($M3_0$) was derived (*A8*) which was subject to a calibration experiment (*A9, E3*) and later was validated by further simulation experiments (*A10, A11* and *E2, E1*, respectively), again based on different wet-lab data. Whereas those experiments and activities can be directly executed, the model ($M3_0$) itself has been composed of two simulation models which have been validated separately [6] and whose simulation experiments have been reused, which again would add a more fine grained account to the provenance model.

3   Towards an PROV Ontology for Simulation Model Development

A PROV ontology defines a specialization of PROV-DM. Our small case study already identified important ingredients of such an ontology: (a)specific types of entities, e.g., data, theories, simulation experiments, and simulation models, (b) specific roles between specific types of entities, e.g., used as input, for calibration, for validation (between data and generation process), used for adaptation, extension, composition (between simulation models and generation process), (c) specific refinement of activities: successive refinement of activities down to a level where simulation experiment specifications define activities and thus are ready to be executed, and (d) specific inference strategies, e.g., warning if the same data have been used for calibration and validation, or validation experiments can be reused among descendants to check consistency. To approach a provenance ontology for simulation models, we are currently applying PROV-DM to additional simulation models in systems biology but also in other domains such as demography. In addition, we explore the potential of the provenance information for consistency checks by reusing simulation experiments across simulation models and studies.

References

1. Grimm, V., Polhill, G., Touza, J.: Documenting social simulation models: the ODD protocol as a standard. In: Edmonds, B., Meyer, R. (eds.) Simulating Social Complexity - A Handbook. UCS, pp. 349–365. Springer, Cham (2017). https://doi.org/10.1007/978-3-319-66948-9_15
2. Groth, P., Moreau, L.: PROV-overview. An overview of the PROV family of documents (2013). https://www.w3.org/TR/prov-overview/
3. Hucka, M., Finney, A., Sauro, H.M., et al.: The systems biology markup language (SBML): a medium for representation and exchange of biochemical network models. Bioinformatics **19**(4), 524–531 (2003)
4. Ludäscher, B., et al.: Scientific workflow management and the Kepler system. Concur. Comput.: Pract. Exp. **18**(10), 1039–1065 (2006)
5. Moreau, L., et al.: The open provenance model core specification (v1. 1). Future Gener. Comput. Syst. **27**(6), 743–756 (2011)
6. Peng, D., Warnke, T., Haack, F., Uhrmacher, A.M.: Reusing simulation experiment specifications in developing models by successive composition - a case study of the wnt/β-catenin signaling pathway. Simul.: Trans. Soc. Model. Simul. Int. **93**(8), 659–677 (2017)
7. Ruscheinski, A., Uhrmacher, A.M.: Provenance in modeling and simulation studies - bridging gaps. In: Winter Simulation Conference 2017, pp. 872–883. IEEE (2017)
8. Wolstencroft, K., et al.: The Taverna workflow suite: designing and executing workflows of web services on the desktop, web or in the cloud. Nucleic Acids Res. **41**(W1), W557–W561 (2013)

Capturing the Provenance of Internet of Things Deployments

David Corsar[(⊠)], Milan Markovic, and Peter Edwards

Computing Science, University of Aberdeen, Aberdeen, UK
{dcorsar,m.markovic,p.edwards}@abdn.ac.uk

Abstract. This paper introduces the System Deployment Provenance Ontology and an associated set of provenance templates. These can be used to describe Internet of Things deployments.

Keywords: IoT deployments · Semantic Sensor Networks Provenance

1 Introduction

There is growing recognition that increasing the transparency of Internet of Things (IoT) devices is key to fostering trust between citizens and the IoT [1, 2]. Within the TrustLens project[1] we are working with members of the public to identify what they want to know about IoT deployments. These end-user requirements are influencing the design of an ontological framework that is being used to represent this information, and make it available for use by tools that enable citizens to pose transparency questions of future IoT deployments.

During our initial discussions, users have highlighted a desire to know what IoT devices are doing, the types of sensors that are part of a device, how accurate the sensors are, and what data are being generated. Information such as this can be described by the Semantic Sensor Network Ontology (SSNO) W3C recommendation [4], which provides formalisms to describe sensors and related concepts in domains such as the Internet of Things. SSNO describes *ssn:Systems*[2], as pieces of infrastructure which may be composed of subsystems; three types (subclasses) of *ssn:System* are defined: *sosa:Sensors*[3], *sosa:Actuator*, and *sosa:Sampler*. Systems implement *sosa:Procedures* that can be used to describe the system's intended operations (e.g. how a sensor will make an observation). SSNO also models system capabilities (e.g. accuracy, expected battery

---

David Corsar's email address for correspondance is d.corsar1@rgu.ac.uk.

The research described here is supported by the RCUK Digital Economy programme award made to the University of Aberdeen; award reference: EP/N028074/1.

[1] http://www.trustlens.org.

[2] Defined by the SSN namespace http://www.w3.org/ns/ssn/, abbreviated to "ssn".

[3] Defined by the SOSA namespace http://www.w3.org/ns/sosa/, abbreviated to "sosa".

© Springer Nature Switzerland AG 2018
K. Belhajjame et al. (Eds.): IPAW 2018, LNCS 11017, pp. 196–199, 2018.
https://doi.org/10.1007/978-3-319-98379-0_18

life), acts (e.g. making an observation), results of those acts (e.g. an observation value), features of interest (the subject of an act), and properties of a feature of interest that can be observed, sampled, or changed.

Our interactions with end-users also highlighted their interest in the activities that may have occurred before and during IoT deployments. For example, whether any community consultation was conducted, who designed the deployment, and if any assessment was made of potential privacy risks. While SSNO includes a *ssn:Deployment* class, it only describes the deployed system and the platform (such as a wall, shelf, etc.) that hosts it, along with any further details about the platform, such as its location. We argue that having additional information about the activities that influenced the deployment would greatly increase its transparency (as desired by users), and assist with interpreting any data generated by the deployed system. For example, knowledge of maintenance activities performed on a sensor may influence an individual's view of the quality of data it generates. This may involve considerations such as when it was last (re)calibrated, its specified accuracy and drift values [3], or whether the surfaces of an air quality sensor have been recently cleaned [5].

This paper presents the Semantic Sensor Network System Deployment Provenance Ontology (SDPO)[4]. SDPO extends PROV-O[5] with a vocabulary for describing deployments of IoT systems as a collection of PROV activities conducted before or during a deployment, the associated agents and entities (e.g. systems, sensors), that have shaped the deployment in some way.

2   Describing IoT System Deployments

SDPO defines the *sdpo:DeploymentRelatedActivity* class, and an initial hierarchy of subclasses representing various types of such activities. SDPO also asserts that: *ssn:Deployment* is a subclass of *prov:Activity*[6]; *ssn:System* is a subclass of *prov:Collection* and *prov:Agent*; and *ssn:hasSubSystem* is a subproperty of *prov:hadMember*. These subsumptions are based on earlier work [3] aligning the non-normative SSNO published by the W3C SSN-XG with PROV-O.

The types of activities defined by SDPO include those that may have been conducted before deployment, such as *sdpo:SystemSelection, sdpo:SiteInspection, sdpo:DeploymentDesign*, and *sdpo:Installation*. Various types of maintenance operations are also defined, based on [5]. These include *sdpo:Calibration, sdpo:Cleaning*, and *sdpo:Replacement* of a system or subsystem. To support developers use SDPO to describe IoT deployments, a set of PROV-TEMPLATES[7] are available for the ProvToolbox library[8] that provide suggested provenance patterns for several types of SDPO deployment related activities[9].

---

[4] Namespace http://www.w3id.org/sdpo/, abbreviated to "sdpo".

[5] Namespace http://www.w3.org/ns/prov#, abbreviated to "prov".

[6] SDPO views a *ssn:Deployment* as an activity during which, for example, a sensor performs the act(s) of making one (or more) observations.

[7] https://provenance.ecs.soton.ac.uk/prov-template/.

[8] https://lucmoreau.github.io/ProvToolbox/.

[9] The templates are available at http://www.github.com/TrustLens/sdpo.

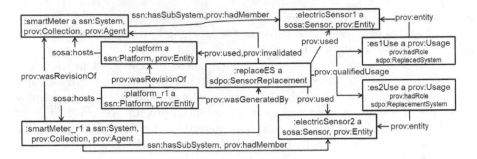

Fig. 1. Provenance record describing the replacement of a sensor in a smart meter.

Figure 1 illustrates an instantiation of the PROV-TEMPLATE designed to capture the replacement of a subsystem. In this example, the sensor *:electric-Sensor1* that monitors electricity consumption as part of a smart meter (*:smart-Meter*) is replaced during the *:replaceES* activity. The roles *sdpo:Replac-ementSystem* and *sdpo:ReplacedSystem* are used to differentiate the function of the two sensors in *:replaceES*. As the sensors are part of the *:smartMeter* system (described in PROV terms as a collection of system entities), a revision of the system is created to reflect the change in collection membership. Consequently, a revision of the platform (*:platform*) hosting the system must be created to reflect that it now hosts *:smartMeter_r1*. As *:smartMeter* and *:platform* cease to exist following the replacement, they are invalidated by *:replaceES*[10]. While not illustrated in Fig. 1, it is expected that *:replaceES* would link to the activity (e.g., a *sdpo:DataReview*) which identified that *:electricSensor1* should be replaced, or to the entity that triggered the replacement (e.g., a fault report).

While SSNO can link an *ssn:System* with the *sosa:Procedure*s (plans) it implements, SSNO does not define how those procedures should be described. Figure 2 illustrates the use of P-PLAN[11] to describe a *sosa:Procedure* as a *p-plan:Plan* that a system will enact during a deployment. P-PLAN describes plans as a series of *p-plan:Step*s that can be linked by *p-plan:Variable*s. In Fig. 2 the first step of the plan (*:plan*) is an *sdpo:Observe* step (a subclass of *p-plan:Step*[12]), which has an output variable *:electricityReading*. This variable is input to the *:uploadReading* step, which will send the reading to the energy supplier. An enactment of this plan is captured in the *:obs1-enactment* provenance bundle, which also illustrates the correspondences between the P-PLAN and SSNO concepts. This information can be used to improve the transparency of the expected behaviour of a device (as described by the implemented plan(s)), and contextualise the device's actual behaviour (as described in the retrospective provenance describing plan enactments). Note, as plans are specific to deployments of individual systems, we do not currently define a set of PROV-TEMPLATES for plans.

---

[10] Note *:electricSensor1* is not invalidated, as it may subsequently be used by a repair or recycling activity.

[11] Namespace http://purl.org/net/p-plan#, abbreviated to "p-plan".

[12] SDPO also defines the steps *sdpo:Sample* and *sdpo:Actuate* corresponding to the *sosa:Sampling* and *sosa:Actuation* acts defined by SSNO.

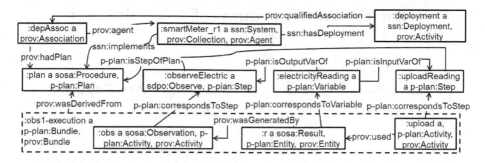

Fig. 2. Example plan for a smart meter to observe and upload the quantity of electricity consumed, and associated retrospective provenance generated during an enactment.

3   Future Work

The plan illustrated in Fig. 2 provides only partial transparency of *:smart-Meter_r1*'s expected behaviour. For example, the plan as shown does not record that the smart meter will observe and upload energy usage every 30 min, as P-PLAN does not presently include the constructs necessary to model repeat processes. We are defining extensions to P-PLAN that will allow us to provide a more representative view of a device's expected behaviour. In addition to repeat processes, our intended extensions include associating constraints with variables. This will, for example, allow a plan to specify that the inputs to an upload step will be all of the readings made in the past 24 h, rather than a single reading.

We are also continuing our user engagement activities, with plans to deploy several IoT devices in public spaces. We are currently developing a software framework that will capture ontological descriptions of these deployments and data generated by the devices. These will be used during co-design sessions involving members of the public, the outcomes of which will guide the development of software tools that allow citizens to explore details about IoT deployments, assist them in understanding the risks and benefits associated with IoT devices, and to assess the quality of the data produced.

References

1. Alliance for Internet of Things Innovation: AIOTI Strategy 2017–2021 (2017)
2. Almeida, V.A.F., Doneda, D., Monteiro, M.: Governance challenges for the internet of things. IEEE Internet Comput. **19**(4), 56–59 (2015)
3. Compton, M., Corsar, D., Taylor, K.: Sensor data provenance: SSNO & PROV-O together at last. In: Proceedings of 7th International Workshop on Semantic Sensor Networks, vol. 1401. CEUR (2014)
4. Haller, A., Janowicz, K., Cox, S., Le Phyoc, D., Taylor, K., Lefrancois, M.: Semantic sensor network ontology. W3C Recommendation, March 2018
5. Williams, R., et al.: Air Sensor Guidebook. U.S. EPA (2014). ePA/600/R-14/159

Towards Transparency of IoT Message Brokers

Milan Markovic[1]([✉]), David Corsar[1], Waqar Asif[2], Peter Edwards[1],
and Muttukrishnan Rajarajan[2]

[1] Computing Science, University of Aberdeen, Aberdeen AB24 5UA, UK
{milan.markovic,dcorsar,p.edwards}@abdn.ac.uk
[2] School of Engineering and Mathematical Sciences, City, University of London,
London EC1V 0HB, UK
{waqar.asif,r.muttukrishnan}@city.ac.uk

Abstract. In this paper we propose an ontological model for document-ing provenance of MQTT message brokers to enhance the transparency of interactions between IoT agents.

Keywords: IoT · MQTT · Provenance

1 Introduction

The Internet of Things (IoT) enables multiple heterogeneous devices and applica-tions to interact with each other using the Internet as a common communication infrastructure. However, these devices bring with them a new set of problems such as security and user data/identity privacy [1]. The concurrent operation of such devices leads to a high risk of data breach where a device capable of com-plex computations can launch an active or a passive attack in a network running weak security protocols [2]. Alongside this, the increasing interest of IoT users in data privacy and new regulations for protecting personal data such as the Gen-eral Data Protection Regulation[1] and the Safe Harbor Framework[2] necessitate greater transparency of IoT systems. This includes user-accessible information on processes utilising the data generated/obtained through IoT devices.

We argue that transparency of interactions between IoT devices (e.g. exchanging of messages) is a critical enabler to support IoT device account-ability, privacy, and data quality assessments. Here, the W3C recommendation PROV [5] could provide means to document causal relationships between agents (i.e. things, data consumers, etc.), activities they perform (e.g. sensing, relaying

The work described here was funded by the award made by the RCUK Digital Econ-omy programme to the University of Aberdeen (EP/N028074/1) and City, University of London (EP/N028155/1).

[1] https://eur-lex.europa.eu/legal-content/EN/TXT/?uri=celex%3A32016R0679.
[2] https://www.ftc.gov/tips-advice/business-center/privacy-and-security/u.s.-eu-safe-harbor-framework.

© Springer Nature Switzerland AG 2018
K. Belhajjame et al. (Eds.): IPAW 2018, LNCS 11017, pp. 200–203, 2018.
https://doi.org/10.1007/978-3-319-98379-0_19

messages), and data entities used and generated. In addition, by documenting the intended actions of agents (i.e. plans) we could also support audit of IoT components in terms of system capabilities and deviations in behaviour.

In this context, message brokers implementing the MQTT standard[3] are commonly used to network groups of IoT devices and software agents[4]. In such networks all communication between clients can be inspected by auditing the connected message brokers. At the same time, malfunctions, misconfigurations or the limited capabilities of message brokers (e.g. not detecting abnormal behaviour such as repeated failed authentication attempts) pose significant security and privacy risks that may result in data loss or breach of data sharing permissions. Provenance records documenting the intended and actual behaviour of message brokers could support discovery of such issues. For example, a provenance query could reveal a list of all agents that had access to a redistributed message which can be checked against a user's policy for data sharing. Further queries could also identify messages that are not being forwarded by the broker (i.e. plans not executed in full), frequent attempts at unauthorised client subscriptions, or clients that are frequently disconnected due to their inactivity without properly closing their connections.

In the remainder of the paper we introduce the MQTT-PLAN ontology, designed to define plans describing the intended actions of brokers upon receipt of different types of MQTT control packets. This can then be used to annotate retrospective provenance records of the broker's actual behaviour, identifying correspondances between the retrospective entities and activities and concepts in the plan. We conclude with a discussion of outstanding challenges and outline our future work.

2   The MQTT-PLAN Ontology

MQTT PLAN[5] defines a vocabulary extending PROV-O[6] and P-PLAN [3] to describe high level abstract plans associated with MQTT brokers; and their corresponding execution traces. The ontology captures information that could be found by inspecting individual MQTT control packets (e.g. message topics) and other information maintained by a broker (e.g. the identity of clients subscribed to receive messages published to each topic, and reasons for client disconnections). In P-PLAN, plans are modelled as sets of variables serving as inputs and outputs of steps. Execution traces are then described using the concepts *p-plan:Entity* and *p-plan:Activity*[7] which

---

[3] http://docs.oasis-open.org/mqtt/mqtt/v3.1.1/os/mqtt-v3.1.1-os.html.

[4] MQTT is a publish/subscribe messaging transport protocol for a client-server communication. The protocol specifies a set of control packets that govern the communication between the client and the message broker residing on a server.

[5] http://w3id.org/mqtt-plan.

[6] https://www.w3.org/TR/prov-o/.

[7] Subclasses of *prov:Entity* and *prov:Activity*.

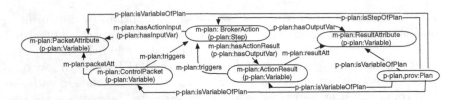

Fig. 1. Main MQTT-PLAN concepts modelled as subclasses of P-PLAN concepts.

are linked to the corresponding plan via *p-plan:correspondsToVariable* and *p-plan:correspondsToStep*. This approach allows for a separation of the abstract plan description from individual execution traces describing instances of enacted processes and associated data. As a result, the interpretation of retrospective provenance is bound to the corresponding plan description. Figure 1 illustrates the main MQTT-PLAN concepts[8]. A step *m-plan:BrokerAction* can be triggered by *m-plan:ControlPacket* and its more descriptive subtypes such as *m-plan:PublishCP*, *m-plan:SubscribeCP*, etc. Subtypes of *m-plan:BrokerAction* such as *m-plan:Subscribe*[9], *m-plan:Publish*[10], *m-plan:Disconnect*[11] are also defined. Control packets can be associated with *m-plan:PacketAttribute*(s) such as *m-plan:TopicName* and *m-plan:Message*. Using property chain axioms associated with *m-plan:hasActionInput* such attributes are inferred as input variables of the *m-plan:BrokerAction*. A broker action can produce an *m-plan: ActionResult* variable, which describes a results object and can also trigger another *m-plan:BrokerAction* step. Such results can be associated with attributes *m-plan:Target*, *m-plan:Reason* and *m-plan:CompletionStatus*. Subtypes of *m-plan:Target*, namely *m-plan:AffectedAgent* and *m-plan:AffectedAgents* define variables which can be instantiated via a retrospective provenance record to describe either a single or group of agents affected by the activity instance corresponding to *m-plan:BrokerAction*. Figure 2 illustrates an example plan describing re-publishing of messages by a message broker and a corresponding execution trace. In this example, a message containing a temperature reading was published under the topic "/temp" by the client *ex:Device1* and was forwarded to the client *ex:Device2* by the agent *ex:Broker*.

Similarly, *m-plan:CompletionStatus* and *mplan:Reason* can be instantiated via the retrospective provenance record to determine whether the broker could complete the activity and the reason if this was not possible. For example, a publish control packet could trigger a publish action which could not complete due to the client being denied access to the topic. A result of this action could also trigger disconnection of the client.

---

[8] MQTT-PLAN concepts are described with the prefix m-plan.

[9] The client sending a control packet triggering this action should be registered to receive messages published under the requested topics.

[10] A message specified in the control packet triggering this action should be forwarded to clients subscribed to the topic under which it was published.

[11] This action should close the connection between a client and a broker.

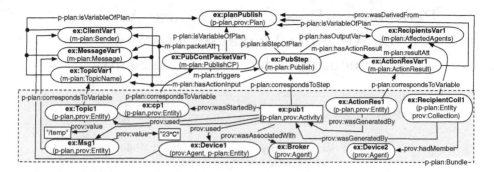

Fig. 2. An example provenance record describing a broker's plan for re-publishing received messages to other clients, and a record of the corresponding execution trace.

3   Discussion and Future Work

In order to keep the vocabulary lightweight, the initial version of the ontology does not cover all of the functionalities specified in the MQTT standard. These include: quality of service tracking, handling of will messages, retaining of messages by the broker, session flags. Username and password flags are also not captured explicitly for security reasons. However, the ontology enables modelling of various plans describing single or multiple broker actions interlinked with their input and output variables. As part of our future work we aim to create a repository of common representations of broker's plans described using MQTT-PLAN to generate further community discussions about their use. We will also evaluate how the lack of support for conditional branches impacts on modelling such plans. Finally, traffic managed by message brokers presents scalability challenges. However, our previous work [4] demonstrated a possible approach using linked data streams. We are currently exploring a means for capturing provenance by extending an open source MQTT message broker in order to evaluate the potential of a stream-based approach for consuming such data.

References

1. Asif, W., Rajarajan, M., Lestas, M.: Increasing user controllability on device specific privacy in the Internet of Things. Comput. Commun. **116**, 200–211 (2018)
2. Bertino, E., Islam, N.: Botnets and internet of things security. Computer **50**(2), 76–79 (2017)
3. Garijo, D., Gil, Y.: Augmenting PROV with plans in P-PLAN: scientific processes as linked data. In: Proceedings of the 2nd International Workshop on Linked Science 2012 (2012)
4. Markovic, M., Edwards, P.: Semantic stream processing for IoT devices in the food safety domain. In: Posters and Demos SEMANTiCS 2016 and SuCCESS 2016 Workshop, Leipzig, Germany (2016)
5. Moreau, L., Groth, P., Cheney, J., Lebo, T., Miles, S.: The rationale of PROV. Web Semant.: Sci. Serv. Agents World Wide Web **35**, 235–257 (2015)

Provenance-Based Root Cause Analysis for Revenue Leakage Detection: A Telecommunication Case Study

Wisam Abbasi[1]([⊠]) and Adel Taweel[1,2]([⊠])

[1] Computer Science, Birzeit University, Birzeit, Palestine
wisam.alabbasi@gmail.com
ataweel@birzeit.edu
[2] Informatics, King's College London, London, UK

Abstract. Revenue Assurance (RA) represents a top priority function for most of the telecommunication operators worldwide. Revenue leakage, if not prevented, depending on the severity of the leakage affecting their profitability and continuity, could cause a significant revenue loss of an operator. Detecting and preventing revenue leakage is a key process to assure telecom systems and processes efficiency, accuracy and effectiveness. There are two general revenue leakage detection approaches: big data analytics and rule-based. Both approaches seek to detect abnormal usage and profit trend behaviour and revenue leakage based on certain patterns or predefined rules, however both are mainly human-driven and fail to automatically debug and drill down for root causes of leakage anomalies and issues. In this work, a rule-based RA approach that deploys a provenance-based model is proposed. The model represents the workflow of critical RA functions enriched with contextual and semantic information that may detect critical leakage issues and generate potential leakage alerts. A query model is developed for the provenance model that can be applied over the captured data to automate, facilitate and improve the current process of root cause analysis of revenue leakages.

Keywords: Debugging · Provenance · Revenue Assurance
Root cause

1 Introduction

The main responsibility of RA analysts is to manage and prevent revenue leakage based on RA methodology [8]. Current RA architectures support revenue leakage detection by applying a series of detective processes consisting of monitoring, summarization, auditing, and investigation [8]. But it is not an easy task to track back to the sources and root causes of a leakage issue manually due to the wide variety of rate plans, products, offers, campaigns, incidents, upgrades and millions or even billions of records in addition to the existence of tiered product plans and flat rates [3]. Therefore, automating the debugging and drill

© Springer Nature Switzerland AG 2018
K. Belhajjame et al. (Eds.): IPAW 2018, LNCS 11017, pp. 204–207, 2018.
https://doi.org/10.1007/978-3-319-98379-0_20

down process would greatly increase performance, ease the auditing process, save operators revenues, provide better analytical experience, better management of data, more accurate reports and leads to an informed future decision making.

On the other hand, provenance is a global term refers to the creation history of an object and to the contextual information related to it [7]. Data Provenance has been applied to the field of computing by defining the origin of processes that have led to a specific state of data product within an information system such as databases and workflows [6]. Scientific research have been conducted in computer science for the purpose of data provenance application upon two major domains, science with the aim of information sharing and validation while preserving copyright and authority aspects [2] and business [1] to achieve data quality, reproducibility, auditability, validation, debugging, accountability, error backtracking, prediction, and forward tracking aspects [5].

Revenue leaks in telecom industry largely affect business profitability and continuity, and there is a critical need in the market for an RA analytics debugging tool as the debugging and drill down processes in current RA architectures are done manually. Therefore, we are proposing a new uniquely provenance data model for this domain, that would help revenue analysts audit their operators traffic in a better way, simplify error tracing back, better management of the data quality, and the provision of a historical record of data products.

2   The Proposed Approach

Provenance data represent semantic and contextual information related to the leakage issue or the telecom usage anomaly. These data are being created automatically based on the processes and sub-processes flow on the RA system. Each RA detective process consists of a number of processing steps and entities.

Figure 1 presents an overview of how the proposed provenance model works. Once an RA detective process starts execution the query model starts capturing semantic and contextual provenance information of each of its sub-processes from connected entities to each process, and store these information into data-oriented workflows as provenance diagrams in a graph database.

Entities that represent source nodes are associated with other entities to provide contextual information related to these nodes such as system logs, incidents and launched offers. The final result data item in the graphical workflow is associated with an entity named public holidays and events based on the date parameter to add more contextual information.

Processes and entities in the provenance diagram are connected using relationships. The relationships are given the properties for backward tracing purpose. Semantic information represented by mapped attributes, and used filters if any are stored at the processing node level.

3   Running Examples

The review of the existing RA systems suggests that they lack the provenance capturing capability to answer the questions of when, where, and why the issue has been introduced and what reason(s) may have caused the revenue leakage issue. The proposed approach has been partially implemented and tested on two revenue leakage scenarios. Initial results show that it can automate the detection and root cause analysis of these scenarios.

Fake (i.e. False Positives) Revenue Leakage Alert: A great increase in voice calls duration with no additional increase in call counts or call charges has been used as an example of an abnormal behavior in the usage monitoring trends, since any additional voice usage must introduce additional fees or charges in the normal case, thus must be investigated by the RA team. The root cause for this behavior is that an offer was launched for local voice calls for prepaid subscribers to get 3 free minutes in each charged call.

Real (i.e. True Positives) Revenue Leakage Alert: A great missing of voice calls in one of the main RA system functions that connects the MSC source node representing the switch and the CCN source node representing the charging system has been used as an example of a real revenue loss as in Fig. 2 and must be investigated immediately by RA team. The root cause for this issue is that calls charging has stopped due to a switch-charging disconnection occurred after an upgrade was done to MSC3 without adjusting its settings properly.

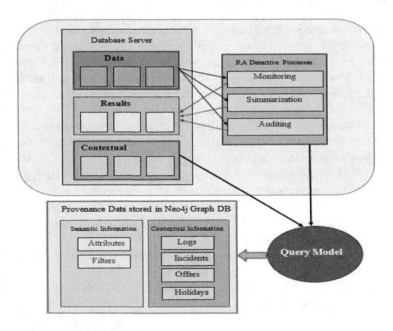

Fig. 1. Proposed provenance-based approach.

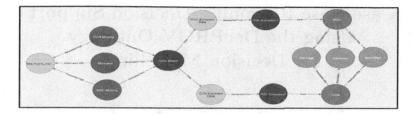

Fig. 2. Real revenue leakage alert scenario provenance graph.

4   Results

We have presented an approach that supports root cause analysis and drill down capabilities in current rules based RA systems. The approach starts by understanding the current state of RA function methodology, processes and approaches, then the current approach was improved through the deployment of logical data provenance and data workflows. For this stage, a preliminary evaluation was conducted to show the potential of the proposed approach and its plausibility on two scenarios, however for the next stage, the evaluation will include several scenarios and enlarged scope. The proposed model has been evaluated based on the accuracy and correctness of answering the questions of how, what, where, and why presented using the debugging and drill down concepts and it has proven its correctness and accuracy depending on the provenance data.

References

1. Curbera, F., Doganata, Y., Martens, A., Mukhi, N.K., Slominski, A.: Business provenance – a technology to increase traceability of end-to-end operations. In: Meersman, R., Tari, Z. (eds.) OTM 2008. LNCS, vol. 5331, pp. 100–119. Springer, Heidelberg (2008). https://doi.org/10.1007/978-3-540-88871-0_10
2. Greenwood, M., et al.: Provenance of e-science experiments-experience from bioinformatics, pp. 223–226 (2003)
3. Revenue assurance how to stop bleeding and start leading. https://clarity.sutherlandglobal.com/blog/accounting-minute/revenue-assurance-how-to-stop-bleeding-and-start-leading/. Accessed 7 Jan 2018
4. Global Telecom Revenue Assurance Survey 2013. http://www.ey.com/Publication/vwLUAssets/Global_telecoms_revenue_assurance_survey_2013/$FILE/Global_revenue_assurance_survey_2013.pdf. Accessed 7 Jan 2018
5. Imran, M., Hlavacs, H.: Provenance in the cloud: why and how? In: The Third International Conference on Cloud Computing, GRIDs, and Virtualization, pp. 106–112. Cloud Computing (2012)
6. Moreau, L.: The provenance of electronic data. Commun. ACM **51**(4), 52–58 (2008)
7. Provenance. https://en.wikipedia.org/wiki/Provenance. Accessed 7 Jan 2018
8. Revenue Assurance. https://en.wikipedia.org/wiki/Revenue_assurance. Accessed 7 Jan 2018

Case Base Reasoning Decision Support
Using the DecPROV Ontology
for Decision Modelling

Nicholas J. Car[(⊠)]

CSIRO Land and Water, Dutton Park, QLD, Australia
nicholas.car@csiro.au
http://people.csiro.au/C/N/Nicholas-Car

Abstract. Decisions are modelled using a new, Semantic Web, specialised provenance ontology. This allows for management in graph databases and common instance components to be globally addressed and thus reused. New decisions are compared to those in a Case Base to provide best-practice advice. This is a Decision Support System (DSS) which also assists other DSS by revealing contemporary practice in standardised ways with details for decision categorisation.

Keywords: Decision modelling · DecPROV · PROV · Provenance
Case-based reasoning

1 Decision Modelling Need and a Domain

Decision Support Systems (DSS) encode expert knowledge and perhaps data for decisions to help users a:ain best practice. Few DSS cater for different decision scenarios or even variations within a scenario.

Fig. 1. A drip irrigation system carrying water to crops via pipes, valves and emitters: modern systems such as these allow for fine-grained irrigation management governed by expert systems. Image curtesy of Irrigation Australia, Pty. Ltd.

© Springer Nature Switzerland AG 2018
K. Belhajjame et al. (Eds.): IPAW 2018, LNCS 11017, pp. 208–211, 2018.
https://doi.org/10.1007/978-3-319-98379-0_21

Standardised decision modelling would allow us to articulate many decision types within a domain and variations within a type consistently perhaps allowing DSS designers to be:er cater for decision ranges.

For irrigation decisions by smallholding farmers, perhaps using systems such as that shown in Fig. 1, we would like to characterise decisions they make in a standardised way, knowing that many factors affect their overall practice [9].

2   Standardised PROV Decision Modelling

DecPROV [2] a specialised version of the PROV Data Model [6] is used to model past decisions. As opposed to other industry or academic decision modelling such as DMN [8] or Decision Modelling Ontology [4], this ontology is both PROV-aligned and uses Semantic Web methods allowing for (Fig. 2):

– Sophisticated modelling of complex decisions
  • The Semantic Web has a large range of interoperable models
  • Whole business processes can be modelled & decisions included
– Describing *why* particular decisions were made in PROV-like terms
– Describing different types of decisions within a domain and categorising them
  with standard taxonomy techniques.

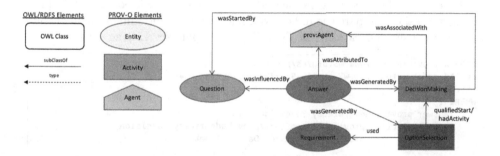

Fig. 2. Classes of DecPROV and their basic relationships. From the ontology documentation at https://promsns.org/def/decprov. DecPROV uses standard PROV-O [5] properties to relate specialised versions of PROV-O classes that describe decision elements in a manner similar to the W3C?s Decision Modelling Incubator Group?s candidate Decision Ontology [7]

3   Case-Based Reasoning with Decisions

A way to provide support for a decision without expert systems is to compare them to previous ones using Case-Based Reasoning [1]. Current cases are matched for similarity to previous one whose results must be known, then best practice advice is offered with the current case then stored for future use. Typically CBR systems use a *cycle*, see Fig. 3, and require a similarity metric to compare cases.

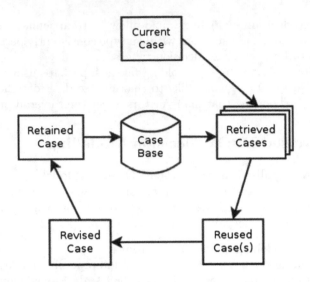

Fig. 3. The CBR cycle, after [1]

Using DecPROV and Semantic Web modelling generally, schema-less RDF triplestores can be used to store decisions and the standardised SPARQL query language used to compare them. For example, a query could find decision outputs (an Answer) sharing datasets of Type X as an input (see Listing 1.1).

```
PREFIX prov: <http://www.w3.org/ns/prov#>
PREFIX rdf: <http://www.w3.org/1999/02/22-rdf-syntax-ns#>
SELECT ?answer
WHERE {
    ?answer prov:wasGeneratedBy ?decision .
    ?optionSelection prov:qualifiedStart/prov:hadActivity ?decision;
                     prov:used/rdf:type :DatasetTypeX .
}
```

Listing 1.1. Example SPARQL query (https://www.w3.org/TR/sparql11-query/) to find a decision using inputs of Dataset Type X

4   Current Work

Currently we are cataloguing and categorising known online irrigation-relevant data sources so decisions using similar input data can be selected for. Without cataloging we can't ascertain data source reuse and without characterisation we can't determine similarity between data sources: multiple, sometimes branded, data sources can deliver similar information.

As we characterise a series of data sources, we are establishing a range of similarity measures to be used in CBR to allow the matching of a Current Case to Past Cases of decisions made. Since the mechanics we are using are RDF triplestores, we are establishing these similarity measures as SPARQL queries.

We are also testing the modelling power of DecPROV: Does it cover all/many irrigation decisions? Does using DecPROV improve data provenance generally to assist with other questions such as those about data quality?

As we characterise decisions made, we are storing anonymised instances of them in a triplestore with a SPARQL endpoint and a wrapping Linked Data layer which publicly lists them with persistent URIs so they can be found, referred to and reused in CBR systems and generally.

5   Future Work

Once a full CBR cycle is implemented, we will begin providing CBR-derived decision support to irrigators. We hope to discover hitherto unknown decision making patterns in irrigation to inform future non-CBR decision support systems. We also hope to expand the use of DecPROV to other decision domains.

References

1. Aamodt, A., Plaza, E.: Case-based reasoning: foundational issues, methodological variations, and system approaches. AICom - Artif. Intell. Commun. **7**(1), 39–59 (1994)
2. Car, N.J.: Modelling causes for actions with the decision and PROV ontologies. In: MODSIM 2017–22th International Congress on Modelling and Simulation, Hobart, Australia (2017). https://www.mssanz.org.au/modsim2017/C2/car.pdf
3. Car, N.J., Moore, G.A.: Bridging the gap between modelling advice and irrigator solutions through empirical reasoning techniques. In: MODSIM 2011–19th International Congress on Modelling and Simulation, Perth, Australia (2011). https://www.mssanz.org.au/modsim2011/B1/car.pdf
4. Kornyshova, E., Deneckère, R.: Decision-making ontology for information system engineering. In: Parsons, J., Saeki, M., Shoval, P., Woo, C., Wand, Y. (eds.) ER 2010. LNCS, vol. 6412, pp. 104–117. Springer, Heidelberg (2010). https://doi.org/10.1007/978-3-642-16373-9_8
5. Lebo, T., Sahoo, S., McGuinness, D.: PROV-O: The PROV Ontology. W3C Recommendation, 30 April 2013. https://www.w3.org/TR/prov-o/
6. Moreau, L., Missier, P. (eds.): PROV-DM: The PROV Data Model. W3C Recommendation, 30 April 2013. https://www.w3.org/TR/prov-dm/
7. Nowara, P.: Decision Ontology. W3C Decisions and Decision Making Incubator Group (2011). https://promsns.org/def/do
8. Object Management Group: Decision Model and Notation (DMN). OMG Specification Formal/2016-06-01, Object Management Group (2016). http://www.omg.org/spec/DMN/1.1
9. Whittenbury, K., Davidson, P.: Beyond adoption: the need for a broad understanding of factors that influence irrigators? Decision-making. Rural Soc. **19**(1), 4–16 (2009)

Bottleneck Patterns in Provenance

Sara Boutamina[1]([✉]), James D. A. Millington[2], and Simon Miles[1]

[1] Department of Informatics, King's College London, London WC2B 4BG, UK
{sara.boutamina,simon.miles}@kcl.ac.uk
[2] Department of Geography, King's College London, London WC2B 4BG, UK
james.millington@kcl.ac.uk

Abstract. A bottleneck, in general, is a point of congestion in a system which impacts its efficiency, productivity and may lead to delays. Identifying and then fixing bottlenecks is an important step in maintaining and improving a system. To detect bottlenecks, we must understand the flow of processes, and dependencies between resources. Thus provenance information is an appropriate form of input to address this matter. In this paper, bottleneck patterns based on provenance graphs are proposed. These patterns are used to define the structures bottlenecks may take based on their classification, and offer a way to detect possible bottlenecks. An example from soybeans distribution is used to illustrate this preliminary work.

Keywords: Bottlenecks · Bottleneck patterns · Provenance graphs

1 Introduction

Bottlenecks can have a great impact on systems leading, for instance, to an increase in the production and distribution times and costs, and hence, a reduction in satisfaction of customers. In global food distribution, for example, detecting bottlenecks in processes can be an important step in solving problems such as preventing food wastage.

There is an ambiguity in the literature regarding the definition of bottlenecks despite the existence of much work, especially in manufacturing, dealing with this topic. In particular, there is a conflation between the definition of bottlenecks and the methods used to detect them (e.g. [1,2]). For instance, in *the inventory definition* [1], bottlenecks are considered to be where there is a queue of the most of work waiting to be processed. This definition focuses on how to identify a bottleneck based on the waiting queue before a station rather than on what independently characterises it. Moreover, the use of different characteristics to describe bottlenecks may lead to different bottlenecks being identified [2]. To have an acceptable definition of bottlenecks, the authors in [3] suggest that it is important to reduce the level of detail integrated in such definition. They propose the following definition: "The bottleneck of a system is the element (node or edge) that limits the system in attaining higher throughput beyond a certain threshold. This threshold is determined by the bottleneck's physical throughput

© Springer Nature Switzerland AG 2018
K. Belhajjame et al. (Eds.): IPAW 2018, LNCS 11017, pp. 212–216, 2018.
https://doi.org/10.1007/978-3-319-98379-0_22

capacity, organizational rules, or operational practices" [3]. It is notable from this that they consider that a bottleneck may occur not only because of physical capacity of a resource, for instance, but also because of the organisation of work at this resource.

In this poster, we present initial work towards specifying bottlenecks in terms of patterns within provenance graphs documenting past performance in a system. First, a classification of bottlenecks is considered, then bottleneck patterns, corresponding to provenance subgraphs, are proposed to match and suit this classification.

The patterns are illustrated using the movement of soybeans between a farmer in Brazil and a consumer in China. A trading company, acting as an intermediary, bought soybeans from the farmer, then transported it to their stores not far from the production area. After that, the soybeans were transported from those stores to port, to be exported to China. This company delegated to two transport companies to transfer soybeans firstly from farm to their storage units, then from these units to port terminal managed by the trading company.

2   Classification of Bottlenecks

In order to determine the forms of pattern to look for in the provenance, we need to first consider the types of bottleneck that can exist. We derive our taxonomy from existing classifications [3]. *Tangible bottlenecks* impede higher system throughput due to physical limitations. System elements that are tangible bottlenecks can be either *active* or *passive*. Active tangible bottlenecks represent elements which can influence system throughput by their own actions and behaviour, such as workers in food distribution. On the other hand, passive tangible bottlenecks are not able to change the throughput themselves, since they do not have the power to do so, but represent other physical limitations, such as streets slowing down transportation due to high traffic. *Intangible bottlenecks* represent processes that prevent higher system throughput, for instance, because of their poor design.

Other ways of classifying bottlenecks exist, not currently translated into provenance patterns in our work. For example, comparable but not quite the same as the above classification, one can distinguish *organisational*, *physical* and *operational* bottlenecks, corresponding to limitations in the way activities are planned, physical capabilities, and the way that work is conducted, respectively. A bottleneck can also be either with an *external* or *internal* locus of control, based on whether the measures used to manage bottlenecks are inside or outside the organisations. We can also classify bottlenecks on whether they are *unavoidable* at points when demand for a resource exceeds its capacity, or *avoidable* when its emergence is due to, for instance, careless preparation.

3   Bottlenecks Patterns

In this paper, we consider that the bottlenecks to be detected are classified as tangible (active and passive) and intangible. To structure and specify these bottlenecks, patterns are proposed which are defined as:

Definition 1. *A bottleneck pattern is a set of rules that apply to a provenance sub-graph indicating whether it presents a bottleneck in the process documented.*

These patterns are specified using PROV which is defined as "a specification to express provenance records, which contains descriptions of the entities and activities involved in producing and delivering or otherwise influencing a given object" [4]. It is based on three main core concepts which are *entities, activities* and *agents* [5]. Entities represent digital, physical or other things; activities are actions dealing with entities to create new ones or to use existing ones; and agents correspond to something that was responsible for an already happened activity, an entity or another agent.

We assume that the provenance graph within which we are trying to detect bottlenecks is representative of the process' past behaviour, or is a representative aggregation of information from multiple provenance documents effectively documenting the process' multiple executions over time. Each entity, activity and agent in a PROV graph can have attributes, which we use to record, for instance, past localised capacity and demand. The way in provenance graphs may be aggregated and the ontology for expressing capacity and demand is beyond the scope of this poster.

For each of the three bottleneck types in the classification, we have a provenance pattern. These are defined informally at this point, but we illustrate their effect with the case study. A bottleneck pattern comprises a *potential bottleneck pattern*, identifying a PROV graph structure within which a bottleneck of the given type may be found, and then rules over the attributes attached to the nodes of the structure, such as demand and capacity, which can be used to confirm the bottleneck exists. Examples of possible bottlenecks, based on the proposed patterns, from the soybeans distribution example are presented in Figs. 1, 2, 3, 4 and 5.

- A potential intangible bottleneck may occur when there is an agent or a number of agents acting on behalf of another agent (e.g. Fig. 1). Moreover, it may occur when there is a collection representing for instance a regulation, and there is at least a member who had business with a non-member (e.g. Fig. 5). *Being a member* of this collection means that the agent had accepted and signed the regulation, and *having a business* means that there is an activity which is associated with at least two agents where one of them is a buyer and the other is a seller.
- A potential passive tangible bottleneck may occur when there is an entity used by one or more activities (e.g. Fig. 2). Moreover, it may occur when there is a collection representing for instance a line of production where the members (such as machines) play a role to define the bottleneck.

– A potential active tangible bottleneck may occur when one or more activities are associated with an agent (e.g. Fig. 3) or when one or more entities are attributed to an agent (e.g. Fig. 4).

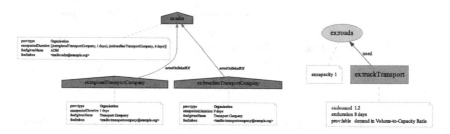

Fig. 1. Agent-agent relationship example

Fig. 2. Entity-activity relationship example

Within the case study, we see bottlenecks matching the rules applied to attributes in the potential bottleneck patterns, illustrated as follows. In Fig. 1, the trading company, ADM, delegated to two transport companies with the goal that soybeans were collected from a farm in one day, and after that reach port terminal in six days. The first company acts according to the set goal, but the second had another goal (9 days), and this discrepancy is an intangible bottleneck. In Fig. 2, roads are a resource shared between activities, with a volume-to-capacity ratio representing the number of vehicles passing through divided by the number of vehicles specified in the designed capacity (if it is greater than 1, then it is over capacity). The farmer was responsible for different entities with damage percentages not to exceed (e.g. the expected percentage of damage in storing bags was 10%, however it was 25%) (Fig. 3), and different activities which would be completed in specific durations (e.g. the expected duration for harvest was 31 days, however it took 40 days) (Fig. 4). As an example of an intangible bottleneck, the Soybean Moratorium (SoyM) [6] is a voluntary agreement to boycott trading soybeans grown on lands deforested after July 2006 in the Brazilian Amazon. SoyM is represented as a collection of companies, traders, etc. who signed it (Fig. 5). Members of this collection had to avoid trading with other parties which did not belong to this collection.

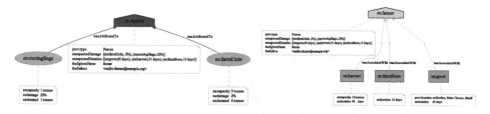

Fig. 3. Agent-entity relationship example

Fig. 4. Agent-activity relationship example

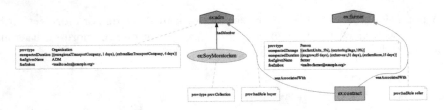

Fig. 5. Collection example

References

1. Lawrence, S.R., Buss, A.H.: Economic analysis of production bottlenecks. Math. Probl. Eng. **1**(4), 341–363 (1995)
2. Li, L., Chang, Q., Ni, J.: Data driven bottleneck detection of manufacturing systems. Int. J. Prod. Res. **47**(18), 5019–5036 (2009)
3. Beer, J.E.: Analysis and management of bottlenecks in supply networks: towards a structured approach to stabilization of inbound material flow (2015)
4. W3C Working Group: PROV Model Primer (2013)
5. Moreau, L., Groth, P., Cheney, J., Lebo, T., Miles, S.: The rationale of PROV. Web Semant. Sci. Serv. Agents World Wide Web **35**, 235–257 (2015)
6. Gibbs, H.K., et al.: Brazil's Soy Moratorium. Science **347**(6220), 377–378 (2015)

Architecture for Template-Driven Provenance Recording

Elliot Fairweather, Pinar Alper, Talya Porat, and Vasa Curcin$^{(\boxtimes)}$

King's College London, London, UK
{elliot.fairweather,vasa.curcin}@kcl.ac.uk

Abstract. Provenance templates define abstract patterns of provenance data and have been shown to be useful when implementing support for provenance capture in existing software tools. Their strength is in exposing only the relevant provenance capture actions through a service interface, whilst hiding the complexities associated with managing the provenance data. We present an architecture for the creation and management of libraries of provenance documents constructed using templates.

1 Introduction

Provenance templates define abstract patterns of provenance data and have been shown to be useful when implementing support for provenance capture in existing software tools. Their strength is in exposing only the relevant provenance capture actions through a service interface, whilst hiding the complexities associated with managing the provenance data. We expand upon the formal model presented earlier in [1] by refining the methods by which provenance fragments generated by such templates are combined and integrated into an overall provenance document, and present an architecture for the creation and management of libraries of such documents constructed using templates.

2 Methodology

A provenance template [1] is a abstract fragment of a provenance document, that may be instantiated using concrete substitutions for variables contained with the template. Variables are of two kinds; identifier variables inhabiting the var namespace which are placeholders for node or relation identifiers, and value variables under vvar, which can be used in the place of an attribute value. A provenance template is itself a valid provenance document and as such allows nodes to be semantically annotated, allowing the inclusion of domain-specific information. Concrete provenance fragments are generated by an algorithm that accepts as input a template and substitution comprised of a set of variable-value bindings, and replaces variables for values in a copy of the template. We now present a system for constructing and managing PROV documents using templates.

© Springer Nature Switzerland AG 2018
K. Belhajjame et al. (Eds.): IPAW 2018, LNCS 11017, pp. 217–221, 2018.
https://doi.org/10.1007/978-3-319-98379-0_23

Document Types. We distinguish three types of document, **target** documents, **template** documents and **fragment** documents. A target document is the document under construction. A system may manage the construction of multiple target documents at any given point. A template document describes a pattern representing a domain action to be replicated within a specific target document. A template document is registered to one particular target document. Call this target document the parent document of the template document. A fragment document is a document to be later merged into a target document, usually constructed by the instantiation of a template belonging to that document. A fragment document is also associated with a single target document, again referred to as its parent. Fragment documents perform a critical role in the document construction.

Metadata. All documents are given a unique identifier and annotated with their type. This is stored separately as metadata and used to index documents in the management system. This metadata also includes which templates and fragments are associated to a target document and namespace data for each document. Metadata can be viewed as consisting of and represented by attribute-value pairs that belong to a document.

Namespace Management. A data document is created empty with a default namespace. Further namespaces may be added at any point. Except for the `ivar`, `vvar` and `pgt` namespaces, a template document may only include namespaces included in its parent document. A fragment document includes the `fragment` namespace used for auditing purposes and during the instantiation process. When a new fragment document is created it also inherits the namespaces of its parent document. New namespaces may not be added to fragment documents. This means that qualified names contained in substitutions given during instantiation must fall within the namespaces of the target document.

Fragment Generation. When a template is instantiated the graph generated is represented as a new fragment document. The generation of new fragments from templates may proceed in two ways, either **simultaneously** as a single step by applying a complete substitution, or **incrementally**, by first applying an initial substitution and then later applying zone substitutions. In both cases, it must be checked that the number of iterations of each zone falls within the bounds of that zone for the final instantiation to be valid. Simultaneous generation is defined algorithmically in Fig. 6 of [1]. Incremental instantiation, however, in contrast to the description given there, is now considered to proceed in such a way that the fragment being generated is always connected. Entry and exit edges of zones are generated at the application of each zone substitution. In the case of serial zones, this requires that entry edges of the zone be repositioned upon each instantiation. Fragment documents are annotated with attribute-value pairs in the `fragment` namespace, as part of the mechanics of incremental instantiation but also for the purposes of auditing and analysis of the construction of the target document.

Merging and Grafting. When instantiation is finished, if the fragment document meets the iteration bound constraints for each zone the fragment is **merged** into the target document. This may result in the **grafting** of nodes. If the identifier of a node in a fragment pre-exists in the target document then that nodes is reused and a **graft** is created, joining the fragment and target documents. If the identifier of a fragment node does not exist in the target document a new node is created in the target. The merging process also adds additional attributes for the purpose of auditing. The validity of the target document is checked against the standard constraints of the PROV model following the merging of a fragment document. This is because the occurrence of grafting can lead to potential violations. If constraints are not met the merge is rolled back and the fragment removed from the target document.

Workflow. We now proceed to give a detailed account of the workflow of the system. In a typical scenario, in order to construct a new document, a user would interact with the system in the following way.

1. Create a new target document Δ
2. Add necessary extra namespaces to target Δ
3. Register templates with target Δ
4. Create a new fragment document Φ belonging to target Δ
   - (a) – by instantiating a template document with a complete substitution
     - i. by instantiating a template document T with an initial substitution
     - ii. and then adding iterations to fragment Φ by instantiating zones of the template T with zone substitutions
     - by importing a standard PROV document
   - (b) Merge fragment Φ into target Δ
5. Analyse and export target Δ or fragments of target Δ.

3   Architecture

We now discuss the architecture of the proposed system with reference to the implementation of the first author. The overall structure of the architecture can be seen in Fig. 1. The core of the system is the model component. Provenance documents are represented as graphs in which vertices and edges are typed and annotated with key-value pairs. The graph itself may also have key-value properties. Serialisation and deserialisation to PROV data formats is accomplished using the parsers provided by ProvToolbox library. Substitutions also form part of the model and parsers to both a proposed PROV-N format and JSON are given in the implementation. The template instantiation algorithm by which new fragment documents are generated from templates and substitutions is also defined within the model component. Storage of data in the system is abstracted by a persistence component to enable the use of different database technologies. By default, a Neo4j graph database is used but a relational database, SPARQL-enabled or alternative graph database could be used either instead or concurrently. The system is accessed via the document management component. This

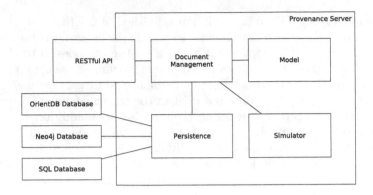

Fig. 1. Architecture

controls and executes operations outlined in the workflow, such as the creation of new target documents, namespace management, the registering of templates, and the generation and merging of new fragment documents. Fragment generation is achieved through interaction with the model component. Operations requiring the import, export or update of document data and metadata are supported via the persistence component. Access to the document management interface is provided via a RESTful web service. Documents and substitutions are passed to and from the server encoded as JSON and analysis is conducted by querying the underlying database. The specifics of a higher-level query interface for the system, agnostic to a particular storage solution, is an area of ongoing research.

4   Conclusions and Future Work

This poster presented an architecture for capturing provenance data using templates. The design is intentionally generic, allowing a similar approach to be applied to any software architecture where it is preferable to capture provenance by mirroring actions from the main software system, rather than embedding it into a shared middleware. Ultimately, our goal is to facilitate the development of provenance back-ends and minimise the overheads involved in integrating provenance capture and utilisation into operational workflows. We have prototyped our architecture based on a decision aid software tool for communicating the risk of recurrent stroke to patients, that is being developed within the stroke theme of the Collaborative Leadership in Applied Healthcare Research and Care (CLAHRC) programme in South London. A key challenge for implementing provenance solutions is how to extract benefit from the captured data, and so, as the next step, we plan to devise user interface solutions for provenance reporting from decision support scenarios and utilise our group's previous experience in the area [2] to conduct a full quantitative and qualitative evaluation.

References

1. Curcin, V., et al.: Templates as a method for implementing data provenance in decision support systems. J. Biomed. Inform. **65**(1), 1–21 (2017)
2. Kostopoulou, O., et al.: Diagnostic accuracy of GPs when using an early-intervention decision support system: a high-fidelity simulation. Br. J. Gen. Pract. **67**(656), e201–e208 (2017)

Combining Provenance Management and Schema Evolution

Tanja Auge[(⊠)] and Andreas Heuer[(⊠)]

University of Rostock, Rostock, Germany
tanja.auge@uni-rostock.de, heuer@informatik.uni-rostock.de
https://dbis.informatik.uni-rostock.de

Abstract. The combination of provenance management and schema evolution using the CHASE algorithm is the focus of our research in the area of research data management. The aim is to combine the construction of a CHASE inverse mapping to calculate the minimal part of the original database — the *minimal sub-database* — with a CHASE-based schema mapping for schema evolution.

Keywords: CHASE algorithm · Data provenance
Schema evolution · Data evolution · Schema mapping
CHASE inverse

1 Introduction

Collecting, recording, storing, tracking, and archiving scientific data is the task of research data management, which is the basis for scientific evaluations on this data. In addition to the evaluation (i.e., a complex database query that we call *evaluation query*) and the result itself, the section of the original database used has also to be archived. Thus, to ensure reproducible and replicable research, the evaluation queries can be processed again at a later point in time in order to reproduce the result.

If the data or the schema of the research database changes frequently, the original database would now have to be *frozen* (permanently stored) after every evaluation carried out on the database. In order to avoid this and in order to avoid massively replicated databases, we want to use provenance management techniques to calculate the minimal part of the database that must be frozen in order to be able to generate the query result again. For this, we want to combine techniques of **why** and **how** provenance [3] with the theory of schema mappings for data integration and data exchange, especially the inverse schema mappings of Fagin [5,6].

In research data management, the path from data collection to publication should be kept comprehensible, reconstructable, and replicable [9]. Since the research database is constantly changing [8] and thus represents a bitemporal database [7], the evolution of data and schemata must interact with the management and archiving of results, the management of the evaluation queries, and

© Springer Nature Switzerland AG 2018
K. Belhajjame et al. (Eds.): IPAW 2018, LNCS 11017, pp. 222–225, 2018.
https://doi.org/10.1007/978-3-319-98379-0_24

the provenance management. Unfortunately, data provenance research has normally been carried out on a fixed database. Two research goals of the project are therefore (1) the calculation of the minimal part of the original research database (we call it *minimal sub-database*) that has to be stored permanently to achieve replicable research, and (2) the unification of the theories behind data provenance and schema (as well as data) evolution.

2   Problem and Poster Description

2.1   Calculation of a Minimal Sub-database

The calculated minimal sub-database should be able to reconstruct the results of the evaluation query under various constraints. The following constraints range from very strict preconditions to weaker constraints:

- The number of tuples of the original relation is retained.
- The sub-database can be homomorphically mapped to the original database.
- The sub-database is an intensional description of the original database.

One specific problem is to decide about the minimal (additional) information that is required for the reconstruction of the sub-database, provided that the query result and the evaluation query is archived. Is it sufficient to pick up a minimum amount of witnesses (*why*-Provenance, [4]) or to calculate the associated provenance polynomials (*how*-Provenance, [10])? Or is it necessary to freeze whole tuples or other parts of the database directly?

The calculation of an inverse query Q_{prov}, which is used to determine the required minimal sub-database, depends on the type of the original query Q and any additional information noted. Thus a *result equivalent CHASE inverse* can be used for the projection [2]. A projection without duplicate elimination can be specified by a *relaxed CHASE inverse* and a simple copy operation by an *exact CHASE inverse* [6]. The homomorphism as a required condition mentioned above is a quite strong constraint which has to be weakened in future investigations [1].

2.2   Unification of Provenance and Evolution

Previous provenance queries Q_{prov} (*where*-, *why*- and *how*-provenance) have usually been processed on a given fixed database S_1 and a query Q. The combination of data provenance with schema and data evolution should enable the evaluation of provenance queries with changing data and schemata (see Fig. 1). By means of an inverse evolution step $\mathcal{E}^{-1}$, the new database J can be transferred to the old schema, if possible. Formally, our evaluation result is calculated by an extended CHASE algorithm, based on ST-TGDs (see below), and an (inverse) provenance query Q'_{prov} should be added in a second step, the BACKCHASE phase. The minimal sub-database I^* (red dashed box) is then computed by chasing the provenance query Q_{prov} into the query result $K^* \subseteq K$ (green box), adding the necessary provenance annotation (such as provenance polynomials).

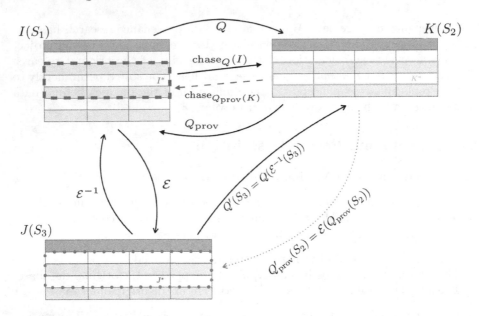

Fig. 1. Unification of provenance and evolution (Color figure online)

Under the schema evolution $\mathcal{E} : S_1 \rightarrow S_3$, the query Q' can be directly calculated as a composition of the original query Q and the inverse evolution $\mathcal{E}^{-1}$:

$$Q'(J(S_3)) = (\mathcal{E}^{-1} \circ Q)(J(S_3)) = Q(\mathcal{E}^{-1}(J(S_3))) = Q(I(S_1)).$$

The new provenance query Q'_{prov} results analogously as

$$Q'_{\text{prov}}(K^*(S_2)) = (Q_{\text{prov}} \circ \mathcal{E})(K^*(S_2)).$$

It is therefore sufficient to memorize one of the two minimal sub-databases $I^*(S_1)$ (red dashed box) or $J^*(S_3)$ (blue dotted box). The other can be calculated with the help of the inverse. In research data management, K^* always corresponds to the entire result database K, i.e. $K^* = K$, since the complete result of the scientific evaluation has to be reproducible. However, general provenance queries can also be processed on subsets of this result (or even on single tuples in the result).

2.3   Query Q

The representation of the evaluation query Q in the form of extended S-T TGDs (*source-to-target tuple-generating dependencies*) or EGDs (*equality-generating dependencies*) allows the application of the CHASE algorithm [5,6]. This incorporates a set of dependencies, here S-T TGDs and EGDs, into a given database instance. The calculation of a CHASE inverse Q_{prov} via the BACKCHASE involves the reconstruction of the minimal sub-database I^* of the original database $I(S_1)$.

2.4 Evolution $\mathcal{E}$

By using the inverse $\mathcal{E}^{-1}$, the old minimal sub-database I^* can be calculated from the current minimal sub-database J^*. For this, the evolution $\mathcal{E}$ and its (exact) inverse $\mathcal{E}^{-1}$ are formulated as S-T TGDs and EGDs and processed by the CHASE algorithm.

2.5 Data Provenance Q_{prov}

The result of the evaluation query Q described by extended S-T TGDs and EGDs can be calculated using the CHASE algorithm. The subsequent construction of the minimal sub-database I^* succeeds by inverting the query Q. This inverse Q_{prov} doesn't necessarily have to correspond to an inverse in the classical sense

$$Q \circ Q_{\mathrm{prov}} = \mathrm{Id},$$

since a *CHASE inverse* can't always be specified [5,6]. In most cases, however, a *result equivalent CHASE inverse* [1,2] can be specified that returns the same result after applying the CHASE algorithm to the original instance I and the minimal sub-database I^* calculated using the BACKCHASE.

References

1. Auge, T., Heuer, A.: Inverse im Forschungsdatenmanagement. In: Proceedings of 30th Workshop Grundlagen von Datenbanken (2018, accepted for publication, to appear). (in German)
2. Auge, T.: Umsetzung von Provenance-Anfragen in Big-Data-Analytics-Umgebungen. Master's thesis, University of Rostock (2017). (in German)
3. Cheney, J., Chiticariu, L., Tan, W.C.: Provenance in databases: why, how and where. Found. Trends Databases **1**(4), 379–474 (2009)
4. Buneman, P., Khanna, S., Tan, W.C.: Why and where: a characterization of data provenance. In: Van den Bussche, J., Vianu, V. (eds.) ICDT 2001. LNCS, vol. 1973, pp. 316–330. Springer, Heidelberg (2001). https://doi.org/10.1007/3-540-44503-X_20
5. Fagin, R.: Inverting schema mappings. ACM Trans. Database Syst. **32**(4), 25-1–25-53 (2007)
6. Fagin, R., Kolaitis, P.G., Popa, L., Tan, W.C.: Schema mapping evolution through composition and inversion. In: Bellahsene, Z., Bonifati, A., Rahm, E. (eds.) Schema Matching and Mapping. DCSA, pp. 191–222. Springer, Heidelberg (2011). https://doi.org/10.1007/978-3-642-16518-4_7
7. Johnston, T.: Bitemporal Data: Theory and Practice. Morgan Kaufmann, Burlington (2014)
8. Bruder, I., Klettke, M., Möller, M.L., Meyer, F., Heuer, A., Jürgensmann, S., Feistel, S.: Daten wie Sand am Meer – Datenerhebung, -strukturierung, -management und Data Provenance für die Ostseeforschung. Datenbank-Spektrum **17**(2), 183–196 (2017). (in German)
9. Heuer, A.: METIS in PArADISE: Provenance Management bei der Auswertung von Sensordatenmengen für die Entwicklung von Assistenzsystemen. In: BTW Workshops. LNI, vol. 242, pp. 131–136. GI (2015). (in German)
10. Green, T.J., Karvounarakis, G., Tannen, V.: Provenance semirings. In: PODS, pp. 31–40. ACM (2007)

Provenance for Entity Resolution

Sarah Oppold[(⊠)] and Melanie Herschel[(⊠)]

IPVS, University of Stuttgart, Universitätsstr. 38, 70569 Stuttgart, Germany
{sarah.oppold,melanie.herschel}@ipvs.uni-stuttgart.de

Abstract. Data provenance can support the understanding and debugging of complex data processing pipelines, which are for instance common in data integration scenarios. One task in data integration is entity resolution (ER), i.e., the identification of multiple representations of a same real world entity. This paper focuses of provenance modeling and capture for typical ER tasks. While our definition of ER provenance is independent of the actual language or technology used to define an ER task, the method we implement as a proof of concept instruments ER rules specified in HIL, a high-level data integration language.

Keywords: Data provenance · Entity resolution · Data integration

1 Motivation

Entity resolution (ER) refers to the problem of identifying duplicates, i.e., multiple representations of or references to a same real-world entity within or across data sources [1]. While numerous different solutions exist, they typically follow the same steps, building a generic ER pipeline.

Provenance may facilitate the understanding and debugging of data processing pipelines. While several provenance types exist for various applications [5], to the best of our knowledge, no solution has been tailored to ER. Here, determining which input data led to a duplicate is not very informative (the data provenance equals the duplicates). Instead, it is more relevant to see how these data affect ER processing. We therefore define a provenance model for ER.

One means to collect ER provenance is to instrument the original program defining ER by modifying it to return, in addition to the ER result, the corresponding provenance. We opt for this solution for two reasons: (i) the modified program can run on the same system as the original program, leveraging any optimizations implemented and (ii) the returned provenance is in the same format as the original output data, facilitating further processing.

In summary, we present a model for provenance describing how data was processed during ER. This model is independent of the actual language or processing engine used to specify and run ER. Indeed, we first abstract ER tasks to algebraic operators to then define provenance on this abstract representation (Sect. 2). In Sect. 3, we discuss how to capture provenance conforming to the abstract model by instrumenting ER rules specified in HIL, a data integration

K. Belhajjame et al. (Eds.): IPAW 2018, LNCS 11017, pp. 226–230, 2018.
https://doi.org/10.1007/978-3-319-98379-0_25

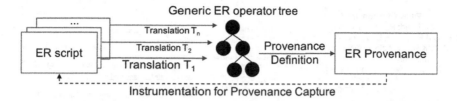

Fig. 1. Overview of the general approach

language developed at IBM [2]. We conclude the paper in Sect. 4 with a summary and an outlook on further research questions.

2   Provenance Model for Abstract ER Pipelines

Figure 1 summarizes our general approach. While many different formalisms to specify ER exist, they typically map to a generic model consisting of algebraic operators. This model forms the basis to define general ER provenance. Conceptually, ER provenance capture can then be achieved by first translating an ER script to the abstract model, to then execute provenance capture defined over this abstract model. This however would entail significant overhead, both in runtime and system complexity compared to running ER alone. A more lightweight solution that we pursue is the instrumentation of ER scripts such that both ER and ER provenance capture run on the original data processing system.

ER tasks typically divide into a pipeline consisting of several common steps (e.g., see [1]). The input comprises two datasets A and B (it is possible that $A = B$). The output are partitions of pairs of entity descriptions (e.g., tuples in relational data) in $A \times B$ such that all entity descriptions in a partition refer to the same entity while no two partitions share entity descriptions referring to the same entity. Considering all pairs in $A \times B$ is computationally prohibitive, so *blocking* prunes pairs from further processing. During *pairwise classification*, the remaining pairs are compared, e.g., using similarity measures or domain-knowledge to ultimately decide whether or not the pair is a duplicate. Finally, *post-processing* views the classifications as a graph where vertices represent entity descriptions and edges connect duplicates. It partitions the graph, handling conflicting classifications (e.g., a, b and b, c duplicates, but a, c non-duplicates) and enforcing additional constraints (e.g., on cardinalities [2]).

Figure 2(a) shows a sample ER rule specified in HIL [2]. The syntax is not important, we use the rule to illustrate the different steps of ER. Here, persons in one source are matched with customers from another source. To avoid comparing all persons with all customers, blocking requires them to have the same ZIP code. Then, persons with same ZIP code are classified as duplicates if they match at least one of two rules (labeled match1 and match2). Finally, a constraint requires that a person can match at most one customer and vice versa. This is enforced during post-processing by pruning pairwise matches violating the constraint.

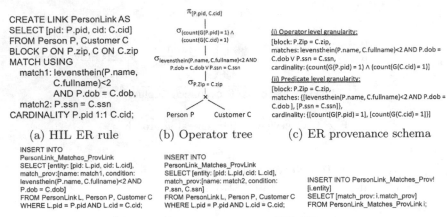

(a) HIL ER rule   (b) Operator tree   (c) ER provenance schema

(d) Provenance capture using HIL EP rules

Fig. 2. Running example

The ER steps described above are common to many different ER solutions, which we can thus map to an abstract representation. We have defined an abstract description of ER pipelines using operators of the Nested Relational Algebra for Bags (NRAB) [3]. Indeed, we want to cover ER both on flat relational and nested data and cannot assume that data is free of exact duplicates. Figure 2(b) illustrates the operator tree for the HIL script shown in Fig. 2(a). For HIL, we have defined a full set of inference rules to map any HIL ER script to an operator tree, similarly to our previous work where we compile PigLatin to NRAB [4]. We cannot cover the details here, but highlight a few principles based on the example. First, we form all pairs of entity descriptions using the Cartesian product ×. Blocking prunes pairs and can thus be modeled using a selection σ. The matching performs pairwise classification that returns only those pairs that satisfy either of the match conditions, resulting in a selection operator with a complex predicate in DNF. Finally, the constraint of the 1:1 cardinality requires both grouping G and selection based on the size of groups. The ER rules in HIL return pairs of duplicates, which translates to the final projection π.

Given ER pipelines defined by trees of NRAB operators with clear semantics, data provenance (i.e., why- and how-provenance) [5] is a candidate choice for ER provenance. However, it focuses on data flow, which is not informative for ER, as the provenance of a duplicate pair simply consists of the pair members. Instead, we propose to capture the control flow of the pipeline. More specifically, we record, at each processing stage, the results of function calls, comparisons etc. in addition to data valuations. For efficiency and understandability reasons, we define two granularities of ER provenance: (i) the granularity of operators and (ii) the granularity of individual predicates in the operator parameters. Figure 2(c) shows the schema of the provenance at these two granularities for our running example. An example instance of the second granularity is $[70569 = 70569, \{[1 < 2, 5/29/60 = 6/29/60], 123\text{-}45\text{-}678 = 123\text{-}45\text{-}678\}, 1 = 1]$.

This evaluates to $[true, \{[true, false], true\}, true]$, clearly indicating that the duplicate was found based on match2 only, as unequal dates let match1 fail.

3   Implementing Provenance Capture for HIL ER Rules

As motivated previously, we opt for program instrumentation to capture provenance for ER. As a proof of concept, we have formalized and implemented the instrumentation of HIL scripts [2] that allow the specification of ER rules, illustrated in Fig. 2(a). Our implementation supports the full set of HIL ER rule clauses (not all are illustrated here). Given a HIL script with an ER rule, we generate additional entity population (EP) rules. These rules are an integral part of the HIL language and will, when executed, produce the provenance conforming to our general ER provenance. Figure 2(d) shows EP rules generated for the sample HIL ER rule of Fig. 2(a). Capturing the necessary provenance using HIL constructs requires several intermediate steps, the final provenance being stored in the result labeled *PersonLink_Matches_Prov*. A detailed discussion is out of the scope of this paper, but the example showcases the complexity of instrumenting HIL for provenance capture.

4   Conclusion and Outlook

This paper presented a framework for defining and capturing provenance for typical ER pipelines. We showed how ER pipelines consisting of several common steps map to trees of algebraic operators. We then defined ER provenance over this abstract ER representation, thus providing a language-independent provenance model. To capture ER provenance in practice, we showed how to instrument a particular language to specify ER, namely HIL ER rules to capture ER provenance conforming to our model.

In the future, we plan to extend provenance capture to further data integration tasks from both a language-independent and a HIL specific perspective. Further important issues for making provenance capture practical and relevant for users are runtime optimizations and provenance visualization, exploration, and querying.

Acknowledgements. The authors thank the German Research Foundation (DFG) for financial support within project D03 of SFB/ Transregio 161. This research was also partly funded by an IBM Faculty Award.

References

1. Christen, P.: Data Matching: Concepts and Techniques for Record Linkage, Entity Resolution, and Duplicate Detection. Data-Centric Systems and Applications. Springer, Heidelberg (2012). https://doi.org/10.1007/978-3-642-31164-2
2. Hernández, M.A., Koutrika, G., Krishnamurthy, R., Popa, L., Wisnesky, R.: HIL: a high-level scripting language for entity integration. In: EDBT (2013)

3. Grumbach, S., Milo, T.: Towards Tractable Algebras for Bags. In: PODS (1993)
4. Camacho-Rodríguez, J., Colazzo, D., Herschel, M., Manolescu, I., Roy Chowdhury, S.: Reuse-based optimization for pig latin. In: CIKM (2016)
5. Herschel, M., Diestelkämper, R., Lahmar, H.B.: A survey on provenance: what for? What form? What from? VLDB J. (2017)

Where Provenance in Database Storage

Alexander Rasin$^{(\boxtimes)}$, Tanu Malik, James Wagner, and Caleb Kim

DePaul University, Chicago, IL 60604, USA
{arasin,tanu}@cdm.depaul.edu, {jwagne32,khim85}@mail.depaul.edu

Abstract. *Where* provenance is a relationship between a data item and the location from which this data was copied. In a DBMS, a typical use of *where* provenance is in establishing a copy-by-address relationship between the output of a query and the particular data value(s) that originated it. Normal DBMS operations create a variety of auxiliary copies of the data (e.g., indexes, MVs, cached copies). These copies exist over time with relationships that evolve continuously – (A) indexes maintain the copy with a reference to the origin value, (B) MVs maintain the copy without a reference to the source table, (C) cached copies are created once and are never maintained. A query may be answered from any of these auxiliary copies; however, this *where* provenance is not computed or maintained. In this paper, we describe sources from which forensic analysis of storage can derive *where* provenance of table data. We also argue that this computed where provenance can be useful (and perhaps necessary) for accurate forensic reports and evidence from maliciously altered databases or validation of corrupted DBMS storage.

Keywords: Where Provenance · Database Forensics
DBMS Anti-Tampering

1 Introduction

Where Provenance is defined as the addresses of the data values that were used to evaluate the query. It is similar to *Why Provenance* in tracing query inputs, but focuses on the location of that data. In the relational model, value location is defined as the row (tuple) and the value's location within that row. We propose to extend this concept to support database forensic analysis by computing *where* provenance based on the physical address of data copies in DBMS storage.

Database Management Systems (DBMSes) generate a multitude of data copies as part of their normal operation. For example, a materialized view (MV) stores the pre-computed results of a query drawn from the data tables in order to improve query performance. An index contains a copy of values from the indexed column(s) combined with a pointer back to the source table in order to speed up record access. Many other copies of data are created by DBMS engine actions such as caching, log entries, or internal storage defragmentation.

These and other internal copies of data can be extracted from DBMS storage with the help of *database carving* (briefly described in Sect. 2) and used for

© Springer Nature Switzerland AG 2018
K. Belhajjame et al. (Eds.): IPAW 2018, LNCS 11017, pp. 231–235, 2018.
https://doi.org/10.1007/978-3-319-98379-0_26

evidence of database tampering or storage corruption. Such findings must be supported by a forensic analysis framework that integrates *where* provenance to formalize storage analysis and offer provable results. Recent work by Wagner et al. [1] relied on ad-hoc case analysis (e.g., if the index value does not match the value in table record, report this as a likely indication of tampering) to report malicious activity. Such reports currently require significant effort from forensic analysts – we describe two recent cases that would greatly benefit from integration of *where* provenance into the process of forensic analysis:

Example 1. A consultant from Mandiant/FireEye (a major forensic firm) was working on a case involving a hard drive captured from the suspect. Through manual inspection of drive image, he came to suspect that the drive contained a PostgreSQL database that was uninstalled by the owner. Reconstructing raw data was the first step – but if the case went to court, the analyst could use *where* provenance to prove that the accuracy of reconstructed data report.

Example 2. A forensic analyst from Royal Canadian Mounted Police was investigating a financial fraud case. One of the sources of evidence was a snapshot of RAM from suspect's computer that contained a MySQL database (the snapshot of the hard drive was never recovered in this case). While RAM can contain data from DBMS tables, all of the in-RAM values are *copies* of the original tables. In order to establish MySQL data contents from RAM snapshot with a measure of confidence, a *where* provenance derivation could be used.

In addition to these examples, there are other security and audit applications of *where* provenance that we outline in Sect. 3. Fully deriving and continuously tracking where provenance remains a goal for future work. In this paper, we define the categories of data copies created within all major DBMSes. We consider the causal relationship between the tables and auxiliary structures in DBMS storage, including **active** data, **accessible** data, **abandoned** data.

2   Background and Related Work

Relational databases store data in page units of fixed size – even logs are often stored in system tables. Pages in relational databases (including IBM DB2, SQL Server, Oracle, PostgreSQL, MySQL, Apache Derby, MariaDB, and Firebird) follow the same basic layout structure. The work in [2] described how this layout can be generally parameterized, reconstructed and even automatically learned by loading synthetic data and observing storage behavior. Database page carving (implemented as DBCarver [3]) is a method based on this analysis that reconstructs database file contents without relying on the file system or DBMS. It is also capable of extracting the non-queryable data values, which include: (a) index values and pointers, (b) deleted records, including partially overwritten records, (c) cache contents, including pages and intermediate query results, (d) audit logs.

3   Motivating Where Provenance in DBMSes

A forensic analysts will seek to discover and prove what is or was previously stored in the database tables, or to determine what actions user may have undertaken within the DBMS. While traditional provenance explains query output by investigating the data sources and the computation process of the query, in forensic cases the target of analysis is the data table itself. For each additional data copy (index, MV, RAM), *where* provenance of that copy will serve as support and evidence for contents of the original table.

Figure 1 represents the overall flow of data copying that occurs inside a DBMS engine. After user data is loaded into tables (data loading process can create extra copies in RAM or logs), every access to these tables will cause more copying. A SQL command is initially copied into the audit log; after the query is logged, it proceeds to access the tables. Table access affects several parts of DBMS storage: modifications prop-

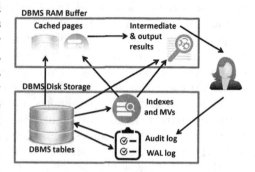

Fig. 1. The causality flow of data in DBMS.

agate into WAL, both read and write access caches pages in RAM (including intermediate results), and all auxiliary structures are cached in a similar manner.

The goal of this paper is to describe the copies that occur along the flow arrows in Fig. 1. Computing *where* provenance (not available in DBMSes) would also require *reversing* the arrows by extrapolating the connection back to the table. For example, a record found in a cached page is evidence of a tuple having been present (at some point) in a source table. The location of the cached record is known, but *where* provenance also needs the link between that copy and the original table record. Note that the original table record may already be *deleted* (can be restored) or even *erased* (cannot be restored) in which case *where* provenance offers evidence for the source data that ceased to exist.

The second application for *where* provenance is tracing back the arrow between audit log and data tables. The idea is that each forensic artifact (e.g., a deleted row) must have been caused by *some* SQL command. User commands (in Fig. 1) recorded in audit log cause changes to data tables. Therefore, if we find a storage artifact (e.g., a deleted row) that does not link back to an audit log command, this could be interpreted as a sign of log tampering.

4   Forensic Evidence in Where Provenance

The three categories of data copies include (1) actively maintained data copies which encompasses indexes, MVs, and cached copies, (2) accessible data copies (not actively maintained, may be out-of-date) including old MV values, audit and WAL logs, and (3) abandoned data copies that consist of all deleted values (in tables, MVs, and indexes), old cached values and discarded DBMS pages.

Once *where* provenance of data copies is computed, it will be unified into a report describing (1) the data values contained within the target of the investigation, (2) the relative confidence in each reported value, and (3) an extrapolated timeline information for each data value.

The target of the investigation can be either user data tables or WAL log. For data tables, Part-#1 would include *every value and every record* for which some evidence of existence (at any time) was identified. This will include data from primary evidence sources (data tables), secondary evidence sources (cached table pages, indexes, MVs), tertiary evidence sources (indexes over MVs, cached index pages), and so on. In cases like Example 2 in Sect. 1 (only RAM data is available), the entire report will be based on secondary evidence or lower.

A reported value may derive from conflicting facts (e.g., on-disk table page and in-RAM cached page disagreeing on what the value was). Part-#2 would therefore seek to unify multiple reports about each value. A value with multiple agreeing sources would have higher confidence; a value with disagreeing or lower tier (e.g., tertiary) sources would have a relatively low confidence. Most importantly, confidence report should include reasons for how it was derived.

Finally, Part-#3 would further annotate all reported values with known timeline information. Evidence of each reported value will be associated with the time range during which it (likely) existed. For example, audit logs may help determine the exact time when the value was created and subsequently deleted.

5 Conclusion

DBMS storage is a rich source of data copies created during normal operations and accessible through forensic analysis. These copies can serve as evidence of database state or proof of DBMS content tampering. *Where* provenance is the mechanism that can create a formal analytical framework to explain and quantify accuracy and of the forensic evidence reliability drawn from storage analysis.

A report of all known data augmented with confidence rating and timeline knowledge will no doubt greatly help forensic and security analysts in their job. Copies of the data are available – but these copies lack the connection to their source; in order to reason about the evidence they offer, copy flow in DBMS storage must be reverse engineered.

Acknowledgments. This material is based upon work supported by the National Science Foundation Grant CNS-1656268.

References

1. Wagner, J., et al.: Carving database storage to detect and trace security breaches. Digit. Invest. **22**, S127–S136 (2017)
2. Wagner, J., Rasin, A., Grier, J.: Database image content explorer: Carving data that does not officially exist. Digit. Invest. **18**, S97–S107 (2016)
3. Wagner, J., Rasin, A., Malik, T., Hart, K., Jehle, H., Grier, J.: Database forensic analysis with DBCarver. In: CIDR (2017)

Streaming Provenance Compression

Raza Ahmad[1], Melanie Bru[2], and Ashish Gehani[1(✉)]

[1] SRI International, Menlo Park, CA, USA
{raza.ahmad,ashish.gehani}@sri.com
[2] Ecole Polytechnique, Palaiseau, France
melanie.bru@sri.com

Abstract. Operating system data provenance has a range of applications, such as security monitoring, debugging heterogeneous runtime environments, and profiling complex applications. However, fine-grained collection of provenance over extended periods of time can result in large amounts of metadata. Xie *et al.* describe an algorithm that leverages the subgraph similarity and locality of reference in provenance graphs to perform batch compression. We build on their effort to construct an online version that can perform streaming compression in SPADE. Our optimizations provide both performance and compression improvements over their baseline.

1 Introduction

Constructing streams of provenance online facilitates a range of real-time applications, including debugging runtime environments and profiling workflows comprised of diverse components. Systems like SPADE [2] are challenged to process, store, and query large streams efficiently within short windows of time. One solution to alleviate the problem is to reduce the size of the provenance metadata before committing it to persistent storage. To this end, several methods have been presented for specific use cases [1,3,4].

Xie *et al.* [5] describe how to store provenance efficiently using techniques from web graph compression. They divide the information contained in a provenance graph into *identity* and *ancestor* information. Identity information is comprised of annotations on edges and vertices. It is compressed using dictionary encoding to eliminate information duplication. Ancestor information describes dependencies between vertices. It consists of a set of edges represented as an adjacency list. This list is encoded using three steps: *reference compression, run-length encoding*, and *delta encoding*. Reference compression finds a reference r for each vertex v, such that their adjacency lists have maximum overlap. This overlap is stored only once with non-overlapping elements stored using run-length encoding and delta encoding. These methods save space by utilizing consecutive subsequences and storing differences between the identifiers of successive elements, respectively.

M. Bru—While visiting SRI.

© Springer Nature Switzerland AG 2018
K. Belhajjame et al. (Eds.): IPAW 2018, LNCS 11017, pp. 236–240, 2018.
https://doi.org/10.1007/978-3-319-98379-0_27

We improve Xie *et al.*'s algorithm with several optimizations. Our implementation provides better performance and compression when compared with the baseline, as shown in Sect. 2.

2 Contributions

We implemented the improvements in SPADE, an open source data provenance framework with a decentralized architecture. In our evaluation, data was collected from Linux Audit over 78 min. It is comprised of 73 thousand vertices and 200 thousand edges. To realize a reproducible stream processing setting, the audit log was replayed in SPADE while performing online compression. We optimize Xie *et al.*'s algorithm as follows:

Bidirectional Traversal: Xie *et al.* only stored the parent information for vertices. This information is insufficient to satisfy common provenance queries efficiently, such as finding all neighbors of a given vertex or finding descendants of a vertex. We include numeric identifiers for both the *parents* and *children* of every vertex. During insertion, we separately compress and store them in the adjacency list.

Reference Selection (ref): During *reference compression*, the reference y for a new vertex x is selected to maximize the overlap between the adjacency lists of x and y. This

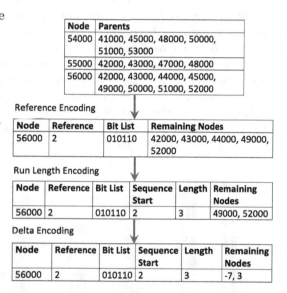

Fig. 1. Three steps of the web compression algorithm by Xie *et al.*, illustrated in a step-by-step example.

overlap is stored in x as a bit list of size equal to that of adjacency list of y. If the size of the adjacency list of y is significantly larger than that of x, space is used to store many zeroes. To improve this, we search for a y that optimizes for the maximum number of 1's and miminum number of 0's in the resultant bit list.

Delta Encoding of Sequences (delta): In the second step of run length encoding, each sequence of consecutive identifiers is encoded using the first vertex's identifier followed by the sequence length, as shown in Fig. 1. However, the starting vertex identifiers could be very large for big datasets, occupying

significant storage for multiple sequences. Hence, we perform delta encoding at
this step as well, storing only the differences between successive starting vertex
identifiers.

Uncompressed Buffer (buffer): During insertion of an edge $e(x, y)$, a fast
lookup of the adjacency lists of previous vertices is needed. Retrieving this information from the disk becomes temporally expensive as database size grows. We
buffer the uncompressed adjacency lists for a subset of vertices. The required
adjacency list of references can then often be found in memory during compression, eliminating the time needed to search the disk and uncompress the
list.

Adjacency List Caching (cache): Even with the above uncompressed buffer,
some queries may need to be resolved using slower persistent storage. We implemented an in-memory cache of compressed adjacency lists to improve performance. When an element is not found in the uncompressed buffer, this cache
is consulted. To maintain consistency, the cache is periodically synchronized
with the underlying database. This allows end user queries to be satisfied while
provenance elements continue to stream into the system.

In the case that the workload is small enough or sufficiently compressible,
the entire adjacency list may fit in memory. This case results in the highest-
performance insertion and querying.

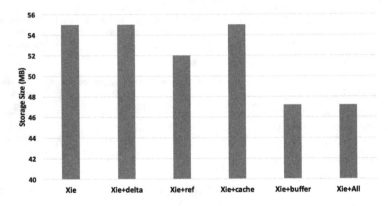

Fig. 2. Effect of individual optimizations on total storage size. *Xie+All* is the case
when they are combined.

We implemented five optimizations and studied their effect on storage size,
insertion time, and query time. The baseline for comparison is our reimplemen-
tation of Xie *et al.*'s algorithm. When all our optimizations are employed, the
size of the compressed provenance significantly decreases when compared to the
baseline, as illustrated in Fig. 2. Our approach improves insertion times by a

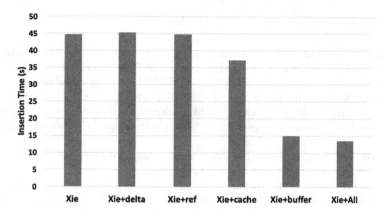

Fig. 3. Effect of individual optimizations on time taken to insert all records in the database.

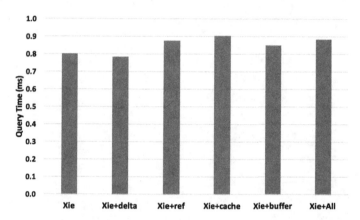

Fig. 4. Effect of individual optimizations on query execution time. Query time is the average time taken to execute 1000 lineage descendant queries of depth 5, starting from randomly chosen vertices.

factor of three, when compared to the baseline, as seen in Fig. 3. This is of particular import in a streaming setting. Finally, we report query time performance in Fig. 4.

Acknowledgements. This material is based upon work supported by the National Science Foundation under Grant ACI-1547467. Any opinions, findings, and conclusions or recommendations expressed in this material are those of the authors and do not necessarily reflect the views of the National Science Foundation.

References

1. Chapman, A., Jagadish, H., Ramanan, P.: Efficient provenance storage. In: 34th ACM International Conference on Management of Data (SIGMOD) (2008)
2. Gehani, A., Kazmi, H., Irshad, H.: Scaling SPADE to "big provenance". In: 8th USENIX Workshop on Theory and Practice of Provenance (TaPP) (2016)
3. Jeannot, E., Knutsson, B., Bjorkman, M.: Adaptive online data compression. In: 11th IEEE International Symposium on High Performance Distributed Computing (HPDC) (2002)
4. Li, X., Xu, X., Malik, T.: Interactive provenance summaries for reproducible science. In: 12th IEEE Conference on e-Science (2016)
5. Xie, Y., Muniswamy-Reddy, K.-K., Feng, D., Li, Y., Long, D.: Evaluation of a hybrid approach for efficient provenance storage. ACM Trans. Storage (TOS), **9**(4) (2013)

Structural Analysis of Whole-System Provenance Graphs

Jyothish Soman[✉], Thomas Bytheway, Lucian Carata,
Nikilesh D. Balakrishnan, Ripduman Sohan, and Robert N. M. Watson

Computer Laboratory, University of Cambridge, Cambridge, UK
{jyothish.soman,thomas.bytheway,lucian.carata,nikilesh.balakrishnan,
ripduman.sohan,robert.watson}@cl.cam.ac.uk

Abstract. System based provenance generates traces captured from various systems, a representation method for inferring these traces is a graph. These graphs are not well understood, and current work focuses on their extraction and processing, without a thorough characterization being in place. This paper studies the topology of such graphs. We analyze multiple Whole-system-Provenance graphs and present that they have hubs-and-authorities model of graphs as well as a power law distribution. Our observations allow for a novel understanding of the structure of Whole-system-Provenance graphs.

1 Introduction

Provenance has become a topic of relevance lately with the advent of multiple systems which augment the existing ones using provenance [1,6]. There are multiple WSP capturing systems which can generate detailed data regarding the interactions happening at the machine level, these are naturally representable as graphs. For such provenance systems, the structure and evolution of the graph are both relevant in the design and optimisation of the storage, analysis and synthetic data generators. This has equivalence in other domains such as webgraphs, social networks, road-networks etc. A large volume of work present in literature support this [2,7]. For example, the work in [7] presents the analysis of the spread of disease in a human-interaction network. This draws parallels with security related WSP research.

With this aim, we present an analysis of provenance graphs. Process traces are taken from a set of running machines, and the structure of the graphs so generated are studied. The results are used to present that the graphs are similar in structure to a well studied class of graphs namely, Power-law graphs. Additionally, we are able to show that they are similar to a Hubs-and-Authorities model of graphs [3] In the rest of the paper, nodes, edges and degree are used to only discuss the graph properties. Degree represents the total number of edges, both incoming and outgoing from a given node.

OPUS and PVM: OPUS [1] is a user space provenance system designed for tracking provenance on a system. For this work, it was used to provide a graph

© Springer Nature Switzerland AG 2018
K. Belhajjame et al. (Eds.): IPAW 2018, LNCS 11017, pp. 241–244, 2018.
https://doi.org/10.1007/978-3-319-98379-0_28

representation of the various interactions on a tracked machine, both implicit and explicit in the form of a graph. In OPUS, a process is considered the active agent, and the changes made by it are tracked. This includes interactions of the process with files and the I/O systems and its communication with other processes using pipes and sockets. OPUS uses Provenance-Versioning-Model (PVM) to handle state changes in entities, this is done with the intention of reducing the number of false dependencies, and de-densifying the resulting graph.

2   Graph Types in WSP

In the current context, two set of graph models are relevant, namely power-law graphs and the Hubs-and-Authorities graph model. In this section, we would discuss them in further detail.

Power-Law Graphs: Power-law graphs have a degree distribution of the form $n(k) = Ax^k$, where $n(k)$ is the number of nodes with a degree k, and A and x are constants. Such graphs also tend to have a tail in the degree distribution. Examples include human-interaction networks such as social-networks, IMDB actors graphs, web-graphs, email graphs, citation graphs and recommendation-networks, to technological graphs such as Autonomous system graphs, web-graphs etc. [4]. Such graphs are also common in time-evolving graphs where interactions (edges) and elements (nodes) are added to an already existing graph.

In machines, such a process is possible as a limited number of processes and files have a higher probability of addition of incoming edges to them. Longer standing processes would accumulate both incoming and outgoing edges. Additionally, files and libraries would have multiple processes linking to them over time. Hence, the number of edges they accumulate would increase, which is in line with the preferential attachment theory.

Hubs and Authorities: In Hubs-and-Authorities (HaA) model of Kleinberg [3], each node can be either a hub or an authority. Hubs are nodes which connect high relevance nodes, and authorities are representative of the immediate neighbourhood. An authority on the other hand would be specialised nodes, and would only have information regarding a specific issue. HaA model also allows for a class of nodes which cannot be classified as either and are disregarded. The equivalent in WSP would be processes being authorities, and files, sockets and other mediums by which they share state being hubs.

The power-law graphs and HaA model together can be used to describe the graphs present in WSP. In Sect. 4, we would present graphs and their structural and property similarities to these two models.

3   Setup

For the generation of the test graphs, single machine-level traces using DTrace running on FREEBSD were taken from multiple machines running varied applications. A total of 9 traces are captured on active machines running multiple processes. OPUS was used to summarise the graphs and to merge nodes from the traces to form a more cohesive view of the traces.

4   Results

The analysis in this section deals with the graph structure, in terms of the degree distribution and general structure of the graph.

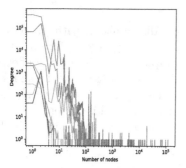

Fig. 1. Degree distribution.

Fig. 2. Graph showing all interactions across 100 connected elements. (Color figure online)

Figure 2 shows a small graph from which dangling nodes and nodes with no outgoing edges are removed. In this graph, the community property of the graph is better visible with two clear groups visible. This graph is similar in structure to the dolphin social network [5]. In the dolphin social network, there are two large groups, one of which is densely connected, and the other one is relatively sparse. In Fig. 2, the purple nodes are processes, red and green are files, and yellow represents sockets. Processes are central to the graph, with files providing bridging connection between the nodes. This is a recurring structure in the graphs studied in this work. From this, we can extrapolate that similar interactions will be present in traces captured from other machines as well.

Figure 1 shows the degree distribution across all the 9 traces. It can be seen that the power law distribution is followed by all the graphs. Do note that versioning causes nodes to version, taking along all the active connections to the next node. Such high degree nodes suggest that certain nodes are able to have active connections to a large subset of the system. From a system stability and security perspective, these are high value nodes, and would need to be stable for a large duration of time. Additionally, such nodes would also add pressure on the storage system, as it would be continuously adding edges, and a graph storage engine which does not coalesce storage for the edges of such nodes, would cause large parts of th storage to be read multiple times.

Effect of Graph Structure on Storage and Analytics: For storage and caching, the presence of high degree nodes can cause significant cache trashing given OPUS like versioning. Access to the properties of the nodes connected to such a high value node would require multiple accesses to the underlying storage. These nodes were added to the system earlier and would have varying lifetimes and hence likely to be stored in different parts of the storage. Thus, a conventional caching mechanism can cause significant cache trashing, as any such access can lead to a large number of cache-evictions.

5   Conclusions

This paper presents that WSP show a power-law distribution, with processes forming the hubs and the other elements connecting the processes forming the authorities. The lifetime of a node in the WSP graph is limited and the effects of such transient nature is also shown. Given the hub-authorities model, the lifetime does not affect the power-law model as long-lasting processes accumulate more edges, and system-critical read-only files do the same. This presents opportunities for not just storage engine, but also to caching, and analysis methods associated with the system.

Acknowledgements. This work is part of the CADETS Project sponsored by the Defense Advanced Research Projects Agency (DARPA) and the Air Force Research Laboratory (AFRL), under contract FA8650-15-C-7558. The views, opinions, and/or findings contained in this paper are those of the authors and should not be interpreted as representing the official views or policies, either expressed or implied, of the Department of Defense or the U.S. Government.

References

1. Balakrishnan, N., Bytheway, T., Sohan, R., Hopper, A.: OPUS: a lightweight system for observational provenance in user space. In: Presented as part of the 5th USENIX Workshop on the Theory and Practice of Provenance. USENIX, Lombard, IL (2013). https://www.usenix.org/conference/tapp13/opus-lightweight-system-observational-provenance-user-space
2. Buldyrev, S.V., Parshani, R., Paul, G., Stanley, H.E., Havlin, S.: Catastrophic cascade of failures in interdependent networks. Nature **464**(7291), 1025 (2010)
3. Kleinberg, J.M.: Hubs, authorities, and communities. ACM Comput. Surv. **31**(4es) (1999). https://doi.org/10.1145/345966.345982
4. Leskovec, J., Kleinberg, J., Faloutsos, C.: Graphs over time: densification laws, shrinking diameters and possible explanations. In: Proceedings of the Eleventh ACM SIGKDD International Conference on Knowledge Discovery in Data Mining, pp. 177–187. ACM (2005)
5. Lusseau, D., Schneider, K., Boisseau, O.J., Haase, P., Slooten, E., Dawson, S.M.: The Bottlenose Dolphin community of doubtful sound features a large proportion of long-lasting associations. Behav. Ecol. Sociobiol. **54**(4), 396–405 (2003). https://doi.org/10.1007/s00265-003-0651-y
6. Muniswamy-Reddy, K.K., Holland, D.A., Braun, U., Seltzer, M.: Provenance-aware storage systems. In: Proceedings of the Annual Conference on USENIX 2006 Annual Technical Conference, ATEC 2006, USENIX Association, Berkeley, CA, USA, p. 4 (2006). http://dl.acm.org/citation.cfm?id=1267359.1267363
7. Newman, M.E.: Spread of epidemic disease on networks. Phys. Rev. E **66**(1), 016128 (2002)

A Graph Testing Framework for Provenance Network Analytics

Bernard Roper[1]($\boxtimes$), Adriane Chapman[1], David Martin[1],
and Jeremy Morley[2]

[1] University of Southampton, Southampton, UK
b.a.roper@soton.ac.uk
[2] Ordnance Survey, Southampton, UK

Abstract. Provenance Network Analytics is a method of analyzing provenance that assesses a collection of provenance graphs by training a machine learning algorithm to make predictions about the characteristics of data artifacts based on their provenance graph metrics. The shape of a provenance graph can vary according the modelling approach chosen by data analysts, and this is likely to affect the accuracy of machine learning algorithms, so we propose a framework for capturing provenance using semantic web technologies to allow use of multiple provenance models at runtime in order to test their effects.

Keywords: Graph · Network · Analytics

1 Introduction

Provenance data describes the events, agents, resources and relationships that have led to the creation of a piece of data or thing and as such is naturally expressed as a graph. Provenance is used in a range of application domains, e.g. geospatial [1–3] and scientific experimentation [4–6]. Some of these applications generate large and complex graphs resulting in a volume of data that is beyond the scope of inspection and query. While some strategies exist [7–9] to simplify their representation for human usability, these techniques are typically made for an individual inspecting a single provenance graph to judge fitness for use of a specific artefact.

Provenance Network Analytics (PNA) is an approach proposed by Huynh et al. [10, 11], which instead attempts to help users assess fitness for use for an artefact by assessing a collection of provenance graphs. In their work, they use a set of provenance specific network metrics [12] adapted from network theory [13]. These are used to summarize a dependency subgraph graph as a feature vector to train machine learning algorithms to predict characteristics of the data artefact for which the provenance has been expressed.

This technique is used in [10] to assess the quality of a map feature from CollabMap, a crowdsourced mapping initiative used for disaster relief planning. Using feature vectors from these provenance graphs, the authors trained a machine learning algorithm to predict user trust ratings with 95% accuracy. They have also tested this in other applications; identifying message types in a disaster response simulation game

© Springer Nature Switzerland AG 2018
K. Belhajjame et al. (Eds.): IPAW 2018, LNCS 11017, pp. 245–251, 2018.
https://doi.org/10.1007/978-3-319-98379-0_29

and identifying owners of PROV-N documents, achieving a high degree of classification accuracy across these domains [11].

However, in [11] the authors note that the model chosen for the provenance could impact the quality of the ultimate machine learning model produced. We replicated this in [14], using PROV graphs generated from Open Street Map (OSM) history data, obtaining only 54% accuracy when attempting to predict the incidence of fix-me tags left by users to indicate issues with the data describing a map feature (Fig. 1).

	OSM [14]	Huynh et al [10]
Analysis goal	Predict prevalence of fix-me tags	Predict user trust ratings
Graph structure	6 relationships,3 vertex types	3 relationships, 4 vertex types
Feature Vector	MFD, #vertices, #edges, diameter	MFD, #vertices, #edges, diameter
ML Technique used	decision tree classifier	decision tree classifier
Target Attributes	fix-me tag	Trusted/uncertain rating
Target flags ratio	50:50	50:50
Most Relevant metrics	diameter	#vertices, #edges
Data sets	Two geographic sets containing 30265 and 97393 features, adjusted to 298 and 1604	Three sets divided by data type: 5175 buildings, 4911 evacuation routes and 3043 route sets
Accuracy of results	54%	95%

Fig. 1. Comparison of techniques between various approaches for machine learning over provenance graphs, and the ultimate accuracy, from [14]

The inability to replicate the classifier accuracy of [10] in [14] could have any number of reasons. While it could be argued that provenance is not useful for making predictions about the characteristics of data, the results obtained from the work by Huynh et al. [10, 11] are sufficient to discount this. Alternatively, the specific characteristic (i.e. the fix-me tag) cannot be predicted by the provenance analytics method. While we cannot discount this entirely, it seems unlikely, as this characteristic is analogous to a user trust rating. Another possibility is that there are errors in the way the machine learning algorithms were used. This is of course possible and will be investigated further during this project. However, there are two important factors which bear deeper investigation:

- The network metrics chosen. It is apparent from the previous Provenance Network Analytics work [11] that these metrics have an impact on the machine learning accuracy and that this varies depending on the type of feature from which the provenance is derived.
- The shape of the extracted subgraphs, defined by the way the provenance is modelled and expressed by analysts. Huynh et al. [11] found that the results from one of the applications they studied, although still useful, were significantly poorer than the other two applications. From visual inspection they noted that the shape of these graphs was quite distinctive and so parameterized their capture method to vary the shape of the graph. Doing so effected the classification accuracy.

The modelling of provenance is something of an art form, and characteristics of a provenance graph can vary depending on the application, use-case, and analysis requirements. E.g. nodes can be abstracted for reasons of confidentiality and data protection [15], or granularity can be varied to manage computing resources [16]. These approaches to the expression of a graph decide its topological characteristics and are likely to influence the effectiveness of PNA. OSM history data presents a variety of ways in which provenance could be extracted to create provenance graphs whose form differs depending on the modelling approach chosen.

For example, Table 1 shows two structurally different graphs of provenance for the same OSM map artefact. The accompanying table shows some graph theoretic measurements and values for MFD (maximum finite distance), a provenance specific measurement used in [10, 11]. The graphs are obviously different in appearance and produce a different set of measurement values (Table 2).

Table 1. Two provenance graphs of an OSM map feature

It is likely that different approaches to provenance modelling will result in variations in the accuracy of machine learning classifiers. To identify any effect, a framework for testing the PNA method using graphs built using a range of modelling approaches is needed. Our contributions in this work are the following:

- We create a provenance extraction framework that allows the shape of a provenance graph to be changed at runtime.
- We showcase the use of this framework on Open Street Maps, and show how an OSM XML history file can be parsed into a history representation that allows any number and shape of provenance graphs to be generated programmatically

Table 2. Metrics from the graphs in Table 1

Metrics	G1	G2	MFD	G1	G2
Nodes	12	8	Entity-entity	1	1
Edges	27	9	Entity-activity	2	2
Components	1	1	Entity-agent	3	3
Diameter	3	5	Activity-entity	0	0
			Activity-activity	0	0
			Activity-agent	2	1
			Agent-entity	0	0
			Agent-activity	0	8
			Agent-agent	1	9

2 A Multi-model Graph Analysis Framework

The system proposed here is related to methods of 'scraping' provenance from log files generated by an application as part of its instrumentation, such as [17, 18]. The diagram in Fig. 2 shows our process, which uses OSM **XML History Data**, which is in the same format as the OSM dataset but contains the state of each map artefact at any stage in the its history, including timestamp, software used, external dataset derivations and an ID of the creator agent. Rather than scraping a specific expression of provenance from the data by parsing, **XSLT** is used to transform it into an **RDF Graph**. This is encoded using OWL and the **PROV-O** ontology, which are used to enrich the data set by entailing more triples to generate a comprehensive and universal provenance graph from which different PROV-DM representations can be extracted.

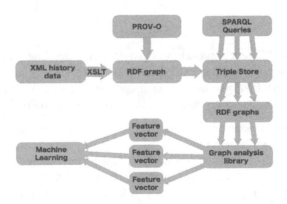

Fig. 2. The framework process

The resulting RDF is added to a **Triple Store** created using the Apache JENA Java libraries. The PROV graphs for map features are obtained using **SPARQL** queries which return **RDF Graphs** as Apache JENA RDF model objects, which can be converted to network graph representations and feature vectors using the JENA-JUNG **Graph Analysis Library**. The **feature vectors** will be used to train a **Machine Learning** classifier.

We capture data with the PROV-DM elements that allow data enrichment by inference using the PROV-O ontology. Figure 3 shows the attribution and derivation relationships of an OSM map artefact. The relationships in bold show provenance that has been explicitly declared in the RDF produced by the XSLT transformation. The other relationships have been inferred by a reasoner using PROV-O.

Fig. 3. Inferred triples in Protégé

We also use a qualified relations design pattern [19] for the provenance relationships, so that each edge is reified into an individual, linked with a qualified relation edge so that more triples can be inferred, creating the simpler wasAttributedTo and wasDerivedFrom relationship.

Once this process is complete, PROV graphs are then extracted using different SPARQL queries to the same set of PROV data as seen in Fig. 4.

This framework allows specification of PROV models using SPARQL. The example above shows two graphs produced by different SPARQL queries run over RDF data extracted from an OSM history file with axioms generated by a reasoner in Protégé [20]. Using feature vectors from results like these we train a ScikitLearn Decision Tree Classifier [21]. This provides a human readable output with information about the significance of the various graph metrics in the classification process, which can be used to help inform the design of other PROV models which can be extracted from the data using SPARQL.

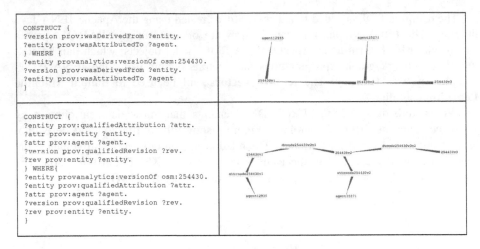

Fig. 4. Two SPARQL queries with their resultant graphs

3   Future Work

Once this framework is completed we will create another XSLT module for use with Ordnance Survey history data and examine other target quality characteristics. We will also explore other machine learning techniques to see if classification accuracies can be improved and if so, whether the decision tree classifier can still be used alongside other algorithms to provide information about the role of the various metrics and different graph morphologies and what insights this might give us into the social worlds and processes of data creation.

Because we are using RDF in a triple store we will be able to update our Provenance dataset as the OSM history is updated. This dataset could be used to produce a provenance powered spatial representation of predicted data quality that updates over time.

References

1. Yue, P., Zhang, M., Guo, X., Tan Z.: Granularity of geospatial data provenance. In: 2014 IEEE Geoscience and Remote Sensing Symposium, pp. 4492–4495 (2014)
2. Maso, J., Pross, B., Gil, Y., Closa, G. (eds.): Testbed 10 Provenance Engineering Report. OGC, 14 July 2014
3. Yue, P., Gong, J., Di, L., He, L., Wei, Y.: Semantic provenance registration and discovery using geospatial catalogue service. In: Proceedings 2nd International Workshop on the Role of Semantic Web in Provenance Management, Shanghai, China, pp. 23–28 (2010)
4. Oliveira, W., Ambrósio, L.M., Braga, R., Ströele, V., David, J.M., Campos, F.: A framework for provenance analysis and visualization. Procedia Comput. Sci. **108**, 1592–1601 (2017)
5. Acar, U., Buneman, P., Cheney J.: A graph model of data and workflow provenance, p. 10 (2010)

6. Miles, S., Groth, P., Branco, M., Moreau, L.: The requirements of recording and using provenance in e-science experiments, p. 15 (2007)
7. Davidson, S., et al.: Provenance in scientific workflow systems, p. 7 (2007)
8. Moreau, L.: Aggregation by provenance types: a technique for summarising provenance graphs. In: Electronic Proceedings in Theoretical Computer Science, vol. 181, pp. 129–144, April 2015
9. Macko, P., Seltzer, M.: Provenance map orbiter: interactive exploration of large provenance graphs, p. 6 (2011)
10. Huynh, T.D., Ebden, M., Venanzi, M., Ramchurn, S.D., Roberts, S., Moreau, L.: Interpretation of crowdsourced activities using provenance network analysis. In: First AAAI Conference on Human Computation and Crowdsourcing (2013)
11. Huynh, T.D., Ebden, M., Fischer, J., Roberts, S., Moreau, L.: Provenance network analytics: an approach to data analytics using data provenance. In: Data Mining and Knowledge Discovery, February 2018
12. Ebden, M., Huynh, T.D., Moreau, L., Ramchurn, S., Roberts, S.: Network analysis on provenance graphs from a crowdsourcing application. In: Groth, P., Frew, J. (eds.) IPAW 2012. LNCS, vol. 7525, pp. 168–182. Springer, Heidelberg (2012). https://doi.org/10.1007/978-3-642-34222-6_13
13. Newman, M.E.J.: Networks: An Introduction. Oxford University Press, Oxford/New York (2010)
14. Roper, B.: Investigating the role of data provenance in assessing variations in the quality of open street map data, MSc, University of Southampton (2017)
15. Missier, P., Bryans, J., Gamble, C., Curcin, V., Danger, R.: *ProvAbs*: Model, policy, and tooling for abstracting PROV graphs. In: Ludäscher, B., Plale, B. (eds.) IPAW 2014. LNCS, vol. 8628, pp. 3–15. Springer, Cham (2015). https://doi.org/10.1007/978-3-319-16462-5_1
16. Pasquier, T., et al.: Practical Whole-System Provenance Capture, pp. 405–418 (2017). arXiv: 1711.05296 [cs]
17. De Nies, T., et al.: Git2PROV: exposing version control system content as W3C PROV. In: Poster and Demo Proceedings of the 12th International Semantic Web Conference, vol. 1035, pp. 125–128 (2013)
18. Ghoshal, D., Plale, B.: Provenance from log files: a BigData problem, p. 290 (2013)
19. Moreau, L., Groth, P.: Provenance: An Introduction to PROV. Morgan & Claypool Publishers, San Rafael (2013)
20. protégé. https://protege.stanford.edu/. Accessed 07 April 2018
21. Pedregosa, F., et al.: Scikit-learn: machine learning in python. J. Mach. Learn. Res. **12**(Oct), 2825–2830 (2011)

Provenance for Astrophysical Data

Anastasia Galkin[1]([✉])[iD], Kristin Riebe[1], Ole Streicher[1][iD], Francois Bonnarel[2],
Mireille Louys[2], Michèle Sanguillon[3][iD], Mathieu Servillat[4],
and Markus Nullmeier[5]

[1] Leibniz-Institute for Astrophysics Potsdam (AIP), Potsdam, Germany
`agalkin@aip.de`
[2] Universitè de Strasbourg, CNRS, Observatoire astronomique de Strasbourg,
Strasbourg, France
[3] LUPM, CNRS, Université de Montpellier, Montpellier, France
[4] Laboratoire Univers et Thèories, Observatoire de Paris, PSL Research University,
CNRS, Paris, France
[5] ARI, Zentrum fuer Astronomie Heidelberg, Heidelberg, Germany

Abstract. In the context of astronomy projects, provenance information is important to enable scientists to trace back the origin of a dataset. It is used to learn about the people and organizations involved in a project and assess the quality of the dataset as well as the usefulness of the dataset their scientific work. As part of the data model group in the International Virtual Observatory Alliance (IVOA) we are working on the definition of a provenance data model for astronomy which shall describe how provenance metadata can be modeled, stored and exchanged. The data model is being implemented for different projects and use cases.

Keywords: Astronomy · Astrophysics · Escience
Data management · Provenance · IVOA

1 Introduction

The Virtual Observatory (VO) is the vision that astronomical datasets and other resources should work as a seamless whole. The IVOA [4] is an organisation that debates and agrees on the technical standards that are needed to make the VO possible.

The goal of the IVOA Data modeling group is to develop a provenance data model which will not only store provenance information but also to find ways

This project is partially funded by BMBF 05A14BAD and 05AI7BA2S. Additional funding is provided by ASTERICS (http://www.asterics2020.eu/), a project supported by the European Commission Framework Programme Horizon 2020 Research and Innovation action under grant agreement no. 653477. Further funding was provided by the German Virtual Observatory (GAVO), the French Virtual Observatory (ASOV OV-France), and Paris Astronomical Data Centre (PADC).

© Springer Nature Switzerland AG 2018
K. Belhajjame et al. (Eds.): IPAW 2018, LNCS 11017, pp. 252–256, 2018.
https://doi.org/10.1007/978-3-319-98379-0_30

to let the astronomical community explore provenance in a interoperable way, linking the provenance information to already existing VO data models and infrastructures.

2 Use Cases for Provenace in Astronomy

For an astronomical data set, provenance can answer questions such as: Which processing steps have been done already? Who was involved in the project? Who can I ask about this data? Is the dataset suited for my research? Which datasets were produced with the same pipeline version? "Forward tracking" is useful to follow the usage within the given domain. Structured provenance metadata helps to find possible error sources such as the version of processing software, telescope configuration, parameter settings.

2.1 Cherenkov Telescope Array

The Cherenkov Telescope Array (CTA) [3] is the next generation ground-based very high energy gamma-ray instrument. Contrary to previous Cherenkov instruments, it will serve as an open observatory providing data to a wide astrophysics community, with the requirement to propose self-described data products to users that may be unaware of the Cherenkov astronomy specificities. Provenance is used to organize the data reprocessing workflow of the pipeline.

2.2 Spectroscopic Surveys

In large spectroscopic surveys (e.g. 4MOST [1]), sections of the sky are scanned to retrieve characteristics of the electromagnetic radiation emitted by cosmological objects, such as stars, black holes or galaxies. The provenance model can help identify adjacent objects on the CCD (an electronic light sensor) for a given 1D spectrum to identify sources of crosstalk.

2.3 APPLAUSE Database - Scanning Historical Photoplates

The APPLAUSE archives [2] host digitized copies of photographic plates from the German astronomical observatories. These items are of particular interest for the study of long-term variability of many types of stars. The provenance usecase here encompasses physical objects such as photographic plates, the scanners and the log book as well as the software processing steps, parameters and the digital outcome of the project - digitized images and identified objects such as stars. The data release 3 is planned to be published in July 2018, provenance metadata are being constructed and will be added in a later addition.

2.4   MUSE Data Reduction Pipeline

The Multi Unit Spectroscopic Explorer (MUSE) [5] is an instrument installed at the Very Large Telescope (VLT) of the European Southern Observatory. The raw data are recorded separately and then transformed into a fully calibrated, science-ready data cube using the MUSE data reduction pipeline [13]. All information is stored in a specific object oriented database [12]. First attempts to describe the provenance information using the W3C model for one final data cube result in metadata containing about 2700 file entities and 270 activities (recipe runs).

2.5   RAVE Survey

RAVE (Radial Velocity Experiment) [6] is one of the largest spectroscopic surveys of Milky Way stars. The final data products are data release tables with properties for half a million stars. These properties are derived from the original raw spectra which are observed by a number of fibres attached to the telescope and were processed in numerous processing steps. If the provenance information contains all the details and intermediate steps, tracking back the provenance for each stellar property through to the original fibre-spectrum, the amount of information becomes overwhelming.

3   Special Requirements in Modelling Provenance in Astronomy

The IVOA provenance data model follows closely the W3C provenance model [7], utilizing entities, activities and agents, and the relevant relations between them. The provenance information use in astronomy has however some specific challenges:

First, the astronomical provenance records are highly complex. A coarse or a detailed view of a provenance model is needed depending on the task where the provenance is used.

Second, many tasks in astronomy are repetitive, e.g. several observations can be performed with the same telescope and instrument, or many simulations are performed using the same code and computing environment, but with slightly varying code parameters. This is normalized by using a special class that abstractly describes the activity. The complex data processing also may require to structure the workflow by combining several activities into one.

Last, activities highly rely on parameters and parameter sets. Parameters have a value and might or might not have a history as well. Thus, parameters could be modeled as entities.

4   Integration into the IVOA Ecosystem

IVOA has built up a well functioning and widely used ecosystem of interoperable services and tools such as Tool for OPerations on Catalogues And Tables (TOP-CAT). One of the main concepts in IVOA is the Table Access Protocol (TAP) [8].

Within the TAP protocol the access is provided for both the database and the table metadata as well as for actual table data. TAP also includes support for synchronous and asynchronous queries as well as support for multiple query languages, mainly the Astronomical Data Query Language (ADQL).

The ProvTAP accesses provenance information accordingly to the TAP standard. The output format is VOTable, the VO standard table output format.

ProvSAP (for Simple Access Protocol) allows the client to request information in a REST framework way with W3C output formats such as PROV-JSON, PROV-XML and PROV-N.

Provenance information can also be directly stored in data files such as images files (FITS) or in VOTables. The standard for it is currently discussed by the IVOA modeling group.

5   Summary

In this document we briefly outlined the development of the IVOA provenance model for the astronomical scientific field. The current IVOA Provenance Data Model is still in development and some core concepts are in discussion now. We welcome and encourage the input of W3C provenance experts to complete the model within the IVOA ecosystem.

For further reading please look at various proceedings, documents and notes, e.g.: [10, 11].

The latest official version of the working draft can be found at [9]. The released versions will be published at the IVOA website [4] in the documents section.

References

1. The 4-metre multi-object spectrograph telescope. https://www.4most.eu/
2. Applause - archives of photographic plates. https://plate-archive.org
3. Cherenkov telescope array. https://www.cta-observatory.org/
4. International virtual observatory alliance (ivoa). http://ivoa.net
5. Muse science - the multi unit spectroscopic explorer. https://muse-vlt.eu/science
6. Rave the radial velocity experiment. https://www.rave-survey.org/project/
7. Belhajjame, K., et al.: PROV-DM: The prov data model. W3C Recommendation, April 2013. http://www.w3.org/TR/prov-dm/
8. Dowler, P., Rixon, G., Tody, D., Demleitner, M.: Table access protocol - version 1.1 (2018). http://www.ivoa.net/documents/TAP/
9. Riebe, K., et al.: The IVOA Data Model Working Group: IVOA Provenance Data Model (2017). http://www.ivoa.net/documents/ProvenanceDM/
10. Riebe, K., Servillat, M., Bonnarel, F., Louys, M., Sanguillon, M.: The IVOA Data Model Working Group: Provenance Implementation Note (2017). http://volute.g-vo.org/svn/trunk/projects/dm/provenance/implementation-note/
11. Servillat, M., et al.: Provenance as a requirement for large-scale complex astronomical instruments. In: ADASS XXVII. ASP Conference Series. ASP, San Francisco (2018)

12. Vriend, W.J.: Porting big data technology across domains. WISE for MUSE. In: Science Operations 2015: Science Data Management - An ESO/ESA Workshop, 24–27 November 2015 at ESO Garching, p. 1, December 2015. https://doi.org/10.5281/zenodo.34624
13. Weilbacher, P.M., Streicher, O., Urrutia, T., Pécontal-Rousset, A., Jarno, A., Bacon, R.: The MUSE data reduction pipeline: status after preliminary acceptance Europe. In: Manset, N., Forshay, P. (eds.) Astronomical Data Analysis Software and Systems XXIII. Astronomical Society of the Pacific Conference Series, vol. 485, p. 451, May 2014

Data Provenance in Agriculture

Sérgio Manuel Serra da Cruz[1]([✉]) [iD], Marcos Bacis Ceddia[1] [iD],
Renan Carvalho Tàvora Miranda[1] [iD], Gabriel Rizzo[1] [iD],
Filipe Klinger[1] [iD], Renato Cerceau[1,2] [iD], Ricardo Mesquita[4] [iD],
Ricardo Cerceau[1] [iD], Elton Carneiro Marinho[5] [iD],
Eber Assis Schmitz[5] [iD], Elaine Sigette[3] [iD], and Pedro Vieira Cruz[1] [iD]

[1] Federal Rural University of Rio de Janeiro, Seropédica, RJ, Brazil
{serra, ceddia}@ufrrj.br
[2] National Agency of Supplementary Health, Rio de Janeiro, RJ, Brazil
[3] Federal Fluminense University, Volta Redonda, RJ, Brazil
[4] SENAI-RJ, Rio de Janeiro, RJ, Brazil
[5] Federal University of Rio de Janeiro, Cidade Universitária, RJ, Brazil

Abstract. Soils are probably the most critical natural resource in Agriculture, and soils security represents a critical growing global issue. Soils experiments require vast amounts of high-quality data, are very hard to be reproduced, and there are few studies about data provenance of such tests. We present OpenSoils; it shares knowledge about data-centric soils experiments. OpenSoils is a provenance-oriented and lightweight e-infrastructure that collects, stores, describes, curates and, harmonizes various soil datasets.

Keywords: Reproducibility · Soil security · Open data · Data quality
Big data

1 Introduction

According to Food and Agriculture Organization (FAO)[1], an agency of the United Nations, the world's population is expected to grow to about 9,6 billion by 2050. Thus, there is widespread concern about the challenges to soil and food systems in meeting the demand of populations for sufficient, affordable, and nutritious food. There are similar concerns about meeting those challenges in ways that agriculture would benefit hugely from common shared global agronomic data spaces.

The modern Agriculture is a data-centric interdisciplinary domain, with the integration of different subjects (from genomics to soil sciences), different scales (from genes to geolocalisation) and, different markets (from local farmers to multinational research teams). The ability to manage and explore these datasets is a crucial issue to tackle the current sustainability challenges. A wide variety of datasets underpin products and processes, which vary in size, complexity, structure, semantics, subject matter and in how they are updated and used.

---

[1] http://www.fao.org/about/what-we-do/en/.

© Springer Nature Switzerland AG 2018
K. Belhajjame et al. (Eds.): IPAW 2018, LNCS 11017, pp. 257–261, 2018.
https://doi.org/10.1007/978-3-319-98379-0_31

Soils are probably the most critical natural resource in Agriculture; they generate environmental, health and socio-economic benefits that are vital to sustaining life on Earth [1]. Soil experiments are indispensable sources of knowledge. Researchers conduct several kinds of soils experiments which are characterized as long-term field experiments (LTE) and short-term (*in vitro* and *in silico*) lab experiments (STE). The LTE have been running for years in many parts of the world for the last 175-years-old (*e.g.* Rothamsted) and need more time to execute the research procedures. On the other hand, STE experiments can be performed in a few weeks or months and have the potential to contribute to the improve LTE. Thus, it is essential to deliver to the agronomic community a novel computing infrastructure that can share raw and curated data and the provenance of STE and LTE and augment the reproducibility of soil experiments. This paper presents a multi-layer e-infrastructure which bring innovations to Soils Science using FAIR principles (Findable, Accessible, Interoperable, and Reusable) [2], W3C PROV-DM[2], open data and semantic web standards.

2   Experiments in Soils Science

Soil Science represents the area that studies the soil (and its properties) as a natural resource, including soil formation, composition, classification, mapping, management and use [1, 3], these properties could be about physical, chemical, biological, and fertility. Soils experiments are costly because the soils are incredibly diverse, and it is necessary to treat them in a specific manner [3]. Any recommendation fits specific soil and weather conditions. Besides, the soil properties have high spatial and time variability. Finally, changes in soil properties can often be proved and quantified only after decades.

The LTE is essential in monitoring and understanding the changes in soil physics or fertility occurring because of long-term agrotechnical operations. Their scientific and practical value is immeasurable and keeps improving over the years. The information about the soils use cannot be replaced by any other means [3]. Additionally, the STE produced much of the data that built the sciences of soil physics, chemistry, and biology [1, 3]. STE often explore soil processes subject to change over decades, topics such as aggregation, weathering, microbial activity, and soil fertility itself. Although STE enriches soil models, most tend to be reductionist, isolating individual components, and do not study the whole soil, with its high-order interactions that become apparent only with time.

3   Open Soils

Data and provenance are the primary and permanent assets in OpenSoils (www.opensoils.org). The architecture is an open, provenance-oriented, and lightweight computational e-infrastructure which rely on layers to store, compute and share curated

---

[2] https://www.w3.org/TR/prov-dm/.

data of (STE and LTE) soils experiments [5]. Figure 1 illustrates a conceptual view and the flow of information in the architecture.

Layer 1 (End-users layer) - hosts on the OpenSoils Web portal; it collects soil data directly from the LTE into OpenSoils database. The specialists can use mobile and web applications (*e.g.*, OpenSoils App, API and Wet Lab tools) to collect the data directly in the fields (LTE experiments) and trace the route of each soil sample sent to chemistry and physics laboratories to be analyzed. Usually, the morphological properties of the soil are analyzed *in situ* by the specialists. OpenSoils app sends raw data to the cloud-based database thought the API. After that, each soil sample is tagged and sent to laboratories where the scientist does wet experiments and execute STE which evaluate specific physic-chemical properties of each soil horizon and selected soil samples are shipped to the UFRRJ's soils museum.

Layer 2 (Services layer) - hosts soil models and data-centric scientific workflows which ingest large amounts of legacy data and analyses the consistency of the incoming data [3].

Layer 3 (Data layer) - stores and describes various soils datasets with metadata. The internal structure supports a diversified degree of data granularity and uses a database named OpenSoilsDB [5, 6] which can store new curated soils data annotated with provenance metadata. Much of the information needed to assure the data quality and to allow researchers to reproduce STE experiments can be obtained by system-atically capturing data provenance [4]. OpenSoilsDB can store provenance from ETL workflows and scripts. ETL Workflow provenance consists of the record of the derivation of a result (*e.g.*, a soil experiment, an image, a map) by a computational process represented as scientific workflows. Script provenance is obtained by running the source code of scripts (*e.g.* R, Pyhton). OpenSoilsDB used W3C PROV-DM recommendation to store provenance and was designed to support the FAIR principles for scientific data management and data stewardship [2]. The principles ensure trans-parency, reproducibility, and reusability of the experiments, facilitating data sharing more systematically.

The database also supports the ingestion of legacy soils data imported through ETL workflows. The layer can store scientific and governance data. Besides, to support open data, we can use general-purpose data repositories (*e.g.*, CKAN, Dataverse, DSpace, Dryad, DataHub).

A specific thesaurus is used to add semantics and annotate soils data, allowing us to link it as RDF triples in WikiData. The thesaurus used in the e-infrastructure is Agrovoc [7], which is a SKOS-XL (Simple Knowledge Organization System eXten-sion for Labels) concept scheme published as LOD (Linked Open Data). It covers several areas of interest of the FAO including food, agriculture and, environment. This thesaurus is used by researchers, librarians, and information managers for indexing, retrieving, and organizing data in agricultural information systems.

Data management is not a target in itself, but a key conduit leading to knowledge discovery and innovation in soil sciences. OpenSoilsDB database stores scientific and governance data. The scientific data aims to serve high quality-assessed, georeferenced soils profiles database to the Brazilian and international communities upon their standardization and harmonization. Each soil profile description recorded in the data-base has more than 43 entities, and 250 attributes to stores the soil properties and soil

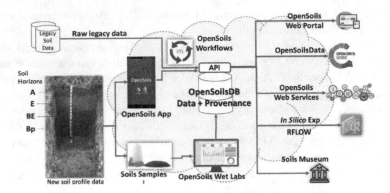

Fig. 1. Overview of the conceptual data-flow in OpenSoils.

experiments (mineralogical, morphological, chemical, physical, and environmental data). Furthermore, the database support data versioning and provenance; stores geo-referenced soil data (text and images) about physic-chemical analytical data from each horizon and soil samples analyzed in wet laboratories.

Data governance is an essential block in the knowledge base of information professionals involved in supporting data-intensive research. Its adoption is advantageous because it is a service based on standardized, repeatable processes, designed to enable the data discovery and the transparency of data-related transformation processes.

Layer 4 (Governance layer) - hosts data licenses, re-use rights, analytical tools, visualization and map generation services that can be connected to other software (*e.g.,* ArcGIS, R or Jupyter) to generate analytical reports, prediction and raster maps. Although received little attention in soils research communities, this layer is foundational for soils security. The prime function of the layer is to improve and maintain the citations and quality of the soils dataset; thus, to be successful at governance, quality must be continuously measured, and the results continuously retrieved by the data and services layers.

4   Concluding Remarks

Maintaining healthy soils is a key to modern agriculture. However, there is still much computational work needed to be developed in soil sciences and more in-depth studies to understand the role of data provenance in Agriculture. We introduced OpenSoils; it is an e-infrastructure which share knowledge about STE and LTE in soils security using FAIR, PROV, and semantic web approaches. The infrastructure is being developed and aims to enhance reproducibility of experiments and deliver high-quality datasets, knowledge and maps based on curated data.

Acknowledgments. This work was supported in part by the Brazilian agencies FNDE/MEC/SESU, PIBIC/CNPq, Petrobras and CYTED networks BigDSSAgro and SmartLogistcs@IB.

References

1. Koch, A., et al.: Soil security: solving the global soil crisis. Glob. Policy **4**(4), 434–441 (2013)
2. Wilkinson, M.D., et al.: The FAIR guiding principles for scientific data management and stewardship. Sci. Data **3**, 160018 (2016)
3. Körschens, M.: The importance of long-term field experiments for soil science and environmental research – a review. Plant Soil Environ. **52**, 1–8 (2006)
4. Cruz, S.M.S., do Nascimento, J.A.P.: SisGExp: rethinking long-tail agronomic experiments. In: Mattoso, M., Glavic, B. (eds.) IPAW 2016. LNCS, vol. 9672, pp. 214–217. Springer, Cham (2016). https://doi.org/10.1007/978-3-319-40593-3_24
5. Cruz, S.M.S., et al.: Towards an e-infrastructure for open science in soils security. In: XII Proceedings on Brazilian E-Science Workshop (BRESCI), pp. 59–66. SBC, Natal-RN (2018)
6. Rizzo, G.S.C., Ceddia, M.B., Cruz, S.M.S.: Banco de Dados Pedológico: Primeiros Estudos. In: 5th Proceedings on Reunião Anual de Iniciação Científica (RAIC), pp. 1–2. UFRRJ, Seropédica (2017). (in Portuguese)
7. Caracciolo, C., et al.: The AGROVOC linked dataset. Seman. Web **4**(3), 341–348 (2013)

Extracting Provenance Metadata
from Privacy Policies

Harshvardhan Jitendra Pandit$^{(\boxtimes)}$, Declan O'Sullivan, and Dave Lewis

ADAPT Centre, Trinity College Dublin, Dublin, Ireland
{harshvardhan.pandit,declan.osullivan,dave.lewis}@adaptcentre.ie

Abstract. Privacy policies are legal documents that describe activities over personal data such as its collection, usage, processing, sharing, and storage. Expressing this information as provenance metadata can aid in legal accountability as well as modelling of data usage in real-world use-cases. In this paper, we describe our early work on identification, extraction, and representation of provenance information within privacy policies. We discuss the adoption of entity extraction approaches using concepts and keywords defined by the GDPRtEXT resource along with using annotated privacy policy corpus from the UsablePrivacy project. We use the previously published GDPRov ontology (an extension of PROV-O) to model provenance model extracted from privacy policies.

Keywords: Provenance · Privacy policy · GDPR

1 Motivation

A privacy policy is a document that outlines information about activities related to personal data, and are notoriously difficult to read [3]. The privacy policy (along with T&C and other documents) is commonly the only available authoritative indication of how personal data is collected and used. Legislations, such as the upcoming General Data Protection Regulation (GDPR), influence what information is required to be mentioned in the privacy policy, but do not provide a uniform structure or mechanism for its declaration.

Research, especially related to technical modelling of privacy, therefore suffers from a lack of structured information about real-world usage of personal data. The UsablePrivacy Project [4] provides a semi-automated annotation of privacy policy based on a combination of crowdsourcing, machine learning and natural language processing. It annotates privacy policy statements to help users identify different data collection and use practices. We propose to extend this approach to identify and automatically extract provenance metadata from privacy policies. This paper describes provenance information present in privacy policies along with approaches towards its identification, extraction, and representation.

© Springer Nature Switzerland AG 2018
K. Belhajjame et al. (Eds.): IPAW 2018, LNCS 11017, pp. 262–265, 2018.
https://doi.org/10.1007/978-3-319-98379-0_32

2   Provenance Metadata

Identification. GDPR is poised to significantly change the type of information made available to the data subject or user regarding activities over their personal data. We discuss identification of provenance metadata using the privacy policy provided by Airbnb Ireland[1], and focus on categories or types of personal data, along with descriptions of activities that relate to how it is collected, used, shared, and stored. The policy contains sections that offer context to its contents. For example, the title of Section 1 refers to collection of information with subsections describing where the information is obtained from. Taking into account such context can be helpful towards heuristics for eventual extraction of provenance metadata. For example, section 1. describes personal information provided when creating a new account. Combining this with the aforementioned context, we can infer that *account information* is a data category with *first name, last name, email address, date of birth* being its types; and *sign-up* is an activity that collects *account information* direct from the *user*.

Extraction Using Keyword-Based Entity Recognition. Manual efforts to extract this provenance information do not scale well across a large number of policies, nor can they be automated. Entity extraction techniques [1,2] can help in identification and categorisation of methods. Identification and extraction can take place by searching for certain keywords known to refer to provenance information. For example, the word "collect" is almost always accompanied with the type of information collected. A starting point for GDPR relevant keywords is the GDPRtEXT ontology [5] that defines GDPR terms and concepts using the SKOS vocabulary.

Extraction Using Machine Learning Models. This approach is similar to the one take by the UsablePrivacy project [4] and requires annotations over a sample corpus to train a machine learning algorithm for automatic entity recognition and extraction. We plan to expand upon the categorisation of privacy policy statements based on published approaches [4,7] with our keyword-based extraction method. For this, the categorisation of statements can be used to identify the type of information contained within the statement. For example, a statement annotated with "First Party Collection/Use" offers the context of a data collection activity, which can be used by the extraction algorithm to identify the contextually relevant terms. Therefore, it may be more performant to train the entity extraction algorithm only on similarly categorised statements as opposed to all statements within policies.

Representation. Provenance metadata expressed using PROV-O concepts are assertions about the past (execution) and should not be used to depict a 'model' or abstraction of how things are supposed to be happen. To this end, we created

---

[1] Accessed 16-APR-2018 https://www.airbnb.ie/terms/privacy_policy.

GDPRov [6], an OWL2 ontology that extends PROV-O and P-Plan (an extension of PROV-O) for modelling data-flows involving consent and data using relevant GDPR terminology. An example representation of the use-case is depicted in Fig. 1 with its representation as RDF triples.

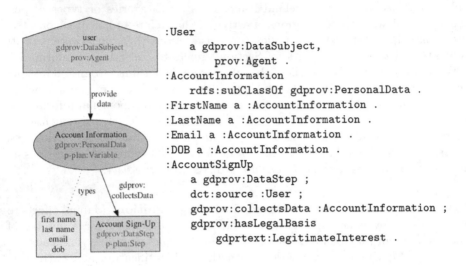

```
:User
    a gdprov:DataSubject,
        prov:Agent .
:AccountInformation
    rdfs:subClassOf gdprov:PersonalData .
:FirstName a :AccountInformation .
:LastName a :AccountInformation .
:Email a :AccountInformation .
:DOB a :AccountInformation .
:AccountSignUp
    a gdprov:DataStep ;
    dct:source :User ;
    gdprov:collectsData :AccountInformation ;
    gdprov:hasLegalBasis
        gdprtext:LegitimateInterest .
```

Fig. 1. Example use-case for representation of information in Airbnb Privacy Policy

3   Potential Applications

Easier Representation of Privacy Policies. Privacy policies, as described earlier, have been notoriously difficult to interpret and understand from the point of view of a generic data subject or user. Efforts such as tl;drLegal3 and UsablePrivacy are good examples of community efforts to mitigate this problem, with UsablePrivacy offering a semi-automated way to annotate privacy policies. Provenance metadata extracted from a privacy policy can be used to augment these efforts through better descriptions and visualisations of how the data is used across different processes. Having a visual representation accompany privacy policies can help users in quickly grasping the gist of the policy.

Approaches Related to Privacy Preferences. Matching a user's privacy preferences with the service is an important topic given the increasing misuse of personal data and the lack of readily available information about data practices. Provenance metadata can augment approaches that try to solve this problem by providing a description of how data is used by the target entity related to the policy. One possibility towards this is using the provenance metadata towards interpreting privacy policies as agreements using Open Digital Rights Language (ODRL). The provenance metadata provides information about what data is collected, how it is used, where/when it is shared. By matching the user's privacy preferences (also expressed as ODRL) with the ODRL privacy policy, it could be possible to express areas that need user attention or those that do not comply with the user's preferences.

4 Conclusion

Through this paper, we presented our early stage work for the identification, extraction, and representation of provenance metadata present in privacy policies. We describe our approach that uses keyword-based entity extraction based on GDPR terms and concepts provided by the GDPRtEXT resource. This approach adopts the machine-learning model used by the UsablePrivacy project to create annotated privacy policies. We represent the extracted provenance metadata using GDPRov, which extends PROV-O and P-Plan, and allows for an abstract model of the policy to be represented. We describe the potential application of this work to augment several important topics related to privacy and data practices.

Acknowledgments. This work is supported by the ADAPT Centre for Digital Content Technology which is funded under the SFI Research Centres Programme (Grant 13/RC/2106) and is co-funded under the European Regional Development Fund.

References

1. Bhatia, J., Breaux, T.D.: Towards an information type Lexicon for privacy policies. In: 2015 IEEE Eighth International Workshop on Requirements Engineering and Law (RELAW), pp. 19–24, August 2015. https://doi.org/10.1109/RELAW.2015. 7330207
2. Bhatia, J., Breaux, T.D.: A data purpose case study of privacy policies. In: 2017 IEEE 25th International Requirements Engineering Conference (RE), pp. 394–399. IEEE (2017)
3. Fabian, B., Ermakova, T., Lentz, T.: Large-scale readability analysis of privacy policies. In: Proceedings of the International Conference on Web Intelligence, WI 2017, pp. 18–25. ACM, New York (2017). https://doi.org/10.1145/3106426.3106427
4. Oltramari, A., et al.: PrivOnto: a semantic framework for the analysis of privacy policies. Semant. Web **9**(2), 185–203 (2018). https://doi.org/10.3233/SW-170283. http://www.medra.org/servlet/aliasResolver?alias=iospress&doi=10.3233/SW-170 283
5. Pandit, H.J., Fatema, K., O'Sullivan, D., Lewis, D.: GDPRtEXT - GDPR as a Linked Data Resource, p. 14. Heraklion, Crete, Greece (2018)
6. Pandit, H.J., Lewis, D.: Modelling Provenance for GDPR Compliance using Linked Open Data Vocabularies, p. 15
7. Tesfay, W.B., Hofmann, P., Nakamura, T., Kiyomoto, S., Serna, J.: PrivacyGuide: towards an implementation of the EU GDPR on internet privacy policy evaluation. In: Proceedings of the Fourth ACM International Workshop on Security and Privacy Analytics, IWSPA 2018, pp. 15–21. ACM, New York (2018). https://doi.org/10. 1145/3180445.3180447

Provenance-Enabled Stewardship
of Human Data in the GDPR Era

Pinar Alper[✉][iD], Regina Becker, Venkata Satagopam, Christophe Trefois,
Valentin Groués, Jacek Lebioda, and Yohan Jarosz

Luxembourg Centre for Systems Biomedicine, 4362 Esch-sur-Alzette, Luxembourg
{pinar.alper,regina.becker,venkata.satagopam,christophe.trefois,
valentin.groues,jacek.lebioda,yohan.jarosz}@uni.lu
https://wwwen.uni.lu/lcsb

Abstract. Within life-science research the upcoming EU General Data
Protection Regulation has a significant operational impact on organisations that use and exchange controlled-access Human Data. One impli-
cation of the GDPR is data bookkeeping. In this poster we describe a
software tool, the Data Information System (DAISY), designed to record
data protection relevant provenance of Human Data held and exchanged
by research organisations.

Keywords: GDPR · Human Data · Provenance

1 Background

1.1 EU General Data Protection Regulation

Today, personal data breach incidents are not only front-page news items, they
are events with highly adverse impact on individuals and the society. In this
regard, a new EU-level legislation, the General Data Protection Regulation
(GDPR) [3], could not have been more timely. GDPR brings increased regulation for organisations utilising personal data. Specifically:

– Organisations are now required to **keep inventory** on the personal data they
  hold: from where, how and under what legal basis the data was obtained, with
  whom it has been shared and the nature data use. This data provenance will
  then serve as the starting point for audits performed by the national Data
  Protection Authorities.
– Individuals have more rights on their data, such as the right to access, right
  to deletion and the right to restriction of the use of their data. GDPR also
  requires that requests for rectification, erasure etc. are passed on to the
  recipients of the data, which means organisations must have a **fine-grained
  (subject-level) traceability of the sharing personal data.**
– Organisations are expected to **take data privacy measures at systems'
  design time.** These include data confidentiality, integrity and availability;

K. Belhajjame et al. (Eds.): IPAW 2018, LNCS 11017, pp. 266–269, 2018.
https://doi.org/10.1007/978-3-319-98379-0_33

data minimisation so that only necessary data attributes are used; storage duration limitations so that data is not kept longer than necessary. Furthermore, GDPR expects **documentation** of security such measures as well as documentation on systematic assessments of data processing setups in terms of data privacy risks (aka "Data Processing Impact Assessment DPIA").

1.2   Stewardship of Human Data

Scientific Data Stewardship refers to "activities for the long-term care of data" to support scientific reproducibility or to enable data sharing [5]. In the context of life-science research, data collected from living human subjects (aka "Human Data") falls under the scope of GDPR as "sensitive personal data". Often, Human Data is solely collected for research and is kept in a pseudonymized fashion (detached from identifying attributes such as name or address). To ensure data-protection Human Data is typically shared via "controlled-access" data catalogues [4]. The common catalogue workflow starts by a study owner submitting a dataset along with descriptive metadata. The second step is the provisioning of a Data Access Committee (DAC) that will be responsible for assessing requests for this dataset in terms of compliance with ethical standards and legal requirements. Data is then advertised in the catalog. Scientists that seeks controlled-access data are required to make a formal application describing the planned study and data use. In addition to the requirements listed in Sect. 1, the stewardship of Human Data further brings the following requirements:

- GDPR allows EU countries to have their own legislative provisions. This leads to the requirement to know if the requested type of data processing is allowed in the country of the requester. Also subjects may disallow the transfer of their data outside the country of collection, or outside the EU. Currently catalogues do not model data use restrictions in detail, instead they rely on DACs to match restrictions against requests. Under GDPR, however, data catalogues will be accountable for granted accesses, therefore detailed consent modelling and conflict detection is necessary.
- Catalogues are typically maintained by life-science institutes that also run their own studies, which may involve Human Data. From the perspective of GDPR, all Human Data needs to be accounted for, regardless of it being a frozen data snapshot in the catalogue or an active dataset in the process of being generated. Henceforth common abstractions and tools are needed to keep inventory of Human Data.

Motivated by these observations, we are developing the Data Information System at ELIXIR Luxembourg.

2   ELIXIR-LU Data Information System

ELIXIR [2] is a pan-European infrastructure for life-science data. ELIXIR-LU is the Luxembourgish node of ELIXIR based at the Luxembourg Centre for Systems Biomedicine (LCSB). ELIXIR-LU hosts a Translational Medicine data

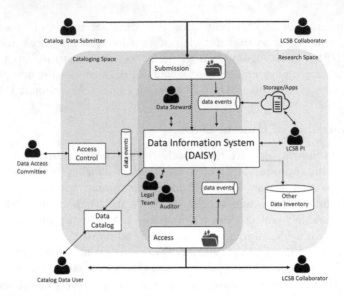

Fig. 1. Data information system overview.

repository as well as a cloud platform and tools to support data integration, analytics and visualisation. ELIXIR-LU Data Information System (DAISY) is a web application that is designed to collect rich provenance on the Human Data held in LCSB for both local research and for the ELIXIR-LU Catalog. Information gets accumulated in DAISY by (1) different stakeholders' manual input and (2) data-events that are generated from loosely coupled applications (depicted in Fig. 1).

- Prior to data's physical arrival to LCSB, we ask submitters to fill in a "Data Information Sheet", which collects essential data protection metadata, such as data use restrictions, data's de-identification method and the legal basis for its processing.
- Data submitted for the catalog undergoes further processing, such as re-pseudonymization, where subject identifiers in data are replaced by catalogue accession numbers, also curation may be performed. These alterations and data storage endpoints are recorded in DAISY by the data steward/curator.
- Access control to data in the catalogue is mediated by an application [1] that facilitates the DAC decision. This application is monitored for information on who has been granted access, and for which duration, all captured in DAISY. This information is complemented with logs of transfers of data to authorised catalog users.
- Access to local-research data is controlled via application/file-system level permissions, through monitoring components DAISY can generate a report on who has access to local data at any given time.
- Documents that guarantee data legality, such as Ethics Approvals, Data Sharing agreements, Consent Templates may be renewed or revised. Such updates are facilitated by manual input of the Legal Team into DAISY. Also data

privacy measures can be recorded by IT Administrators as tags on datasets and any technical documentation, such as DPIA results, can be linked via the content management system.

- The provenance stored in DAISY will be exportable in a standards compliant form. This may be upon request by data subject, by auditor or for transfer of information to other inventories.

In addition to **recording provenance** identified above, DAISY will provide the following features:

- Detection and flagging of conflicts between datasets restrictions and the requests made on those datasets.
- Generation of notifications based data use restrictions. For example notifying the end of data storage durations or legal contracts nearing their end/renewal date, or notifications to data recipients to remind their obligations e.g. co-authorship on publications with data.

3   Future Directions

DAISY is currently under development and is scheduled for an alpha release in July 2018. We are establishing a GDPR working group in ELIXIR. Through this group we hope to refine requirements for DAISY and identify its functions that can be re-used by the ELIXIR community. We plan to make DAISY available as an open source tool.

Acknowledgments. This work was (partially) funded through the contribution of the Luxembourg Ministry of Higher Education and Research towards the Luxembourg ELIXIR Node.

References

1. Brandizi, M., Melnichuk, O., et al.: Orchestrating differential data access for translational research: a pilot implementation. BMC Med. Inf. Decis. Mak. **17**(1), 30:1–30:14 (2017)
2. Crosswell, L.C., Thornton, J.M.: ELIXIR: a distributed infrastructure for European biological data. Trends Biotechnol. **30**(5), 241–242 (2012). https://doi.org/10.1016/j.tibtech.2012.02.002. http://www.sciencedirect.com/science/article/pii/S0167779912000170
3. Regulation (EU) 2016/679 of the European Parliament and of the Council of 27 April 2016 (General Data Protection Regulation). Off. J. Eur. Union **L119**, 1–88 (2016). http://eur-lex.europa.eu/legal-content/EN/TXT/?uri=OJ:L:2016:119:TOC
4. Lappalainen, I., Almeida-King, J., et al.: The european genome-phenome archive of human data consented for biomedical research. Nat. Genet. **47**(7), 692–695 (2015)
5. Wilkinson, M.D., Dumontier, M., et al.: The FAIR guiding principles for scientific data management and stewardship. Sci. Data **3**, 160018 EP (2016). https://doi.org/10.1038/sdata.2016.18

Author Index